A Stage of Emancipation
Change and Progress
at the Dublin Gate Theatre

The excellent essays in this collection add significantly to our knowledge of the Gate Theatre and its social and cultural practices and their contexts.

– Professor José Lanters, University of Wisconsin-Milwaukee

This rich stimulating collection revisions the work of Dublin's Gate Theatre and celebrates how it posed radical challenges to Irish society's social and cultural sore points and no-go-areas. Through a dazzling diversity of case studies in production, performance and theatrical practices the essays argue convincingly for the role of the Gate in confronting audiences with images and impacts that countered attitudes and assumptions about sexuality, gender, class divisions, racialization and Irish (including language) identity.

While the Gate's acknowledged theatrical aesthetics are not neglected, the book stresses the Gate Theatre's achievement in juggling localism and cosmopolitanism with invigorating and engaging tension.

– Dr Cathy Leeney, University College Dublin

A Stage of Emancipation is full of outstanding theatre scholarship from emerging and established voices. It provides fascinating insight into the role that the Dublin Gate Theatre has played in promoting social, economic, and cultural change within Irish society since the late 1920s. Most notably, it highlights the valiant efforts by key figures in the theatre's history to bring marginalised stories and progressive attitudes to the Irish stage. This is an enormously valuable book for students, academics, and practitioners alike.

– Dr Fiona McDonagh, Mary Immaculate College

This collection makes room to breathe in Irish theatre – allowing us to inhale the extraordinary diversity of identities and artistry which were embodied on the Gate stage. Our eyes are opened once again to these forgotten legacies which challenge singular concepts of nation and society, transforming not only our understanding of the past but liberating our approach to theatre now.

– Dr Melissa Sihra, Trinity College Dublin

A Stage of Emancipation

*Change and Progress
at the Dublin Gate Theatre*

edited by
Marguérite Corporaal
and
Ruud van den Beuken

LIVERPOOL UNIVERSITY PRESS

First published 2021 by
Liverpool University Press
4 Cambridge Street
Liverpool
L69 7ZU

Copyright © 2021 Liverpool University Press

The right of Marguérite Corporaal and Ruud van den Beuken to be identified
as the editors of this book has been asserted by them in accordance with the
Copyright, Designs and Patents Act 1988.

An Open Access edition of this book is available on the
Liverpool University Press website and the OAPEN library.

British Library Cataloguing-in-Publication data
A British Library CIP record is available

ISBN 978-1-80085-951-7 cased
ISBN 978-1-80085-610-3 limp

Typeset by Carnegie Book Production, Lancaster
Printed and bound by CPI Group (UK) Ltd, Croydon CR0 4YY

Contents

Acknowledgements   vii

List of Illustrations   ix

List of Contributors   xi

1. Introduction: A *Stage* of Emancipation   1
   Marguérite Corporaal and Ruud van den Beuken

Part I: Liberating Bodies

2. Queering the Irish Actress: The Gate Theatre Production of
   Children in Uniform (1934)   25
   Mary Trotter

3. Maura Laverty at the Gate: Theatre as Social Commentary in
   1950s Ireland   39
   Deirdre McFeely

Part II: Emancipating Communities

4. 'Let's Be Gay, While We May': Artistic Platforms and the
   Construction of Queer Communities in Mary Manning's
   Youth's the Season—?   57
   Grace Vroomen

5. Images and Imperatives: Robert Collis's *Marrowbone Lane*
   (1939) at the Gate as Theatre for Social Change   77
   Ian R. Walsh

6. Authenticity and Social Change on the Gate Stage in the
   1970s: 'Communicating with the People'   91
   Barry Houlihan

Part III: Staging Minority Languages

7. Micheál mac Liammóir, the Irish Language, and the
   Idea of Freedom   113
   Radvan Markus

8. The Use of Minority Languages at Dublin's Gate Theatre and
   Barcelona's Teatre Lliure   131
   Feargal Whelan and David Clare

Part IV: Deconstructing Aesthetics

9. Mogu and the Unicorn: Frederick May's Music for the
   Gate Theatre   151
   Mark Fitzgerald

10. Tartan Transpositions: Materialising Europe, Ireland, and
    Scotland in the Designs of Molly MacEwen   167
    Siobhán O'Gorman

Part V: Contesting Traditions in Contemporary Theatre

11. From White Othello to Black Hamlet: A History of Race
    and Representation at the Gate Theatre   189
    Justine Nakase

12. Bending the Plots: Selina Cartmell's Gate and Politics of
    Gender Inclusion   207
    Marguérite Corporaal

Index   221

Acknowledgements

The editors of this book would like to thank Professor Ondřej Pilný, Charles University Prague, and Professor Patrick Lonergan of the National University of Ireland, Galway, co-directors of the Gate Theatre Research Network, for their support in the completion of this volume. We are especially obliged to the Netherlands Organisation for Scientific Research (NWO) for an Internationalisation in the Humanities grant (236-40-001/3789) in support of establishing 'The Gate Theatre Research Network: Cosmopolitanism, Cultural Exchange and Identity Formation' and funding its activities and meetings; and to Radboud University Nijmegen, the National University of Ireland, Galway, and Charles University, Prague, for co-funding the project.

We are very grateful to Christabel Scaife at Liverpool University Press for her assistance in bringing this book to publication, to David Clare for his insightful feedback on its Introduction, and to Ricardo Reitsma and Aafke van Pelt for assisting us during various stages of copy-editing. We are particularly thankful to the anonymous readers for their carefully considered comments, which have been extremely useful in finalising the structure of the book.

A special note of thanks is due to the Gate Theatre's directorate, and Celena Madlansacay at Narrative, for helping us to obtain permissions to reproduce images from theatre productions. Additionally, we are grateful to Scottish Registry of Tartans, the University of Glasgow Library, and the Archives and Special Collections and the Digital Gate Archive at NUI Galway for granting permission to use images from their collections as illustrations. Every effort has been made to trace the copyright holders and obtain permission to reproduce all third-party material.

Illustrations

Cover image. Ruth Negga as Hamlet, directed by Yaël Farber at the Gate Theatre, Dublin. Photograph by Chris Sutton. Image reproduced with permission of the Gate Theatre, Dublin and Narrative.

Figure 1. Brian Phelan and Chloe Gibson on the set of *The Signalman's Apprentice*, 1971, courtesy of the Gate Theatre Digital Archive, Hardiman Library, NUI Galway.   101

Figure 2. Set design by Robert Heade for *The Signalman's Apprentice*, 1971, courtesy of the Gate Theatre Digital Archive, Hardiman Library, NUI Galway.   105

Figure 3. Purple and gold Bracken tartan designed by Molly MacEwen for the Edinburgh Festival production of *The Highland Fair* (1951), by permission of the Scottish Registry of Tartans.   169

Figure 4. Sketch of a stage backdrop featuring three birds holding a flower garland, by Molly MacEwen (undated), by permission of the University of Glasgow Library, Archives and Special Collections. The same design appears in the Dublin Gate Theatre Archive and the Charles Deering McCormick Library, Northwestern University, where it is linked to Micheál mac Liammóir's *Home for Christmas* (1950).   173

Figure 5. Production image of *The Thrie Estaites*, Assembly Hall, Church of Scotland, Edinburgh (1948), by permission of the University of Glasgow Library, Archives and Special Collections.   179

Figure 6. Sketches of period costumes by Molly MacEwen for three merchants played by James Gilbert, Randolph Kennedy, and Sam D. Stevenson in the Citizens' Theatre Company's production of *The Thrie Estaites*, Assembly Hall, Church of Scotland, Edinburgh (1951 revival), by permission of the University of Glasgow Library, Archives and Special Collections.   180

Figure 7. Molly MacEwen's design for the Citizens' Theatre Company production of *Douglas* (1950), by permission of the University of Glasgow Library, Archives and Special Collections. 181

Figure 8. Sketch of a female period costume, by Molly MacEwen (undated), by permission of the University of Glasgow Library, Archives and Special Collections. 183

Figure 9. Stephanie Dufresne in Nancy Harris's *The Red Shoes*. Photograph by Ste Murray. Image reproduced by permission of the Gate Theatre, Dublin. 212

Contributors

Ruud van den Beuken is Assistant Professor of English Literature at Radboud University Nijmegen (the Netherlands). He was awarded the 2015 New Scholars' Prize (Irish Society for Theatre Research), and he held a Visiting Research Fellowship at the Moore Institute (National University of Ireland, Galway) in 2018. He is the Assistant Director of the NWO-funded Gate Theatre Research Network. He has published articles in *Irish Studies Review* (2015) and *Études irlandaises* (2018), and contributed chapters to *The Gate Theatre, Dublin: Inspiration and Craft* (Carysfort / Peter Lang, 2018), and *Navigating Ireland's Theatre Archive: Theory, Practice, Performance* (Peter Lang, 2019). He has also co-edited various volumes, including *Irish Studies and the Dynamics of Memory: Transitions and Transformations* (Peter Lang, 2017) and *Cultural Convergence: The Dublin Gate Theatre, 1928–1960* (Palgrave Macmillan, 2021). His monograph *Avant-Garde Nationalism at the Dublin Gate Theatre, 1928–1940* was published by Syracuse University Press in 2020.

David Clare is Lecturer in Drama and Theatre Studies at Mary Immaculate College, University of Limerick. He previously held two Irish Research Council-funded post-doctoral fellowships based at NUI Galway's Moore Institute. Clare's books include the monograph *Bernard Shaw's Irish Outlook* (Palgrave Macmillan, 2016), and the edited collections *The Gate Theatre, Dublin: Inspiration and Craft* (Carysfort / Peter Lang, 2018) and *The Golden Thread: Irish Women Playwrights (1716–2016)*, which is forthcoming (Liverpool University Press, 2021). Additionally, he has published essays related to Gate Theatre productions of works by Oliver Goldsmith, Mary Manning, Christine Longford, Maura Laverty, Samuel Beckett, and Mark O'Rowe. Clare is the curator of the Irish Research Council (IRC)-funded database www.ClassicIrishPlays.com.

Marguérite Corporaal is Full Professor of Irish Literature in Transnational Contexts at Radboud University Nijmegen, the Netherlands. She is a

Director of the Gate Theatre Research Network, funded by the Dutch Organisation for Scientific Research (NWO). She was the principal investigator of the project *Relocated Remembrance: The Great Famine in Irish (Diaspora) Fiction, 1847–1921*, for which she obtained a Starting Grant for Consolidators from the European Research Council (2010–15). Corporaal was recently awarded a prestigious NWO-Vici grant for her project *Redefining the Region: The Transnational Dimensions of Local Colour* (2019–24). Furthermore, she is the PI of *Heritages of Hunger*, which is funded as part of the Dutch research council NWO's NWA programme (2019–24). Among her recent international publications are her monograph *Relocated Memories of the Great Famine in Irish and Diaspora Fiction, 1847–70* (Syracuse UP, 2017); *The Great Irish Famine: Visual and Material Culture* (co-edited, Liverpool UP, 2018); *Travelling Irishness in the Long Nineteenth Century* (co-edited, Palgrave, 2017).

Mark Fitzgerald is senior lecturer at TU Dublin Conservatoire. He was executive editor of *The Encyclopaedia of Music in Ireland* (UCD Press, 2013) and he co-edited *Music and Identity in Ireland and Beyond* (Routledge, 2015). He is the author of *The Life and Music of James Wilson* (Cork University Press, 2015) as well as articles on Modernism, Frederick May, Gerald Barry, Ferruccio Busoni and W.B. Yeats. In 2016 he was awarded a Trinity College Long Room Hub Visiting Fellowship during which period he reconstructed the score of Frederick May's *Symphonic Ballad*. He is Executive Editor of the *Journal of the Society for Musicology*, Ireland.

Barry Houlihan is an archivist at the Hardiman Library, National University of Ireland, Galway. He has worked on a range of theatre archive and digital access projects, including the Abbey Theatre and Gate Theatre digital archives, the Druid Theatre Company archive, and the Galway International Arts Festival, as well as a number of ongoing oral history projects around social change, activism and, memory. He lectures in a number of disciplines including drama and theatre studies, history, children's studies, digital archives, and digital media at NUI Galway. He has published in many international journals and books on topics relating to theatre history and digital performance, and is the editor of *Navigating Ireland's Theatre Archive: Theory, Practice, Performance* (Peter Lang, 2019).

Radvan Markus is senior lecturer in the Irish language and literature at Charles University, Prague. He is the author of *Echoes of the Rebellion: The Year 1798 in Twentieth-Century Irish Fiction and Drama* (Peter Lang, 2015) and numerous articles and essays on twentieth-century Irish-language prose.

His current research interests include the work of Máirtín Ó Cadhain and modern Irish-language drama. A translator from Irish to Czech, his annotated translation of Ó Cadhain's *Cré na Cille* (2017) won the prestigious Magnesia Litera award. He is a board member of the European Federation of Associations and Centres of Irish Studies (EFACIS).

Deirdre McFeely is a former Adjunct Lecturer at Trinity College Dublin. She is the author of *Dion Boucicault: Irish Identity on Stage* (Cambridge UP, 2012), and was the recipient of IRC scholarships for her doctoral and post-doctoral work on the playwright. She is a contributor, (with Cathy Leeney, on the work of Maura Laverty) to *The Golden Thread: Irish Women Playwrights 1716–2016*, forthcoming with Liverpool University Press. She undertook post-doctoral research on the IRC-funded project 'Shakespeare's Plays in Dublin, 1660–1904,' and has contributed articles to various volumes on theatre history.

Justine Nakase completed her PhD at the National University of Ireland, Galway, where she was an Irish Research Council postgraduate scholar. Her dissertation *Performing Scalar Interculturalism: Race and Identity in Contemporary Irish Performance* used intercultural performance studies to examine the relationship between racial and national identities, focusing on mixed race and minority ethnic Irish individuals in theatre, sport, and dance. Her publications include articles in *Scene* and *New Hibernia Review* and chapters in *Methuen Drama Handbook of Performance and Interculturalism* (Methuen, 2020), *Interculturalism and Performance Now* (Palgrave, 2019), and *Performance in a Militarized Culture* (Routledge, 2017). She is also a co-editor of the forthcoming two-volume edited collection *The Golden Thread: Irish Women Playwrights (1716–2016)* (Liverpool University Press, 2021).

Siobhán O'Gorman is a Senior Lecturer and MA Theatre Programme Leader at the School of Fine & Performing Arts, University of Lincoln. She is co-editor of a special double issue on Performance and Ireland of the international journal *Scene* (2021) and a special issue of *RISE* on the Gate Theatre. She is also on the editorial board of *Studies in Costume & Performance* and on the executive committee of the Irish Society for Theatre Research. With Charlotte McIvor, she edited the first book to focus on devised performance within Irish contexts, *Devised Performance in Irish Theatre: Histories and Contemporary Practice* (Carysfort, 2015). She was part of the curatorial team for the Irish exhibition at the Prague Quadrennial in 2015, and her monograph, *Theatre, Performance and Design: Scenographies* *in a Modernizing Ireland*, is forthcoming with Palgrave Macmillan. Her work has also appeared in several edited collections and such journals as *Irish Studies Review, Studies in Theatre and Performance*, and the *Journal of Adaptation in Film and Performance*.

Mary Trotter is an Associate Professor of English and Interdisciplinary Theatre Studies at the University of Wisconsin–Madison. She is the author of two monographs: *Ireland's National Theaters: Political Performance and the Origins of the Irish Dramatic Movement* (Syracuse UP, 2001) and *Modern Irish Theatre* (Polity, 2008). Her current research project, *Actresses and Activists: Feminism, Nationalism and Theatricality in Early Twentieth-Century Ireland*, examines the ways several notable Irish women negotiated the relationship between their labour as theatre performers and their political activism during a period rife with social and political change, locally and internationally. She is an Editorial Advisory Board Member for *Modern Drama* (2007–present), and was President of the American Conference for Irish Studies (2013–15).

Grace Vroomen is a Research MA student at Radboud University Nijmegen and Creative Director and co-founder of Underground Theatre. Her bachelor's thesis focused on the transnational influence of the Gate Theatre on the American playwright Elmer Rice. She recently completed a research internship at the archives of NUI Galway, where she curated and digitised the Joe Vaněk Archive of Theatre and Opera Design. She has, moreover, been active as a director and playwright for several successful student and amateur productions, including *Warhole*, an adaptation of Müller's *The Hamletmachine*, and *Generation Lost*, inspired by Golding's *Lord of the Flies*. Most recently, she produced and directed a revival of Christine Longford's *Tankardstown*, which toured Limerick and Nijmegen in February and March 2020.

Ian R. Walsh is Lecturer in Drama and Theatre Studies at NUI Galway. He was awarded a PhD from University College Dublin in 2010 and has worked as a freelance director of both theatre and opera. He has published widely on Irish theatre in peer-reviewed journals and edited collections. His monograph *Experimental Irish Theatre: After W.B. Yeats* was published in 2012 by Palgrave. Other publications include *The Theatre of Enda Walsh* (Carysfort / Peter Lang, 2015) co-edited with Mary Caulfield, and *Cultural Convergence: The Dublin Gate Theatre, 1928–1960* (Palgrave, 2021), co-edited with Ondřej Pilný and Ruud van den Beuken. He has worked as a theatre reviewer for *Irish Theatre Magazine* and for RTÉ Radio

1. Publications on the Gate Theatre include 'Hilton Edwards as Director: Shade of Modernity' in *The Gate Theatre Dublin: Inspiration and Craft* (Carysfort / Peter Lang, 2018) and 'Irish Theatre: A Director's Theatre' in *The Palgrave Handbook of Contemporary Irish Theatre and Performance* (Palgrave, 2018).

Feargal Whelan has published and presented widely on the work of Samuel Beckett and on twentieth-century Irish drama. He is a co-director of the Samuel Beckett Summer School at Trinity College Dublin and has also collaborated with Mouth on Fire Theatre Company on its annual Beckett in Foxrock performances. Book chapters and papers are included in *Staging Beckett in Ireland and Northern Ireland* (Bloomsbury, 2016), *Estudios Irlandeses* (2017), *Beckett and Modernism* (Palgrave, 2018), *The Gate Theatre* (Carysfort / Peter Lang, 2018), and *Beckett and Politics* (Palgrave, 2020). He is a board member of the Samuel Beckett Society and is the editor of its magazine *The Beckett Circle*.

Introduction

A *Stage* of Emancipation

Marguérite Corporaal
and Ruud van den Beuken

In his introduction to *Irish Drama and Theatre since 1950* (2019), Patrick Lonergan outlines the genealogy of the #WakingTheFeminists movement, which began as a contestation of how the Abbey's 2016 Waking the Nation programme marginalised female playwrights and directors, but quickly expanded to raise awareness about the precarious position of women in the Irish theatre scene more generally. By also charting earlier attempts to challenge gender inequalities, Lonergan reveals a disturbing history of forgetfulness, if not outright disregard, so that 'each iteration [of defiance] occurred as if for the first time.'[1] Indeed, in the face of this negligence by both historiographers and the wider cultural sector, Lonergan appeals to 'theatre scholars [to] think about the choices we make when we document the past.'[2]

The present volume takes this plea to heart in an attempt to recover these and other types of marginalised histories and to demonstrate how the Dublin Gate Theatre played various emancipatory roles in Irish culture and society over the course of its long history. Founded in 1928 by Hilton Edwards, Micheál mac Liammóir, Desirée 'Toto' Bannard Cogley, and Gearóid Ó Lochlainn, the Gate quickly became a cosmopolitan mecca in the strongly insular Irish Free State. As Robert Hogan already described in his contribution to the demi-centenary Festschrift *Enter Certain Players* (1978), their new venture provided Ireland with 'expertise and craft, education and a honing of taste, a growth of urbane tolerance and a lessening of parochialism, a series of masterpieces that inspired terror,

---

[1] Lonergan, *Irish Drama and Theatre*, 4.
[2] Lonergan, *Irish Drama and Theatre*, 5.

a series of nonsenses that evoked delight.'[3] The catholicity of Hogan's enumeration – and his stress on the emancipatory quality of the Gate's efforts – is also illustrated in a more comic vein by an incident that the architect Michael Scott recounts in the same volume. When the Gate acquired the Rotunda's concert wing in 1930, mac Liammóir told Scott that he wanted the toilet doors to be 'painted black with the words "Fir" and "Mna" in gold leaf,' but a building inspector protested that the English words for *men* and *women* should be used instead. Mac Liammóir's response illustrates a particularly tenacious streak to his cosmopolitan sentiments: 'Micheál was so insensed [*sic*] at the Corporation's insistence on English that he instructed the painter to put the two words in eight languages.'[4]

While this retaliation might seem rather capricious, it is actually emblematic of the emancipatory remit that the Gate accorded itself: to promote multiplicity and to embrace difference, especially when it flies in the face of authority.[5] Two of the most important achievements of the Gate as a socio-political – rather than purely cultural – project in this regard include creating a covert safe space for gay and lesbian actors in a country that did not decriminalise homosexuality until 1993, and putting women centre stage both literally and figuratively. Meriel Moore, Coralie Carmichael, and Betty Chancellor, for example, were the Gate's leading actors for many years, while the violinist Bay Jellett directed the orchestra and the playwright Mary Manning edited the Gate's official journal, *Motley*, for its entire run.[6] By escaping the mainstream of Irish society, which designated the place of women as 'within the home' in an infamous article of the 1937 Constitution, women could find a degree of freedom and appreciation at the Gate that was largely unimaginable in most other societal contexts.[7] This contrast also serves to contextualise the intense camaraderie that Manning, who was also one of the Gate's most successful original playwrights, describes in retrospect: 'There was a freshness, a joyousness about it which matched the spring of our own years when the writers, the directors, the actors and the design all merged together in perfect unison.'[8] Such conjunctions are also reflected in many

---

[3] Hogan, Untitled, in *Enter Certain Players*, 18.

[4] Scott, Untitled, 20.

[5] Van den Beuken, *Avant-Garde Nationalism*, 206–9.

[6] See also Van den Beuken, *Avant-Garde Nationalism*, 60, 208.

[7] Quoted in Luddy, 'A "Sinister and Retrogressive" Proposal,' 194. See also Meaney, O'Dowd, and Whelan, *Reading the Irish Woman*, 196–97.

[8] Manning, Untitled, 37.

contributions to this volume, which not only pay tribute to the significant roles that women played throughout the Gate's history as directors, actors, stage designers, and playwrights, but also establish how intersections of class, ethnic, sexual, and linguistic identities at the Gate enabled emancipatory community formation.

As Nicholas Allen has argued, then, it is important to place the Dublin Gate Theatre in a larger societal framework, since its 'background in experimental theatre [...] fed from the energy of a culture whose political space was not yet accepted as the proper forum for active debate.'[9] His claim that 'the Gate Theatre was a central location for projects that tried to refigure Ireland after revolution' likewise offers an important reminder of the politicised nature of the Gate's incursion into the Dublin cultural scene.[10] This book accordingly emphasises the emancipatory potential of such theatrical ventures, thereby seeking to further consolidate the recent academic recognition of the Gate's infrastructural importance to Irish theatre and society more generally. The last few years have seen the publication of the first book-length studies of the Gate: the collections *The Gate Theatre, Dublin: Inspiration and Craft* (edited by Clare, Lally, and Lonergan, 2018) and *Cultural Convergence: The Dublin Gate Theatre, 1928–1960* (edited by Pilný, Van den Beuken, and Walsh, 2021) as well as the monograph *Avant-Garde Nationalism at the Dublin Gate Theatre, 1928–1940* (Van den Beuken, 2020).[11] At the same time, it must be acknowledged, as Cathy Leeney does with regard specifically to the way women are framed in Irish theatre, that rediscovering marginalised identities is only the first step in redressing historiographical wrongs. Indeed, the greater difficulty lies in truly realising – in both senses of the word – 'how reassessment in gender terms has the potential to unbalance existing models of how Irish theatre operated, has energized or stultified the fluid thing that is the nation.'[12]

Such acknowledgements of – and interventions in – the fraught relationship between cultural infrastructures and marginalised (or otherwise contested) identities have characterised important recent developments

---

[9] Allen, *Modernism, Ireland, and Civil War*, 98. See also Van den Beuken, 'MacLiammóir's Minstrel and Johnston's Morality,' 12.

[10] Allen, *Modernism, Ireland, and Civil War*, 109. See also Van den Beuken, 'MacLiammóir's Minstrel and Johnston's Morality,' 12.

[11] For a more detailed discussion of the Gate's academic reception, see Pilný, Van den Beuken, and Walsh, 'Introduction,' 2–4; and Van den Beuken, *Avant-Garde Nationalism*, 6, 24–33, 207.

[12] Leeney, 'Women and Irish Theatre before 1960,' 269.

in the field of Irish theatre studies. Donald E. Morse's introduction to *Irish Theatre in Transition* (2015) offers a concise characterisation of this sea change: discussing Christopher Murray's seminal scholarship, he comments on how key issues in Irish drama have been changing 'from national identity, faith and cultural values to economics, sex, gender, and demographics.'[13] The concomitant 'renegotiation and pluralizing of Irish theatrical traditions' that Melissa Sihra has advocated and spearheaded with regard to the roles and positions of women has also been politicised in the Northern Irish context by Fiona Coleman Coffey, who argues, for example, that 'women's dramatic writing and performance have often contradicted mainstream narratives [of the Troubles].'[14]

There is, then, a sense of multiplicity, of disputing monolithic constructions of meaning and power, that marks a wide array of recent Irish theatre scholarship. To a large extent, this hermeneutic stance is inherent to its emancipatory politics, as Fintan Walsh's intersectional approach to the performance of queerness in Irish theatre also demonstrates. Walsh interprets 'the affective and phenomenological work that the interconnected experiences of dissent and disorientation do' in the productions that he analyses 'both as symptoms of exclusion and upheaval, but also as strategies of resistance and sustenance, which can effect real social, cultural and political change.'[15] While the conceptual fluidity of queerness intrinsically posits a challenge to authority, Michael Pierse has shown that literature and drama that engage with trenchant class divides can be equally ex-centric: 'The fiction and plays of working-class Dublin after O'Casey represent an enduring lineage of class struggle through art, a literary disruption, contestation and subversion of the established order.'[16] A final important illustration of this critical approach to hegemonic structures is provided by Charlotte McIvor's research on the performance of migrant identities in the Republic of Ireland. McIvor's simultaneous adoption and contestation of new interculturalism as a theoretical paradigm allows her to establish 'how community can be appropriated as a discourse by the state, but still used as a site of performative protest from below.'[17]

---

[13] Morse, 'Introduction: *Irish Theatre in Transition*,' 2.
[14] Sihra, 'Introduction: Figures at the Window,' 10; Coffey, *Women in Northern Irish Theatre*, 5.
[15] Walsh, *Queer Performance*, 16.
[16] Pierse, *Writing Ireland's Working Class*, 257.
[17] McIvor, *Migration and Performance*, 18. See also McIvor's problematisation of new interculturalism in a global(ised) context in 'Introduction: New Directions?' 1–16, 22–23.

There is a clear emancipatory thrust, then, behind such ground-breaking scholarship, and this volume seeks to extrapolate this approach in a diachronic manner to scrutinise how the Dublin Gate Theatre has functioned as an infrastructural hub in this regard: for over ninety years, dramatic engagements with marginalised identities of all kinds have taken place on its stage. At the same time, it must be acknowledged that this is not a straightforward endeavour, and that the *change* and *progress* that the subtitle of this book signals have not been unequivocal or ubiquitous. Many theatre scholars and practitioners will know that in November 2017, the Board of the Gate Theatre commissioned a report on workplace conditions during Michael Colgan's tenure as the Gate's director (1983–2017) after the *Irish Times* published on a wide range of allegations that had been made by former staff members.[18] A few months later, the resulting report found that there was 'a case to answer' regarding inappropriate behaviour, abuse of power, and undermining the dignity to work.[19]

In light of these issues, it should be stressed that the title of this volume aims to reflect the precarious nature of change and progress: as the various chapters will illustrate, there have been many different impulses transforming the Gate into a stage of emancipation, but it is no less important to realise that this project is always only *at* a stage, and that the dangers of regression, complicity, and exclusion are real and tangible. The title is thus aspirational, not blindly celebratory: it is an invitation to recognise and assess the emancipatory endeavours of people as diverse as Micheál mac Liammóir and Selina Cartmell, Mary Manning and Brian Phelan, whose efforts to foster progress and change should provide vital warnings against complacency in such matters.

Gender, History, and Power: On and Off the Stage

Of course, any attempt to facilitate such revisions must be predicated on a broader understanding of both the historicity of Irish theatre and the power dynamics that enforce marginalisation more generally. While this volume focuses on different types of emancipation – including contexts of class, ethnicity, sexuality, and language – the ways in which the politics of gender have been contested throughout the history of Irish theatre offer particularly salient insights into the processes involved in fostering emancipation. One striking fact, for example, is that the first performance

---

[18] Mackin and Gallagher, 'Seven women allege abuse and harassment by Michael Colgan.'

[19] Cunningham, 'Gate Theatre: Confidential Independent Review,' 10.

of a play in English by a woman writer took place in Dublin rather than London. Katherine Philips's translation of a play by Pierre Corneille, *Pompey, a Tragedy*, originally intended as closet drama, was performed at Dublin's Smock Alley Theatre in 1663, a production arranged and directed by Philips's Irish friend, Roger Boyle, the Earl of Orrery.[20] Remarkably, this was a few years before the first play by a woman writer made it to the London stage: Frances Boothby's *Marcelia; or the Treacherous Friend* (1669).

Indeed, the Smock Alley Theatre played a significant role in advancing the careers of eighteenth-century female actors and dramatists as well. Eliza Haywood began her career at this prestigious Dublin playhouse around 1714, performing in, among others, Thomas Shadwell's adaptation of Shakespeare's *Timon of Athens*, before moving to London around 1716.[21] Additionally, Welsh-born but Dublin-raised Elizabeth Griffith made her acting debut as Juliet in 1749 on the Smock Alley stage, of which her father Thomas Griffith was the manager.[22] Afterwards, she became a very successful dramatist for Drury Lane and Covent Garden during the 1760s and 1770s. Peg Woffington is another famous actress who performed at the Smock Alley Theatre, with David Garrick, after she had previously played parts at the Theatre Royal and the Lilliputian Theatre in Dublin.[23]

During the early nineteenth century, Sydney Owenson, Lady Morgan, contributed a libretto to the comic opera *The First Attempt of the Whim of a Moment*, which was performed at the Theatre Royal on 11 March 1807.[24] As her father had worked as an actor-manager in Ireland for years and she had accompanied him during tours across the country, it was not entirely unexpected that Owenson would find a stage for her work as well. Her close friend Alicia Sheridan Le Fanu, who came from a family of actors and dramatists, wrote a five-act comedy that made it to the London stage: *Sons of Erin; or Modern Sentiment*. The play was performed at the Lyceum in 1812 and aimed to counter current stereotypes about the Irish in England. While Le Fanu did not write for the Irish public stage, we know that she had held 'plays in the drawing room of

---

20 See Corporaal, 'Katherine Philips: *Pompey, a Tragedy*,' 158–62.

21 Meaney, O'Dowd, and Whelan, *Reading the Irish Woman*, 42–43. See also Ingrassia, *Authorship, Commerce, and Gender in Early Eighteenth-Century England*, 190.

22 Finberg, 'Introduction,' xxvii.

23 See, amongst others, Curtis, *Temple Bar*, chapter 13. Many thanks to David Clare for this suggestion.

24 Donovan, *Lady Morgan and the Politics of Style*, 62.

Le Fanu house on Cuffe Street in Dublin' for years prior to this public performance of her comedy.[25]

During the rest of the nineteenth and early twentieth century, Irish women's drama often did not make it to the professional stage. Instead, women's plays appeared in print or were performed in the setting of private theatricals. While Eva Gore-Booth was closely associated with W.B. Yeats, the many plays she wrote (which often re-explored gender representations in Irish mythology) were not staged by the Irish Literary Theatre. *A Daughter of Eve* (1891), a political burlesque, was written for private performance at her family home, Lissadell House. Plays such as *The Triumph of Maeve* (1902) and *The Buried Life of Deirdre* (1908–12) came out in print posthumously in 1930.[26] Maud Gonne played the lead role in the premiere staging of W.B. Yeats's and Lady Gregory's *Cathleen Ni Houlihan* at Theresa's Hall, Clarendon Street on 2 April 1902.[27] However, her play *Dawn* only found its way to audiences in print, in *The United Irishmen* of 29 October 1904, and remained unstaged. This was due to her resignation as vice president of the Irish National Theatre Society as a result of its gender-biased enactments of Irish peasant women, and her granting the exclusive rights of performance to Inghinidhe na hÉireann.[28]

The fact that *Dawn* was never performed on the public stage unfortunately means that it had less impact in its day than, for example, W.B. Yeats's *The Countess Cathleen*, which also first appeared only in published form in three editions in 1892 and 1895,[29] but was staged on 8 May 1899 as the inaugural production of the Irish Literary Theatre. Gonne's play is set in a village in the northwest of Ireland at a time of severe famine, which has been designated by some critics as the 1898 Mayo famine during which Maud Gonne herself offered relief,[30] but which might as well refer to the Great Famine (1845–49). The opening of the one-act play evokes the memory of the notorious relief schemes, showing that Mike O'Hara and Neil Durkan, who have been 'nine hours on the works, and the hunger on us all the while,' only receive a small bag of Indian meal and are close to collapsing from fatigue and weakness.[31] The

[25] Taylor, 'Sydney Owenson, Alicia Sheridan Le Fanu and the Domestic Stage of Post-Union Politics,' 158.

[26] Leeney, *Irish Women Playwrights, 1900–1939*, 61–62.

[27] Sihra, 'Introduction: Figures at the Window,' 7–8.

[28] Quinn, 'Ireland/Herland,' 898.

[29] For a detailed discussion of these published versions see, amongst others, Morash, '"Where All Ladders Start,"' 119–37.

[30] See Meaney, *Gender, Ireland and Cultural Change*, 50.

[31] Gonne, *Dawn*. All references are to this digital edition.

play, however, primarily focuses on the plight of Bride and her daughter Brideen. Abandoned by their son and brother Seumas, who has joined the British Army, and by Brideen's husband Eoin, who is seeking his fortune in the New World, the two women have been chased from their land by the 'Stranger' – a character epitomising both the Anglo-Irish Ascendancy and British imperial rule – and are facing deprivation and famine.

As Antoinette Quinn points out, the tableaux of which the play consists 'invite a symbolic reading,'[32] and Bride can clearly be interpreted as a Cathleen Ni Houlihan figure representing the emerald isle who calls for people's commitment to fight for the return of her lands: she is called 'Bride of the Sorrows' by old Michael and described by him as a 'queen' to whose 'service' he has commited himself and to whom he has 'been faithful.' Foregrounding how men who take up the fight for Ireland, personified by Bride's husband and son Patrick and old Michael, lose their lives while others, such as Seumas, betray the nation's cause, the famine can be read as the backdrop to Gonne's promotion of a dawning era in which the Irish will reclaim their land, with 'bright swords … that clash the battle welcome.' While Gonne's nationalist play seems to be similar to Yeats's and Gregory's *Cathleen Ni Houlihan* in its politics and directions as well as its allusions to a female mythological figure as an emblem for masculine sacrifice, Gonne revises gender roles in significant ways. As Joseph Valente observes, *Dawn* presents a 'double-woman formula,'[33] with on the one hand a feminine Ireland that can always be regenerated when people defend her rights, and on the other hand the image of the faithful female subject in the form of the daughter Brideen, who is more loyal to Ireland than her brother or husband.

Despite its political engagement, Gonne's work remained marginalised, and this is also true for other early twentieth-century Irish women writers: in many cases, it is at best uncertain whether their plays were ever performed. For example, the Cork dramatists Geraldine Cummins and Susanne R. Day wrote *Fidelity* (1914), a play dealing with rigid social structures and the limited choices available to women, but, as Melissa Sihra points out, there are no reviews available, so it seems likely that the play was never performed.[34] At the same time, the actor-director Florence Farr was instrumental to the success of the Irish Literary Theatre, while Lady Augusta Gregory contributed significantly to the repertoire of the Abbey Theatre as a playwright in her own right, but also by seeking out suitable

---

[32] Quinn, 'Ireland/Herland,' 898.
[33] See Valente, *The Myth of Manliness in Irish National Cuture*, 112.
[34] Sihra, 'Introduction: Figures at the Window,' 14.

drama by other authors.[35] Her own plays and her astute management helped to keep the Abbey afloat in its early days. Nonetheless, the role of women as actors, directors, designers, and playwrights in those early years of the Abbey was limited. While surviving prompt books suggest that Dorothy Macardle's *Ann Kavanagh* (1922) was produced by the Abbey, as Cathy Leeney states, her plays *Witch's Brew* (1928) and *Fenian Snow* (1924) were rejected by this theatre.[36] In 1932 she found a stage for *Dark Waters* at the Gate – her only play to be performed there – but, sadly, and symptomatically, no copies of the text seem to have survived.[37] Interestingly, the early years of the Gate saw more women turning to this theatre rather than the Abbey: Mary Manning, who had been trained at Sara Goodall's theatre school at the Abbey as an actor, chose to have her drama performed at the Gate, while Christine Longford designed costumes, managed productions, and wrote plays such as *Mr Jiggins of Jigginstown* (1933) for the Gate.

From our contemporary perspective, the recent repeal of the Eighth Amendment (2018) and the legalisation of same-sex marriage in the Republic of Ireland (2015) and Northern Ireland (2020) have marked significant strides in the acceptance of marriage equality as well as societal recognition of women's autonomy over their own bodies. However, we must also realise that, in preceding decades, Irish theatre had already adopted a leading position in fuelling debates over birth control, abortion, and the constraints faced by queer communities. One of the most prominent cases of an Irish theatre production stirring controversy was the Pike's staging of Tennessee Williams's *The Rose Tattoo* as part of the first Dublin Theatre Festival in 1957. Before its first performance, director Brendan Smith had received letters from the League of Decency complaining about the upcoming production, because the play advocated birth control.[38] As reconstructed by Patrick Lonergan, the company was formally accused of obscenity when the play's run began, allegedly because the Irish police accused the Pike of using a condom on stage.[39]

Themes such as restrictions on birth control and abortion would go on to be addressed in Irish theatres more frequently in recent times. Bill Whelan and Arthur Riordan's *The Train* (2017), staged at the Abbey, is a

---

[35] Remport, *Lady Gregory and Irish National Theatre*, 10–11.

[36] Leeney, *Irish Women Playwrights, 1900–1939*, 102–3.

[37] Leeney, *Irish Women Playwrights, 1900–1939*, 104. See also Van den Beuken, "'Three Cheers for the Descendancy!'", 142, for examples of lost plays.

[38] Sweeney, *Performing the Body in Irish Theatre*, 43.

[39] Lonergan, *Irish Drama and Theatre since 1950*, 50.

comedy focusing on a group of forty-seven women who travel from Dublin to Belfast in 1971 in order to get contraceptives forbidden in the Republic. Marina Carr's *The Mai*, set in the Midlands, performed at the Abbey in October 1994 and revived by the Peacock in 1995, critiques the gatekeepers of morality in Ireland by depicting how a group of women ostracise the character Beck on the basis of rumours of her aborted pregnancy.[40] Just a few years earlier, Patricia Burke Brogan had addressed related issues of societal exclusion and incarceration in *Eclipsed* (Punchbag Theatre, 1992), which is set in a Magdalen Laundry in the 1960s. This time-frame recalls one of the most controversial plays in its own time, Máiréad Ní Ghráda's *An Triail*. First performed at An Damer on 22 September 1964, it appears initially to stage the court case of Máire Ní Chathasaigh, a young single mother who, rejected by society, kills her child and then commits suicide. However, as the play progresses. it becomes clear that this Irish-language play rather puts the restrictive society in which she lived on trial.[41]

The problems that women face with regard to legal restrictions on abortion are also central to Amanda Coogan's *The Fountain* (2001) and Tara Flynn's *Not a Funny Word* (2017). Coogan's performance during *Marking the Territory*, a three-day international performance event at the Irish Museum of Modern Art, dramatises the tragic story of Ann Lovett, a fifteen-year-old who died while giving birth alone in a grotto in Granard, Co. Longford in 1984.[42] *Not a Funny Word* is an autobiographical monologue, staging Flynn's account of having to travel out of Ireland for an abortion. Likewise, the stage adaptation of Roddy Doyle's *The Snapper* (2018) centres on Sharon, who becomes pregnant and refuses to name the father. When the possibility of abortion is mentioned, the play deviates from the original novel in that it is 'not wholly repudiated,' nor compared to murder, as Peter Crawley claims.[43] Its theme is very similar to Rachel Trezise's *Cotton Fingers*, which premiered at the Belfast MAC in May 2019, and centres on a nineteen-year-old Belfast girl who becomes pregnant against her will. Aoife embarks on a journey to Wales to terminate her pregnancy – a theme that is still relevant in Northern Ireland, where abortion was only decriminalised in October 2019.

---

[40] See also Sihra, *Marina Carr*, 81.
[41] See De Fréine, 'On Trial.'
[42] Mannion, 'Live Art in Ireland,' 95.
[43] Crawley, 'The Snapper Review.'

Volume Outline

Part I of this volume – 'Liberating Bodies' – demonstrates how this ongoing engagement of Irish theatre-makers with issues surrounding contraception and abortion also extends to the Gate Theatre. As Deirdre McFeely's chapter demonstrates, the Gate has a long-standing tradition of addressing issues related to female sexuality and birth control that go back to the early 1950s. McFeely shows how Maura Laverty's trilogy of Gate plays *Liffey Lane* (1951), *Tolka Row* (1951), and *A Tree in the Crescent* (1952) were well ahead of their time in their portrayal of women and their reproductive rights. *Tolka Row* in particular was revolutionary in its frank discussion of the rhythm method of birth control at a time when the Censorship of Publications Act prohibited any books and periodicals advocating the prevention of conception. Furthermore, the play problematises women's lack of control over procreation as well as finances, thereby criticising the ways in which existing gender roles aggravate the plight of lower middle-class women, even as issues of gender and class inequality also intersect on various levels.

The Gate's productions of Maura Laverty's controversial plays illustrate how the theatre, under the directorship of Edwards and mac Liammóir, was willing to invest in the promotion of female dramatists as well as plays that sought to subvert gender expectations. Further evidence of this policy can be found in the fact that the Gate imported foreign drama by female playwrights that was pioneering in its exploration of queer sexualities. An example in case is the Gate's production of *Children in Uniform* (1934), a German play by Christa Winsloe that Mary Trotter examines in her contribution to this volume. Theatre, as Simon Shepherd writes, is concerned with the social, political and moral values attached to bodies.[44] Mary Trotter's chapter accordingly illustrates how the physical presence of leading female actors such as Ria Mooney and Betty Chancellor in this homoerotically charged German play created a production that shifted existing moral perceptions, and was inspiring to both liberal Dublin playgoers and to the actors themselves. Indeed, the queer dramaturgy of Winsloe's play allowed the Gate to create a space for queering the increasingly oppressive notions of gender both on and off most Irish stages in the 1930s. In contrast to the Abbey, which became more conservative by the 1930s, Trotter argues, the Gate was offering talented women not only the opportunity to expand their range as actors, but also roles that challenged existing notions of femininity and heteronormative sexuality, thus liberating female bodies on stage.

---

[44] Shepherd, *Theatre, Body, Pleasure*, 1.

The fact that the Gate was groundbreaking in both creating space for the work of upcoming female dramatists and addressing alternative sexualities also becomes clear from its production of Mary Manning's *Youth's the Season–?* on 8 December 1931. Although Manning had been trained as an actor at the Abbey, she found the experimental Gate a more suitable platform for her artistic visions.[45] Her very successful black comedy *Youth's the Season–?* not only provided alternative models of femininity through the character of Deirdre (who has no romantic conceptions at all of love and marriage), but also touches upon queer sexuality. In Part II, 'Emancipating Communities,' Grace Vroomen's chapter discusses how the implied sexual Otherness of characters such as Toots, Desmond, and Terence intersects with their conflicted gender identities. Furthermore, as Vroomen notes, queerness operates on various levels in the play, and also figures in terms of social isolation and artistic disconnection. While Manning's play satirises Dublin's vapid middle class and its values, it also critically interrogates the lack of space that the Irish Free State grants to deviating forms of masculinity.

Staging Manning's tragicomedy and Winsloe's tragedy in the 1930s, the Gate was clearly at the vanguard of exploring alternative sexualities. As Brian Singleton observes, addressing homosexuality on the Irish stage was a fraught process until relatively recently. Thomas Kilroy's *The Death and Resurrection of Mr Roche* (Olympia Theatre at the Dublin Theatre Festival, 1968), Brian Friel's *The Gentle Island* (Olympia Theatre, 1971), and Micheál mac Liammóir's *Prelude in Kazbek Street* (Gate Theatre, 1973) were plays that paved the way in this regard, followed by Aidan Mathews' *Diamond Body* (Operating Theatre, 1984).[46] In the 1990s, the canon of queer drama was significantly expanded by the work of Geraldine Aron. Her play *The Stanley Parkers*, produced by Druid in 1990, stages a mature Irish-Greek gay couple lying in bed, for instance.[47] Frank McGuinness's dramatic oeuvre also played a fundamental role in staging homosexuality, and in 2002 he wrote a play, commissioned by and staged at the Gate, about the gay relationship of its founders, Edwards and mac Liammóir. This play, *Gates of Gold*, looks at mac Liammóir's final days and celebrates homosexual love.[48] In view of the Gate's pioneering role in representing homosexuality, both through the drama it produced and in light of the lifestyle of its founders, this play was a fitting tribute to its emancipatory politics.

[45] Leeney, *Irish Women Playwrights, 1900–1939*, 127.
[46] Singleton, *Masculinities and the Contemporary Irish Theatre*, 110. Many thanks to David Clare for his useful comments on this section.
[47] Singleton, *Masculinities and the Contemporary Irish Theatre*, 111.
[48] Lojek, *Contexts for Frank McGuinness's Drama*, 578.

While Vroomen's chapter engages with a play that can thus be shown to stand in a larger tradition of contesting the marginalisation of queer identities, Part II also comprises two chapters that emphasise the Gate's role in emancipating other types of marginalised identities. Both Ian R. Walsh and Barry Houlihan write about the ways in which productions on the Gate stage drew attention to the living conditions of financially precarious social groups. In the summer of 1939, at a time of high unemployment and dire housing conditions in Dublin, the Edwards–mac Liammóir Company produced *Marrowbone Lane*, a play written by the outspoken paediatrician Robert Collis. Walsh analyses this play as a piece of theatre for social change. As Walsh reveals, *Marrowbone Lane* not only explicitly staged the intense suffering and harrowing circumstances of the working-class inhabitants of Dublin's tenements, but also stimulated the creation of a fund that contributed, *inter alia*, to the Fairy Hill Home established in Howth, Co. Dublin, for the treatment of children from Dublin's tenements who suffered from tuberculosis, and to the formation of the National Association for Cerebral Palsy, known today as Enable Ireland.

Barry Houlihan's chapter engages with the production and presentation of plays at the Gate Theatre that reflected political concerns relating to working-class identities during the 1960s and 1970s, of which *The Signalman's Apprentice* (1971) by Brian Phelan, directed by Chloe Gibson, was most prominent. In his discussion, Houlihan specifically focuses on the important work done by Phelan and Gibson in bringing socialist and feminist agendas to the Gate stage. Gibson especially is an often-overlooked figure in the study of direction at the Gate, and this chapter illustrates how her artistic contributions helped shape the Gate's societal engagement. While Irish and Northern Irish working-class drama, such as, for instance, Frank McGuinness's *The Factory Girls* (the Abbey, 1982) and Christina Reid's *Tea in a China Cup* (the Lyric, Belfast, 1983) have received much acclaim,[49] Gate plays that foreground class struggle and poverty in such poignant ways deserve further critical attention. One such play focusing on Dublin tenement life would also include Maura Laverty's *Liffey Lane*, produced by Edwards and mac Liammóir in May 1951.

The Gate's commitment to championing marginalised communities is also borne out by its engagement with issues of language. In *Speaking in Tongues: Languages at Play in the Theatre* (2009), Marvin Carlson examines the politicisation of minority languages by theatre companies, arguing that the function of speech as an instrument of 'cultural control' has encouraged

---

[49] For further reading, see Pierse, ed. *A History of Irish Working-Class Writing.*

theatres in postcolonial societies to give a stage to marginalised, indigenous languages.[50] Ireland's theatrical history reveals that especially the period between the foundation of Douglas Hyde's Gaelic League (1893) and the early years of the Free State saw a significant rise in drama in Irish. Douglas Hyde's *Casadh an tSúgáin*, performed at the Gaiety Theatre on 21 October 1901,[51] is generally considered to have been the first professional stage production in Irish as well as the Irish Literary Theatre's first 'peasant' play. This production was preceded by amateur productions in Irish, such as the staging of P.T. MacGinely's *Eilís agus an Bhean Déirce* by Inghinidhe na hÉireann at the Antient Concert Rooms, Dublin, in August of that year.[52]

Often acting groups or playhouses that committed to staging plays in the Irish language initially relied on translations of international plays into Irish. This was certainly the strategy of Galway-based theatre An Taibhdhearc (1928), the country's first Irish-language theatre, which often relied on translated plays for its stage productions in its early days. Nonetheless, as Christopher Morash notes, the theatre's opening play was *Diarmuid agus Gráinne*, written and directed by Micheál mac Liammóir, and An Taibhdhearc was soon 'nurturing a whole new generation of Irish-language playwrights.'[53]

Mac Liammóir's strong involvement in An Taibhdhearc in Galway ran parallel with the foundation of the Gate Theatre, and, while leading the Gate with Hilton Edwards, he would write many essays as well as translating plays into Irish. Additionally, the fact that the Gate opened its stage to the Irish-language company An Comhar Drámaíochta reveals that we should also examine the Gate's role in the emancipation of minority languages. It is therefore vital to compare the Gate as an emancipatory stage for minority languages to the work conducted by theatres such as the Peacock and An Damer in the 1960s. The two chapters in Part III, 'Staging Minority Languages,' are devoted to this largely under-researched aspect of the Gate's long history. Radvan Markus's chapter assesses various aspects of mac Liammóir's engagement with the Irish language, as well as his promotion of translation as a means to enrich Irish-language drama, in the context of his defence of the autonomy of art. As Markus reveals, mac Liammóir's support for Irish drama actually incorporated a critique of nationalism. In a paradoxical way, mac Liammóir envisaged opportunities

---

[50] Carlson, *Speaking in Tongues*, 105.
[51] Murphy, *Hegemony and Fantasy in Irish Drama*, 44, 48.
[52] Morash, *A History of the Irish Theatre*, 121.
[53] Morash, *A History of the Irish Theatre*, 178.

for reconciling localism and cosmopolitanism by integrating a local minority language with avant-garde artistic experimentation inspired by international models.

Feargal Whelan and David Clare subsequently discuss Micheál mac Liammóir's collaboration during the early Gate years with An Comhar Drámaíochta, which saw him directing translations of plays originally written by Anton Chekhov, Sacha Guitry, Gregorio Martínez Sierra, and Molière, among others. What is more, their contribution draws relevant and hitherto unexplored analogies between the Gate as a theatre of cultural and language emancipation and Barcelona's Teatre Lliure. As Whelan and Clare observe, both theatres benefitted from the central involvement of female, LGBTIQ+, and migrant theatre-makers, and both have promoted translations of international, cosmopolitan drama in the local minority language.

In this sense, their chapter also points forward to future possibilities of placing the Gate Theatre in a broader trans-European context of drama companies that put language emancipation on their artistic and political agendas. One could think, for example, of the Théâtre Populaire Breton, established in Sainte Anne d'Auray in 1909 by Job Le Bayon and Louis Cadic,[54] as well as the Théâtre populaire de Bretagne, founded in 1963 by Jean Moign and contributor to many regional theatre festivals.[55] Another example of a theatre that could be compared to the Gate as a stage of language emancipation is the Frisian Tryater, which, since its foundation in 1965, has played a prominent role in shaping regional identities through engagements with international repertoire, including Frisian adaptations of plays by John Osborne, Jean-Paul Sartre, Henrik Ibsen and Shakespeare, as well as in providing a platform for original plays in the Frisian language.[56]

Part IV, conversely, incorporates *non*-textual engagements by analysing the deconstructive aesthetics that underlie intersections between various artistic practices and the politics of identity. As both chapters in this section reveal, the Gate offered key opportunities to the female stage designer Molly MacEwen and the homosexual composer Frederick May, who in turn shifted aesthetic boundaries in significant ways. In his chapter, Mark Fitzgerald addresses the contributions that May – a student of Ralph Vaughan Williams – made to the Gate's productions of Padraic Colum's *Mogu of the Desert* (1931) and Denis Johnston's *A Bride for the*

---

[54] Wardhaugh, *Popular Theatre*, 88–101.
[55] Cadiou, *Emsav*, 4.
[56] Dykstra et al., 'Van Steen des Aanstoots tot Boegbeeld,' 263–302.

Unicorn (1933). As a young gay Irishman, May had to navigate a cultural infrastructure in which opportunities for composers were scarce, but at the Gate he was given the chance to develop his talents in a new field, as well as to experiment with musical forms in a high-profile setting. Siobhán O'Gorman completes this section with a chapter that questions received ideas about mac Liammóir's artistic centrality at the Gate. Indeed, she reveals that Molly MacEwen, a Scottish-born designer, produced a wide range of scenography for the Gate, from *Hollywood Pirate* in 1938 to *The Importance of Being Oscar*, mac Liammóir's famous one-man show about Wilde, in 1960. O'Gorman not only charts MacEwen's work at the Gate, but also outlines her legacy to the Scottish cultural revival more broadly after the Second World War.

The fifth and final part of this book – 'Contesting Traditions in Contemporary Theatre' – takes a flight in time, launching us into the present era of Selina Cartmell's artistic directorship. The two chapters in this part of the book discuss recent Gate productions: Yaël Farber's adaptation of *Hamlet* (2018) and Nancy Harris's *The Red Shoes* (2017), which is based on Hans Christian Andersen's fairy tale of the same name. In her introduction to *Feminist Theatrical Revisions of Classic Works* (2009), Sharon Friedman discusses the phenomena of genre-bending and plot revision in adaptations of classical works as 'deconstructive approaches to probe constructions of gender.'[57] This bending of plots and genre is what also characterises Harris's *The Red Shoes*, as Marguérite Corporaal reveals. In her chapter, she shows how Nancy Harris's reworking of Hans Christian Andersen's fairy tale for a contemporary audience exposes the at times brutal class and gender politics of the original narrative, while maintaining an engagement with traditional concepts of sin, resilience, and recovery. Harris's production lays bare gender and class inequalities that persist in present-day Ireland, but the play also stresses the role of ethnic bias and its intersections with gender stereotyping, as protagonist Karen's mother is judged even more severely because of her exotic background. Corporaal also discusses Farber's *Hamlet* production, starring Irish-Ethiopian actress Ruth Negga, in connection with issues of marginality, empowerment, and processes of in- or exclusion, demonstrating how particular aspects of the staging open the play up to interpretations of contemporary gender roles in relation to politics and globalisation.

Justine Nakase also addresses Farber's important *Hamlet* production, but instead focuses on issues of ethnicity. As Nakase argues, Negga's casting can be read as an acknowledgement of Ireland's increasingly

---

[57] Friedman, 'Introduction,' 1.

diverse population, and demonstrates a willingness to engage with new understandings of what it means to be Irish. Furthermore, her chapter situates Ruth Negga's *Hamlet* performance in the Gate's long history of Shakespeare productions, tracing four distinct iterations of racial performance on the Gate stage: cross-racial appropriation, imported authenticity, hidden histories, and emerging interculturalism. Performances of *Othello* during the Edwards–mac Liammóir years, and an adaptation of *Jane Eyre* (2003) under Michael Colgan's artistic directorship, as well as its revival with the casting of Black Irish actors Mary Healy and Donna Anita Nikolaisen as Bertha Mason, are analysed in this regard.

As this final part of the book reveals, then, cultural diversity and social emancipation can very well be expected to remain on the Gate Theatre's political agenda for years to come. After all, as Fintan O'Toole already wrote in the *Irish Times* of 30 June 2012, 'the long-term effects of inward migration will start to make themselves felt as the children of migrants become performers, directors and writers.'[58] Just as in the days of Edwards and mac Liammóir, Gate productions are travelling abroad: in February 2020, Ruth Negga and the rest of the *Hamlet* started their New York tour, which was unfortunately cut short by the Covid-19 pandemic. The fact that Cartmell chose to tour this specific production in a city known for ethnic diversity suggests that the Gate also seeks to contribute to discussions about race beyond Ireland. Furthermore, the aborted 2020 season was also set to exhibit such multiplicity: it opened with a reimagined version of *Medea* by Kate Mulvany and Anne-Louise Sarks, directed by Oonagh Murphy, followed by Nancy Harris's *Our New Girl*, which only had a short run before theatrical venues were shut down. Innovative stagings of Lillian Hellman's *The Little Foxes*, directed by Blanche McInture, and Seán O'Casey's *The Shadow of a Gunman*, directed by Louise Lowe, had to be cancelled altogether. Nevertheless, as Cartmell has stated in the *Irish Times*: 'I hope the staging of these important plays by four talented women can guide us towards being stronger and more courageous in our own lives.'[59] This volume illustrates both the historical dimension of this commitment to emancipation of all kinds – and certainly future engagements with other forms of inequality, societal marginalisation, and quests for liberation will follow suit.

---

[58] O'Toole, 'If Ireland has changed so much, why hasn't theatre kept pace?'
[59] Falvey, 'Ruth Negga takes Hamlet to New York.'

Bibliography

Allen, Nicholas. *Modernism, Ireland and Civil War*. Cambridge: Cambridge University Press, 2009.

Cadiou, Georges. *Emsav: Dictionnaire critique, historique et biographique: Le mouvement breton de A à Z*. Spézet: Coop Breizh, 2013.

Carlson, Marvin. *Speaking in Tongues: Languages at Play in the Theatre*. Ann Arbor: University of Michigan Press, 2009.

Coffey, Fiona Coleman. *Women in Northern Irish Theatre, 1921–2012*. Syracuse, NY: Syracuse University Press, 2016.

Corporaal, Marguérite. 'Katherine Philips: *Pompey, a Tragedy*.' In *Reading Early Modern Women*, edited by Helen Ostovich and Elizabeth Sauer, 158–62. London: Routledge, 2004.

Crawley, Peter. 'The Snapper Review: Fuzzy Memories with Intriguing Adjustments.' *Irish Times*, 21 June 2018. https://www.irishtimes.com/culture/stage/the-snapper-review-fuzzy-memories-with-intriguing-adjustments-1.3538805.

Cunningham, Gaye. 'Gate Theatre: Confidential Independent Review.' Dublin Gate Theatre. 1 March 2018.

Curtis, Maurice. *Temple Bar: A History*. Dublin: The History Press, 2016.

De Fréine, Celia. 'On Trial: The Challenge of Exploring on Stage the Lives of Irish Women.' *Breac* 4, no. 2 (2017). https://breac.nd.edu/articles/on-trial-the-challenge-of-exploring-on-stage-the-lives-of-irish-women/.

Donovan, Julie. *Lady Morgan and the Politics of Style*. Bethesda & Dublin: Academica Press, 2009.

Dykstra, Waling, et al. 'Van Steen des Aanstoots tot Boegbeeld: Toneel, Kleinkunst, Film vanaf 1860.' In *Zolang de Wind van de Wolken waait: Geschiedenis van de Friese Literatuur*, edited by Teake Oppeweal et al., 263–302. Amsterdam: Bert Bakker, 2006.

Falvey, Deirdre. 'Ruth Negga takes Hamlet to New York in Gate Theatre's 2020 Season.' *Irish Times*, 5 December 2019. https://www.irishtimes.com/culture/stage/ruth-negga-takes-hamlet-to-new-york-in-gate-theatre-s-2020-season-1.4105681.

Finberg, Melinda C. 'Introduction.' In *Eighteenth-Century Women Dramatists*, edited by Melinda C. Finberg, ix–xlvii. Oxford: Oxford University Press, 2001.

Friedman, Sharon. 'Introduction.' In *Feminist Theatrical Revisions of Classic Works: Critical Essays*, edited by Sharon Friedman, 1–14. Jefferson, NC: McFarland, 2009.

Gonne, Maud. *Dawn*. 1904. www.arts.gla.ac.uk/STELLA/C16/texts/MAUD GONNE/Dawn.rtf.

Hogan, Robert. Untitled. In *Enter Certain Players: Edwards–Mac Liammoir and the Gate 1928–1978*, edited by Peter Luke, 13–18. Dublin: Dolmen Press, 1978.

Ingrassia, Catherine. *Authorship, Commerce, and Gender in Early Eighteenth-Century England*. Cambridge: Cambridge University Press, 1998.

Leeney, Cathy. *Irish Women Playwrights, 1900–1939: Gender and Violence on Stage*. Oxford: Peter Lang, 2010.

Leeney, Cathy. 'Women and Irish Theatre before 1960.' In *The Oxford Handbook of Modern Irish Theatre*, edited by Nicholas Grene and Chris Morash, 269–85. Oxford: Oxford University Press, 2016.

Lojek, Helen Heusner. *Contexts for Frank McGuinness's Drama*. Washington, DC: CUA Press, 2004.

Lonergan, Patrick. *Irish Drama and Theatre since 1950*. London: Methuen, 2019.

Luddy, Maria. 'A "Sinister and Retrogressive" Proposal: Irish Women's Opposition to the 1937 Draft Constitution.' *Transactions of the Royal Historical Society* 15 (2005): 175–95.

Mackin, Laurence, and Conor Gallagher. 'Seven women allege abuse and harassment by Michael Colgan.' *Irish Times*, 4 November 2017. https://www.irishtimes.com/news/ireland/irish-news/seven-women-allege-abuse-and-harassment-by-michael-colgan-1.3279488.

Manning, Mary. Untitled. In *Enter Certain Players: Edwards–mac Liammoir and the Gate 1928–1978*, edited by Peter Luke, 35–39. Dublin: Dolmen Press, 1978.

Mannion, Una. 'Live Art in Ireland.' In *The Palgrave Handbook of Contemporary Irish Theatre and Performance*, edited by Eamonn Jordan and Eric Weitz, 93–113. Basingstoke: Palgrave, 2018.

McIvor, Charlotte. 'Introduction: New Directions?' In *Interculturalism and Performance Now: New Directions?*, edited by Charlotte McIvor and Jason King, 1–26. London: Palgrave Macmillan, 2019.

McIvor, Charlotte. *Migration and Performance in Contemporary Ireland: Towards a New Interculturalism*. London: Palgrave Macmillan, 2016.

Meaney, Gerardine. *Gender, Ireland and Cultural Change: Race, Sex and Nation*. London: Routledge, 2012.

Meaney, Gerardine, Mary O'Dowd, and Bernadette Whelan. *Reading the Irish Woman: Studies in Cultural Encounters and Exchange, 1714–1960*. Liverpool: Liverpool University Press, 2013.

Morash, Christopher. *A History of the Irish Theatre, 1601–2000*. Cambridge: Cambridge University Press, 2002.

Morash, Christopher. '"Where All Ladders Start": Famine Memories in Yeats's *Countess Cathleen*.' In *Global Legacies of the Great Irish Famine: Transnational and Interdisciplinary Perspectives*, edited by Marguérite Corporaal et al., 119–37. New York: Peter Lang, 2014.

Morse, Donald E. 'Introduction: The *Irish Theatre in Transition*.' In *Irish Theatre in Transition: From the Late Nineteenth to the Early Twenty-First Century*, edited by Donald E. Morse, 1–9. Basingstoke and New York: Palgrave Macmillan, 2015.

Murphy, Paul. *Hegemony and Fantasy in Irish Drama, 1899–1949*. Basingstoke: Palgrave, 2008.

O'Toole, Fintan. 'If Ireland has changed so much, why hasn't theatre kept pace?' *Irish Times*, 30 June 2012. https://www.irishtimes.com/culture/tv-radio-web/if-ireland-has-changed-so-much-why-hasn-t-theatre-kept-pace-1.1069909.

Pierse, Michael, ed. *A History of Irish Working-Class Writing*. Cambridge: Cambridge University Press, 2018.

Pierse, Michael. *Writing Ireland's Working Class: Dublin after O'Casey*. London: Palgrave Macmillan, 2011.

Pilný, Ondřej, Ruud van den Beuken, and Ian R. Walsh. 'Introduction: Cultural Convergence at Dublin's Gate Theatre.' In *Cultural Convergence: The Dublin Gate Theatre, 1928–1960*, edited by Ondřej Pilný, Ruud van den Beuken, and Ian R. Walsh, 1–13. London: Palgrave Macmillan, 2021.

Quinn, Antoinette. 'Ireland/Herland: Women and Literary Nationalism, 1845–1916.' In *The Field Day Anthology of Irish Writing*, Vol. 5, edited by Angela Bourke et al., 889–98. Cork: Cork University Press, 2002.

Remport, Eglantina. *Lady Gregory and Irish National Theatre: Art, Drama, Politics*. Basingstoke: Palgrave, 2018.

Scott, Michael. Untitled. In *Enter Certain Players: Edwards–mac Liammoir and the Gate 1928–1978*, edited by Peter Luke, 19–20. Dublin: Dolmen Press, 1978.

Shepherd, Simon. *Theatre, Body, and Pleasure*. London: Routledge, 2013.

Sihra, Melissa. 'Introduction: Figures at the Window.' In *Women in Irish Drama: A Century of Authorship and Representation*, edited by Melissa Sihra, 1–22. London: Palgrave Macmillan, 2007.

Sihra, Melissa. *Marina Carr: Pastures of the Unknown*. Basingstoke: Palgrave, 2018.

Singleton, Brian. *Masculinities and the Contemporary Irish Theatre*. Basingstoke: Palgrave, 2011.

Sweeney, Bernadette. *Performing the Body in Irish Theatre*. Basingstoke: Palgrave, 2008.

Taylor, Colleen. 'Sydney Owenson, Alicia Sheridan Le Fanu and the Domestic Stage of Post-Union Politics.' In *Ireland, Enlightenment and the English Stage, 1740–1820*, edited by David O'Shaughnessy, 146–65. Cambridge: Cambridge University Press, 2019.

Valente, Joseph. *The Myth of Manliness in Irish National Cuture, 1880–1922*. Chicago, IL: University of Illinois Press, 2011.

Van den Beuken, Ruud. *Avant-Garde Nationalism at the Dublin Gate Theatre, 1928–1940*. Syracuse, NY: Syracuse University Press, 2020.

Van den Beuken, Ruud. 'MacLiammóir's Minstrel and Johnston's Morality: Cultural Memories of the Easter Rising at the Dublin Gate Theatre.' *Irish Studies Review* 23, no. 1 (2015): 1–14.

Van den Beuken, Ruud. '"Three cheers for the Descendancy!": Middle-class Dreams and (Dis)illusions in Mary Manning's *Happy Family* (1934).' In *Navigating Ireland's Theatre Archive: Theory, Practice, Performance*, edited by Barry Houlihan, 141–57. Oxford: Peter Lang, 2019.

Walsh, Fintan. *Queer Performance in Contemporary Ireland: Dissent and Disorientation*. London: Palgrave Macmillan, 2016.

Wardhaugh, Jessica. *Popular Theatre and Political Utopia in France, 1870–1940: Active Citizens*. Basingstoke: Palgrave, 2017

PART I
Liberating Bodies

• 2 •

Queering the Irish Actress

The Gate Theatre Production of *Children in Uniform* (1934)

Mary Trotter

The year 1934 offered good opportunities for women artists at the Gate Theatre, Dublin. The company produced actress[1] and director Ria Mooney's adaptation of *Wuthering Heights*, in which she also starred. The Gate also staged *Happy Family*, a new drama by Mary Manning, whose play *Youth's the Season–?* had been well received by Dublin audiences in 1931. Women also held positions of power and responsibility off-stage and in theatre administration. Mary Manning, for example, worked as the lead editor of *Motley*, the Gate Theatre's journal, and Daisy 'Toto' Bannard Cogley served on its board of directors. New women practitioners were getting their chance behind the scenes as well. In December of 1934, nineteen-year-old Mairin Hayes became the Gate's assistant stage manager, a technical position usually held by men.

I am indebted to the editors of this volume for their excellent comments to a draft of this work. I am also very grateful to the staff at the Deering Special Collections at Northwestern University for their guidance through the rich resources of the Dublin Gate Theatre Archive.

[1] While theatre practitioners and researchers increasingly use the gender-neutral term 'actor' for performers of all genders, I use the term 'actress' here to note the universal use of the term in 1930s Western theatre. I also use this term to highlight assumptions inherent in early twentieth-century theatre circles that read the female actor as fundamentally different than her male counterpart, and how that gender differentiation often translated into lack of access for women to particular kinds of agency in rehearsal, roles in performance, and power in theatre administration. These inconsistencies across theatre traditions have been discussed widely in such works as Wandor's *Carry On Understudies* and the recent report of the #WakingTheFeminists movement.

However, one of the more extraordinary opportunities for women at the Gate that year came with the decision to produce *Children in Uniform* by the queer feminist Prussian author Christa Winsloe. Known today for its homoerotic subtext, brought vividly forward in Leontine Sagan's 1931 film version of the play,[2] and certainly present in its theatrical performances in London and New York before coming to Dublin, it is not surprising that the Gate Theatre chose to take on Winsloe's drama for its artistically and culturally progressive Dublin patrons.[3] But what made *Children in Uniform* even more unusual for the Dublin theatre scene in the 1930s – or any other decade – was the fact that the play provided so many good roles for women. In the 1930s, as today, plays with several leading parts for women, featuring fully developed women characters or plots that do not centre around male characters, were rare. Remarkably, *Children in Uniform* has over thirty roles, many of them complex, and an all-woman cast. Even the group that performed music during the intervals, the Gate Theatre Trio, was made up entirely of women during the play's performance.[4] The Gate production of *Children in Uniform* gave many of Dublin's finest actresses an opportunity to play in ensemble with one another on a scale unprecedented in the Irish dramatic movement to that date.

Staging this play thus reflected the Gate's respect for its women actors, and an opportunity for them to show their craft outside the parameters of traditional women's roles on Irish stages in early twentieth-century

---

[2] Fest, 'Yesterday and/or Today,' 457–71.

[3] The German film of this play, *Mädchen in Uniform* (1931) created a great stir internationally and is still regarded as one of the first lesbian films, thanks largely to the queer eye of its director, Leontine Sagan. The teenaged girls are played by women in their twenties in the film, which also makes the homosociality of the girls' adolescent exuberance toward one another and their young teacher more obvious than it would be with younger actors. In 1932 the English translation of the play was produced in London, with Joyce Bland playing Von Bernberg and twenty-three-year-old Jessica Tandy as Manuela. That same year, the play, under the title *Girls in Uniform*, was produced on Broadway, and touted by *New York Times* critic Brooks Atkinson (in '"Maedchen in Uniform") for its casting of young amateurs in the student roles, including a 'shop girl' playing the lead, Manuela. Reviews of these theatrical productions in mainstream newspapers praise Winsloe's play as the tragedy of an oversensitive girl in a strict boarding school, signalling its homoerotic subtext to those in the know, but not commenting directly on it.

[4] According to the programme for *Girls in Uniform*, the Gate Theatre Trio featured three women musicians: Bay Jellett (violin and director), Cathleen Rogers (piano), and Gretta Smith (cello).

Ireland. It also provided the Gate with a vehicle to explore ideas about female homosociality and sexuality that were pointedly counter both to the Abbey Theatre's aesthetic, and to the increasingly conservative mainstream culture of 1930s Ireland. By producing a performative, all-woman critique of patriarchy and heteronormativity's impact on Prussian schoolgirls in Weimar Germany, the Gate Theatre created a space for its audiences not only to rethink particular notions of gender normativity, but also to imagine a feminist theatre practice outside the patriarchal confines of most modern drama to that date. Thinking of Jill Dolan's notion of utopia in performance, or the potential of theatre 'to inspire moments in which audiences feel themselves allied with each other, and with a broader, more capacious sense of a public, in which social discourse articulates the possible, rather than the insurmountable obstacles to human potential,'[5] the Gate Theatre performance of *Children in Uniform* created a space to imagine both more inclusive ways to think about gender and sexuality, and more complex ways to think about both women characters in drama and women actors on stage.[6]

The Gate as an Alternative Theatre in 1930s Dublin

The Gate Theatre's reputation as an outlet for international avant-garde performance and frank discussions of sexuality in conservative Ireland is certainly confirmed by this production. Research by historians and critics such as Joan FitzPatrick Dean, Elaine Sisson and others has brought to light the important influence of the Irish artistic counter-culture in the 1920s on Irish theatre, art and literature in the 1930s, pointing out that the Gate Theatre was an exceptionally productive space for women playwrights and designers that emerged from this alternative Dublin scene. They have also brought to the fore the Gate's roots in other arts and cultural organisations, such as the Dublin Drama League, An Taibhdhearc, and

---

5 Dolan, *Utopia in Performance*, 2.

6 In her ground-breaking book, *Utopia in Performance*, Jill Dolan theorises how theatre can create moments of *communitas* for audiences. She describes utopian performatives as 'small but profound moments in which performance calls the attention of the audience in a way that lifts everyone slightly above the present, into a hopeful feeling of what the world might be like if every moment of our lives were as emotionally voluminous, generous, aesthetically striking, and intersubjectively intense.' Such moments are plentiful in the Gate Theatre production of *Children in Uniform*, and many more of their plays in the 1930s. Dolan, *Utopia in Performance*, 5.

cabaret.[7] These works point out that while women played major roles in the counter-cultural movement, their influence can be difficult to trace.

For instance, by following the work of Madame Bannard Cogley in establishing the Studio Arts Club in the 1920s, Elaine Sisson has uncovered 'a largely lost and invisible socio-cultural network of artists, actors, singers, bohemians, gay men and women, atheists, feminists, communists, refugees and general misfits,' many of whom 'turn up in the Gate Theatre Playlists from 1928 onwards' as actors, designers, directors, and writers. 'This circle of thinkers,' Sisson argues, 'unlike the generation that had gone before (Yeats, Markievicz, Pearse, etc.) are not engaged in formal politics; instead they are engaged in shaping a new cultural iteration: connected to Europe, modern, energised artists and activists.'[8] The often pointedly queer aspects of production and performance among this group created spaces for artists outside the growing cultural conservatism taking hold in 1930s Ireland.[9] But the Gate had to be careful to articulate its queer sensibilities in oblique, coded ways. As theatre producer Phyllis Ryan, a teenager during this period, recalled, 'the Abbey Theatre was known as the "Monastery" by those sophisticates who favoured the Gate. But the Gate people were also inhibited as far as the spoken word was concerned when the subject was delicate, and although sex might be lurking underneath, limits were imposed.'[10] Gender and sexuality norms could be challenged in performance, as long as the challenge was not directly identified as such.

Although not publicly addressed in reviews at the time of its performance at the Gate, *Children in Uniform*'s non-binary gender possibilities were not only sexual, but political and social as well. The play absolutely fitted the bill for the kind of work to which this new generation of artists inhabiting the Gate aspired. It was European, its modernity suited mac Liammóir's and Edwards's production aesthetic, and it gave company actors excellent material with which to practise their craft. However, *Children in Uniform* did more than push the envelope of acceptability for representations of sexuality in 1930s Dublin. It also gave Irish women performers an opportunity to expand for Dublin audiences – and for themselves – the range of possibilities for the expression of women's experience on stage.

---

[7] Examples of this research in the Gate Theatre's relationship to other avant-garde movements include Sisson, 'Experimentalism and the Irish Stage,' 39–58; Sisson, 'Experiment and the Free State,' 11–28; Dean, *All Dressed Up*; and Meaney, O'Dowd, and Whelan, 'Sexual and Aesthetic Dissidences,' 196–217.

[8] Sisson, 'Experiment and the Free State,' 18.

[9] See Dean, *Riot and Great Anger* and Pilkington, *Theatre and the State in Ireland*.

[10] Ryan, *The Company I Kept*, 34.

Leading lights of the Dublin theatre scene took the main roles in this production. Ria Mooney, then thirty-one, and with several iconic roles to her name, played the headmistress.[11] Coralie Carmichael, also in her thirties and a long-standing leader in the Gate Theatre and the liberal artistic scene that surrounded it, played the role of the beloved Fräulein Von Bernberg. The twenty-four-year-old Betty Chancellor, who had performed several romantic leads at the Gate, played the teenaged Manuela. Other well-known faces in the cast included Hazel Ellis, Geraldine Fitzgerald, and Ann Dowling. As mentioned above, when these actresses played their roles in *Children in Uniform*, the Gate Theatre audience would have recognised them not only as bodies performing a theatrical role, but known persons, whose choices, gestures, and presence on the stage echoed audience members' knowledge of them personally and/or memories of their performance in other theatrical roles. To see so many actresses on stage in a play completely devoid of male roles, and without male influences directly informing the plot, was to see a radical alternative to the male-dominated theatre canon. As the audience watched these actors perform a play about women's queer desire, they also saw the actresses on stage queer Dublin theatre's largely heteronormative theatrical canon, making visible not only the quality but the sheer number of actresses in 1930s Dublin who were ready to work and who wanted to tell modern stories.

Indeed, the celebrity status of several of the actors in Dublin theatre circles – particularly Ria Mooney, Coralie Carmichael, Betty Chancellor, and Mary Manning – urged the audience to address any connection or dissonance between the actress's professional career and her identification with previous roles, and the character she now played. The script of the play imagines a naïve child falling in love with an idealistic teacher. In performance, the audience saw actresses playing the characters that the text described. However, on another level they also saw Betty Chancellor, an actress in her twenties known for ingenue roles like Ophelia in *Hamlet*, playing an adolescent girl falling in love with her teacher and dorm mistress played by Coralie Carmichael, an actress in her thirties who had performed the titular character in Wilde's *Salome*. For an audience intimately familiar with a company actress's work beyond the performance currently before

---

[11] In addition to her prominent work at the Abbey and the Gate, Mooney spent 1928–30 as a member of New York's Civic Repertory Theatre. Led by the Eva Le Gallienne, and featuring queer artists such as Alla Nazimova (whose dramatic fashion sense Mooney emulated for some time), the Civic gave Mooney the opportunity to work in an atmosphere of female leadership, gender inclusivity, and sexual open-mindedness. See Mooney, 'Players and the Painted Stage,' 3–120.

them, an actress's connection to previous characters and types she had played would inevitably shadow audience interpretation of her current performance. The audience for *Children in Uniform* at the Gate, then, saw a teenaged girl develop a crush on her adult teacher, but they also saw, on some level, Ophelia fall in love with Salome.

Children in Uniform thus illustrates how the Gate Theatre production of this play offered not only a (potentially) queer perspective on female sexuality, but also – and more importantly – queered particular notions of female gender performance that had come to be ossified in the growing Irish realist/naturalist canon, and the performance of gender in Irish everyday life. By reading how Gate Theatre actors tested those limits on stage, we can gain insight into the effect of these plays on audiences eager to challenge the conservative status quo.

Children in Uniform's Queer Feminism

Children in Uniform was written by Christa Winsloe, a queer Prussian aristocrat, who became a writer in the 1920s and died serving in the French resistance during the Second World War. Originally titled *Gestern und Heute* (*Yesterday and Today*), Winsloe's 1930 drama reflects not only the tragic death of an emotional young girl, but also the cruelty of the Prussian educational system that Winsloe experienced in her own childhood, and that system's roots in defunct cultural practices. Set in Weimar Germany, the play follows the tragic demise of Manuela, a fifteen-year-old girl sent away to a boarding school that was devoted to using strict discipline to promote the values expected of women who may marry military officers; namely 'Kirche, Küche, Kinder' [church, kitchen, children].[12] Throughout the play, the children are reminded of their duty to serve the nation as wives and mothers. Thus, we see not only the tragedy of the girls' stifled individuality and desire for affection, but also the irony of their preparing for life in a military cultural tradition undermined by modernity and usurped by encroaching fascism.[13]

---

[12] Ironically, this Prussian phrase about women's special role in the state as upholders of morality, homemakers, and mothers resonates with the growing religion-based gender conservatism in 1930s Ireland.

[13] Deeney argues that readings by British critics of the play as a critique of German culture, rather than sexuality, helped get the work past the UK's strict censorship laws for public theatre performances. He argues that the licence to perform the play in London 'was demonstrably influenced by the Advisory Committee, particularly by Bonham Carter's view that Manuela's actions were an indictment of an "uncompromisingly German education system. From the Censor's position

Manuela manages to make friends with other girls at the school and develops a close bond with her teacher and dorm mistress, Fräulein Von Bernberg. Von Bernberg is liked more than other teachers because although she is strict, she can also be kind, and she kisses each girl in her dormitory good night every evening. On her first night at the school, Manuela shivers with anticipation at being kissed by Fräulein Von Bernberg, having not been kissed good night since her mother's death years before. Later in the play, Manuela remarks that she is too nervous to answer questions in Von Bernberg's classes because she is so eager to please her. Throughout the script, the stage directions instruct the actor playing Manuela to shiver with anticipation when speaking of or being near Von Bernberg. Von Bernberg, understanding Manuela's sensitive nature and reduced economic circumstances, realises that she needs special care. Although she warns Manuela not to tell the other girls since she cannot show preference, she does assure her that 'I think about you very much,'[14] thus solidifying Manuela's belief that she has a special personal relationship with her teacher.

While nervous around Van Bernberg, Manuela shows confidence in her boy-like behaviour at school. Manuela's non-conforming attitudes towards gender expectations are shown throughout the play in her enjoyment of playing male roles and her disinterest in heteronormative sexual relationships. When her dancing instructor engages her in a minuet and '[s]he dances as gentleman to the old lady,'[15] Manuela relishes the moment. But she is dismissive of situations that place her in a heteronormative feminine role, such as receiving a secret letter containing a proposal of marriage from her fencing instructor. When another girl, finding the letter romantic, asks Manuela if she is going to answer it, Manuela replies with absolute disdain: 'It's bad enough I've had to read it. And I have to give up my fencing lessons.' She also remarks that seeing her instructor again 'would make her quite sick.'[16] Manuela's distress lies not in receiving a marriage proposal from a man many years her senior, but rather in no longer being able to practise a male-identified sport. Compared to Manuela's exuberant desire for her female teacher's

---

– it is important to heed that the Lord Chamberlain was an official of the royal household – Children in Uniform played into the axiom of British supremacy during an auspicious period in German and European history."' Deeney, 'Censoring the Uncensored,' 222.

[14] Winsloe, *Children in Uniform*, 42.

[15] Winsloe, *Children in Uniform*, 16.

[16] Winsloe, *Children in Uniform*, 38.

passion, her dismissal of the opportunity and/or the threat of having an adult man willing to 'rescue' her from the drudgeries of school life by making her a wife point to a gender identity in Manuela that was more interested in close relationships with women than culturally sanctioned intimacy with one man.

In Act Two, we see another example of Manuela's identification with traditionally male social roles when she performs the theatrical role of Nerestan (a male knight in armour) for a school festival before students and staff. One of the servants at the school comments on how well Manuela played the part and how 'her voice sounded so deep – not a bit like her own voice,'[17] implying that the performance transformed her into her role as the manly young knight she portrayed. Still dressed as a knight after the performance, but in a 'breeches role' costume with 'silver armour' and 'unbound hair'[18] that ironically highlights her female frame, Manuela basks in the praise of her fellow students and their reports of how the teachers admired her. She brushes off the news that the headmistress, Fräulein Von Nordeck, commented that Manuela had 'nice legs,' since that 'had nothing to do with the role.' But she is thrilled to learn of Fräulein Von Bernberg's response: 'ILSE: That was a queer do! The Bernberg never said a word (*Manuela shrinks*) But she looked my dear! Oh, she looked ... her eyes!'[19] Manuela is dismissive of Von Nordeck finding her exposed legs pretty in her 'breeches role' costume designed to show off her feminine frame. But she longs for Von Bernberg's attention, and seems, based on Ilse's interpretation, to have been the object of her teacher's silent gaze, offering the audience the opportunity to project into Von Bernberg's silence the teacher's approval, or perhaps even her desire, for Manuela.

At the meal served to the girls after the performance (where they are unusually unsupervised) one of the servants accidentally serves a very strong alcoholic drink and Manuela becomes intoxicated. After several minutes of joyful celebration among the girls, the drunk Manuela, in her excitement, reveals to the other girls the secret that Fräulein Von Bernberg gave her one of her own chemises, and announces that Von Bernberg 'loves me! ... and I will serve her ... life has no other meaning.'[20] The headmistress and other teachers overhear Manuela's expression of devotion for her teacher, including the gift of an undergarment, and they break up the girls' party

---

[17] Winsloe, *Children in Uniform*, 44.
[18] Winsloe, *Children in Uniform*, 44.
[19] Winsloe, *Children in Uniform*, 44.
[20] Winsloe, *Children in Uniform*, 52.

as the headmistress declares 'Scandalous!'[21] Manuela faints from drink and excitement and is sent to the infirmary.

In Act Three, a hungover and upset Manuela awakens in the infirmary, where she is admonished for her behaviour by the headmistress. Manuela runs to Fräulein Von Bernberg's room for comfort, where Von Bernberg receives her even though she has been warned not to speak to the girl. When Manuela learns that she is to be punished with solitary confinement, and no longer allowed to speak to either her classmates or with Von Bernberg, she is devastated. Aware of Manuela's distress and her naïveté about the sexual connotations of her remarks among the other schoolgirls the evening before, Von Bernberg tells Manuela, 'You must not love me so much. It is wrong. It is harmful – it is a sin.'[22] Manuela rushes from the room, and Von Bernberg is about to follow her when the headmistress appears and admonishes the younger teacher for disobeying her orders. They argue about the military discipline imposed on the girls, but are interrupted when another teacher bursts in to inform them that Manuela has jumped from a window to her death. The headmistress closes the play with the response to the news that they will say the girl's death was an accident, thus covering up the school's failure to keep their student safe, as well as any question of Manuela's non-conformity to the school's patriarchal status quo.

The Gate Theatre Production

The Gate Theatre production of this drama was a tremendous success, with an extended run. Reviews, likewise, were positive, but relatively short and generally focused on the quality of the acting,[23] with no real commentary on any potentially queer readings on the work. As in mainstream reviews of the *Children in Uniform* productions in London and New York, reading the play as a condemnation of the cruelty of Prussian aristocratic boarding schools trumped considerations of homosociality or homosexual desire in the play. One reviewer of the Gate production commented in *The Evening Standard*, however, that the acting was superb, but read the girls in the

---

[21] According to the Gate Theatre prompt copy of the script, Edwards changed the line from 'Scandalous!' to 'A scandal!' in his 1934 production of the play. I believe this switch from an adjective to a noun to describe the event shows how, in the Gate Production, Von Norbeck is less angry about Manuela's behaviour as indecent than she is with the idea that it will cause public outrage if it is revealed. Winsloe, *Children in Uniform*, 52.

[22] Winsloe, *Children in Uniform*, 69.

[23] Meaney, O'Dowd, and Whelan, 'Sexual and Aesthetic Dissidences,' 214.

play as mentally unstable, stating that 'the play would have been more convincing had the girls been a more normal type' and that 'Manuela, superbly played by Betty Chancellor, is a sensitive, imaginative child, but she is morbid, and it is the weakness of her own character more than the stern, loveless system of the school that drives her to her death.'[24] The review's pathologising of Manuela's desire, blaming her suicide on a 'weakness of character,' reflects the homophobia inherent in mainstream Irish culture at the time and helps explain why other reviewers, more sensitive to the drama's consideration of same-sex desire, chose to focus on acting technique over content.

Most Gate Theatre patrons, however, would have been perfectly aware of *Children in Uniform*'s queer sexual overtones in performance because of the content of the play and the context of seeing members of Dublin's arts scene performing it on stage. Others may have also seen the 1931 film adaptation of the play. Although there is no film record of the Gate Theatre's production, stills from the play, along with the prompt book listing blocking, lighting, and sound cues, give insight into how the production played up expressionist elements in the drama to highlight the conflict between Manuela's innocent exuberance and sexual awakening and her forced repression by a suffocating educational system that was designed to uphold patriarchal, heteronormative social structures.

The prompt book and photographs of the Gate production also show how well-suited *Children in Uniform* was to the Gate's aesthetic. While the West End and Broadway productions of the play chose more realistic stage designs, Hilton Edwards let loose with his powerfully dramatic lighting style, relying heavily on expressionistic shadow effects. In several images from the Gate production, we see the students cringing in disciplined lines, while the headmistress's shadow towers above them on the back of the set. The stage itself was largely bare of decoration, adding to the feel of spartan poverty at the school, with a small light hanging above the centre stage, and simple set pieces such as a chest, tables, and beds placed on and off as the scenes required. The superb use of light and shadow in performance reminds the viewer of the inner life and strong emotions of the characters, even as they are forced to circumscribe their bodies to the strict discipline of school life.

The sound design of the production likewise added to the expressionist feel of the play. Hilton Edwards, who directed the production while mac Liammóir designed sets and costumes, replaced the acoustic bell used in the original play with the insistent, jarring, electric sound. This bell rang

---

[24] See the review 'Children in Uniform,' published in *Evening Herald*.

at key times throughout the drama, including the beginning and ending of each act, underlining the sense of discipline to the clock and subservience to the system expected not only of the students but also the school staff. Edwards likewise used the sound of a military drum and marching feet to reflect the rigour of the school structure. The third, and perhaps most malevolent of the sound effects representing school discipline, is that of the headmistress's cane. The prompt book includes Hilton Edwards's very precise instructions about when the headmistress would pound her cane on the floor. Ria Mooney, who played this role, was directed by Edwards to start pounding her cane before appearing on stage so that the sound of her approach could appear all the more intimidating.

The headmistress's pounding cane was also used to emphasise her speech. For instance, in the text, the play ends with the headmistress declaring Manuela's suicide 'an accident,'[25] announcing her cover-up for Manuela's death as a verdict and rewriting the painful truth of the situation and her complicity in it to suit the violence of a system that led a pupil of her school to suicide. To emphasise the forcefulness of the headmistress's declaration, however, Edwards added repetition to the final line in the prompt book and included thick horizontal lines noting when the actor was to strike her cane on the floor as she walks off-stage. In the Gate Theatre production, according to the prompt book, Von Nordeck declares (using her cane for emphasis), 'We'll tell [our school patron] there has been an accident (knock) an accident (knock) accident (knock. knock. knock. knock).'[26]

Edwards expanded this final scene beyond the scripted dialogue and blocking to add to the pathos of the situation and make palpable to the audience the depth of Von Bernberg's grief. In the original script, the headmistress and Von Bernberg are alone in the latter's room. In the Gate production, the students file into the room amid the confusion around Manuela's death; then, when the headmistress declares her verdict on Manuela's death and leaves the room, the girls, spiritually defeated, form a line behind her and trail out of the room, as the sound effect of drums fills the auditorium. Edwards gives the last gesture of the play to Coralie Carmichael as Von Bernberg who, left standing alone in her room after all have filed out, collapses onto a table. The scripted ending, leaving Von Bernberg and the headmistress standing along together on stage, makes the two women unhappy allies left to return order to the school after Manuela's death. The Gate Theatre's production choice, however, shows Von Bernberg's

[25] Winsloe, *Children in Uniform*, 72.
[26] Winsloe, *Children in Uniform*, 72.

alienation from and abjection to Von Nordeck's rigid adherence to the status quo. Unable to return to the decorum shown by the other teachers and students, who return to the rigid formalities of drums, walking sticks and straight lines, Von Bernberg's collapse betrays her inability to uphold the patriarchal tradition of *Kirche, Küche, Kinder* for her wards, or for herself.

It is tempting to read the climax of Winsloe's play as a conservative social corrective for the intrinsic queerness of the text, so that Manuela's death pathologises her resistance to gender norms and proves what *The Evening Standard*'s review of the play called her 'morbidity.' But Hilton Edwards's addition of Von Bernberg's physical collapse reads against that interpretation, showing instead a moment of empathy for Manuela and the potential for future resistance. Such a reading may indeed have served as a fig leaf for the play for the uptight reader, offering an example of how the Gate had to work within 'limits' when approaching 'delicate manners.'[27] But in performance, before an alert audience, the readings were likely quite different, seeing in the production moments filled with potential for the audience to commune with the actors and one another in imagining a 'utopian performative,' where actresses were serious actors, and where all love was love.

One of the scenes in the Gate production of *Children in Uniform* with the most potential to make a space for a queer feminist imagination of theatre – that is, the best chance of creating a 'utopian performative'[28] – occurs during Act II of the play, when the students, some still dressed in their costumes after performing *Zaire*, celebrate during their post-show dinner. The girls' conversation quickly turns to the age-old argument about the nature of acting, and why the occupation is especially fraught for women:

> EDELGARD: (*rather out of her depth*) But Manuela, would you honestly like to be an actress?
> MANUELA: (*dreamily*) Yes, I should! It's strange – you are yourself and not yourself. You are really another person, yet you laugh and cry like yourself.
> ILSE: Well, you can laugh and cry without acting.
> MANUELA: No, Ilse, never ... enough!
> ILSE: But why not?
> MANUELA: Because one may never show what one feels –
> ILSE: I don't get that.

---

[27] Ryan, *The Company I Kept*, 39.
[28] Dolan, *Utopia in Performance*, 5.

MANUELA: Well, in the first place it's not well bred. Father
   says to me: "Never show your feelings. It's not even decent."
ODA: Is that so – well then – *you* must have indecent feelings!
MANUELA: (*surprised*). I? Indecent feelings?
MARGA: (*reprovingly*). Oda, you must be mad! Don't judge
   others by your own standard!
ANNA: Really! What does she mean? …
… TRIESCHKE: Girls, don't make a row!
MANUELA: (*topping them*). Nobody's making a row! We're all
   good friends here, aren't we? And if Oda wants to know, I
   only understand beautiful and ugly feelings. What indecent
   feelings are, I don't know. (*rising*). Your health, Oda!
ODA: (*rising.*) Your health, Manuela![29]

In this moment, Winsloe puts into the mouth of Oda the old anti-theatrical
argument that actors – particularly women actors – are untrustworthy,
immoral, and thus separate from respectable social networks. But she also
shares through Manuela's words (spoken by Betty Chancellor on a stage
filled with other actresses and no men) the potential to explore and inhabit
new ideas, new emotions, new ways of being. Manuela has the last word
and the girls toast one another. While the moment is short-lived in the
play, it does embody a homosocial space in which feelings are categorised
only as beautiful or ugly and hierarchical ideas of decency and indecency
do not hold sway. As queer and queer allied spectators watched a stage
full of Gate Theatre actresses perform this scene, inside a theatre space
that served as a vital outlet for queer bodies to create community through
art, it is likely that members of the audience imagined themselves on stage
around that table of joyful schoolgirls, and joined in Manuela's toast.

Bibliography

Atkinson, Brooks. '"Maedchen in Uniform" Becomes "Girls in Uniform" on the
   Stage.' *New York Times*, 31 December 1932. 10.
'Children in Uniform.' *Evening Herald*, 11 April 1934. 3.
Dean, Joan FitzPatrick. *All Dressed Up: Modern Irish Historical Pageantry*. Syracuse,
   NY: Syracuse University Press, 2014.

---

[29] The actors onstage in this scene in 1934 were Noel Delany (Oda), Geraldine
   Fitzgerald (Ilse), Betty Chancellor (Manuela), Dorrie Monson (Edelgard), Rosemary
   Molloy (Marga), Sheila May (Anna), Mairin Hayes (Trieschke), and Peggy Pelissier
   (José). See 'Programme for *Children in Uniform*.'

Dean, Joan FitzPatrick. *Riot and Great Anger: Stage Censorship in Twentieth-Century Ireland.* Madison: University of Wisconsin Press, 2004.

Deeney, John F. 'Censoring the Uncensored: The Case of Children in Uniform.' *New Theatre Quarterly* 16, no. 3 (August 2000): 219–26.

Dolan, Jill. *Utopia in Performance: Finding Hope in the Theatre.* Ann Arbor: University of Michigan Press, 2005.

Fest, Kerstin. 'Yesterday and/or Today: Time, History and Desire in Christa Winsloe's *Mädchen in Uniform*.' *German Life and Letters* 65, no. 4 (October 2012): 457–71.

Meaney, Gerardine, Mary O'Dowd, and Bernadette Whelan. 'Sexual and Aesthetic Dissidences: Women and the Gate Theatre, 1929–60.' In *Reading the Irish Woman: Studies in Cultural Encounters and Exchange, 1714–1960*, edited by Gerardine Meaney, Mary O'Dowd, and Bernadette Whelan, 196–217. Liverpool: Liverpool University Press, 2013.

Mooney, Ria. 'Players and the Painted Stage, Part One.' *George Spelvin's Theatre Book* 1, no. 2 (Summer 1978): 3–120.

Pilkington, Lionel. *Theatre and the State in Ireland: Cultivating the People.* London: Routledge, 2001.

'Programme for *Children in Uniform* at the Gate Theatre, Dublin, April 1934.' Book 9, The Dublin Gate Theatre Archive, 1928–79. Deering McCormick Library Special Collections. Evanston, IL: Northwestern University.

Ryan, Phyllis. *The Company I Kept.* Dublin: Townhouse, 1996.

Sisson, Elaine. 'Experiment and the Free State: Mrs. Cogley's Cabaret and the Founding of the Gate Theatre, 1924–1930.' In *The Gate Theatre, Dublin: Inspiration and Craft*, edited by David Clare, Des Lally, and Patrick Lonergan, 11–28. Oxford: Peter Lang, 2018.

Sisson, Elaine. 'Experimentalism and the Irish Stage: Theatre and German Expressionism in the 1920s.' In *Ireland, Design and Visual Culture: Negotiating Modernity, 1922–1992*, edited by Linda King and Elaine Sisson, 39–58. Cork: Cork University Press, 2011.

Wandor, Michelene. *Carry on Understudies: Theatre and Sexual Politics.* New York: Routledge, 1986.

Winsloe, Christa. *Children in Uniform.* Translated by Barbara Burnham. London: Samuel French, 1933.

Maura Laverty at the Gate

Theatre as Social Commentary in 1950s Ireland

Deirdre McFeely

Micheál mac Liammóir wrote a consoling letter to Maura Laverty from Paris when he heard that *Lift Up Your Gates* (1946), the third of her four published novels to fall foul of Ireland's Censorship of Publications Board, had been banned.[1] While no specific reason was given for this ban other than the general classification of indecent or obscene, it is likely that Laverty's portrayal of the social realities of tenement life in 1940s Dublin did not sit comfortably with Ireland's carefully cultivated self-image as a primarily rural but modern nation. Laverty would return to this theme when scripting *Our Country*, Ireland's first political campaign film, for Clann na Poblachta's 1948 election efforts.[2] The film highlights some of the many problems facing Ireland, particularly urban Dublin, after sixteen years of Fianna Fáil rule, and attempts were made by that party to block the film's distribution. Despite official distaste for subject matter, such as urban poverty and tuberculosis, that reflected badly on the State more than twenty-five years after its inception, Hilton Edwards saw the dramatic potential offered by Laverty's portrayal of tenement life, first suggesting it as material for a movie but later requesting that Laverty adapt *Lift Up Your Gates* for the stage.[3]

Edwards offered Laverty her first playwriting opportunity at a time when the work of female playwrights was scarce on both the Gate and Abbey stages. He also afforded her the liberty to present her form of social realism in a forum that was, in the main, beyond the official

---

[1] Fitz-Simon, *The Boys*, 169.
[2] O'Leary and Stafford, *Our Country*.
[3] Fitz-Simon, *The Boys*, 170.

censorship of the state, or that found ways to navigate the strict scrutiny
to which the printed word was subjected. He would later reap rewards
because, as Christopher Fitz-Simon points out, it was Laverty's subsequent
association with the Gate Theatre that kept it financially afloat during the
1950s. Opening as *Liffey Lane* on 12 March 1951, the play quickly drew
comparison from the critics with Seán O'Casey's Dublin plays, the *Irish
Press* stating on 5 November 1951 that the play 'is the voice of Dublin at
the moment and … it may be said that Mrs Laverty is the only authentic
Dublin voice since O'Casey.'[4] It also drew large crowds to the Gaiety
Theatre; its success prompted Edwards to ask Laverty for a second work,
and she obliged with *Tolka Row*.[5] Laverty's concern with social conditions
and class is clear from that play's press publicity that outlined her plan to
write a series of six plays, each one a step higher on Dublin's social ladder.[6]

Tolka Row features the Nolan family and their neighbours, the
Feeneys, who have left tenement life behind to live in one of the new
council estates built by Dublin Corporation. The Nolans' home 'is one
of a thousand similar houses in a slum-clearance scheme on the fringe
of Dublin,' the name Tolka suggesting a location adjacent to that river
on Dublin's northside.[7] Laverty presents an insightful engagement with
social issues that were not raised in public discourse, particularly those
encountered by women, including financial struggles, marital breakdown,
and lack of control over marital fertility. Laverty's treatment of the subject
of birth control in *Tolka Row* is the focus of this chapter, which considers
a conversation about the rhythm method of birth control that takes place
between Mrs Nolan and Mrs Feeney. Women's reproductive rights at
that time were under the strict control of the Catholic Church, and birth
control was a taboo subject. Therefore, David Clare correctly claims with
regard to the play that Laverty is 'unafraid to include controversial subject
matter' and that 'she tackles Irish gender politics in a very direct manner.'[8]

---

4 *Irish Press*, 5 November 1951.
5 Edwards and mac Liammóir split from the Longfords in 1936, resulting in the
   establishment of two separate companies: Dublin Gate Theatre Productions and
   Longford Productions. Use of the Gate Theatre was shared, each company having
   it for six months a year. It is for this reason that both *Liffey Lane* and *Tolka Row*
   premiered at the Gaiety Theatre, with revivals taking place at the Gate Theatre.
6 Laverty wrote only one more play: *A Tree in the Crescent* opened at the Gaiety
   Theatre on 13 October 1952, for Dublin Gate Theatre Productions, directed by
   Edwards. In subsequent years Laverty made reference to a fourth play, *The Flowing
   Bowl*, but it would appear that this play was never completed.
7 Laverty, *Tolka Row*. Unpublished manuscript. Stage directions, n.p.
8 Clare, 'Reflections on Classic Gate Plays,' 32.

At a time when publications that referred to birth control were subject to censorship, Laverty used the stage as the medium to address that subject in a very public manner.[9] Produced by Edwards and starring mac Liammóir, *Tolka Row* epitomises the output of the Dublin Gate Theatre in terms of its championing of social emancipation. That this play could have been produced by any other company, particularly the Abbey, in 1950s Ireland is inconceivable.

Women's Domestic Burden: Children and Laundry

On International Women's Day in 2009, the Vatican declared via its official newspaper that the washing machine had contributed most to the emancipation of Western women.[10] As we approached the millennium, other media sources suggested, more realistically, that it was the pill first, followed by the washing machine, that had most improved the lot of women in the twentieth century: both had relieved the burden that large families and laundry placed on women throughout the last century. It also suggests a, perhaps obvious, correlation between access to reliable forms of birth control and laundry: the lack of the former usually results in more of the latter. Incongruous as it may seem, in *Tolka Row* Maura Laverty brings together these issues of laundry, birth control (or, more importantly, the lack thereof), and the Catholic Church in Irish life in the 1950s.

Tolka Row is a play firmly rooted in an urban and female domestic space. Rita Nolan keeps the home for her husband, Jack, and two of her adult children, Sean and Peggy. Additionally, Jack's sister, Statia, has lived with them for their twenty-five years of married life, and Rita's father, Dan, has recently come to live with them after giving up his rural cottage. Tensions are running high in an already overcrowded house when the Nolans' eldest child, Eileen, returns home from England, having left her husband and her unhappy marriage. While living in Tolka Row represents social progression for its residents, three generations living in a small house puts the working-class family under pressure. It is Rita, as the person solely responsible for domestic affairs, who struggles to accommodate the family's practical and emotional needs. In an overcrowded house, she suffers a loss of control over her home space and her family: a stressful situation for someone whose domain is the domestic sphere. She loves her

---

[9] It is possible that the discussion of birth control in *Tolka Row* was a factor in the playscript not being published. However, Laverty's other two plays, *Liffey Lane* and *A Tree in the Crescent*, were also not published.

[10] RTÉ, 'Washing Machines Liberated Women?'

father (played originally by Micheál mac Liammóir to great acclaim), but struggles with his presence in her home all day long, as she explains to Mrs Feeney: 'Anything to get him out from under my feet for a minute, I wouldn't hurt his feelings for the world. But you know how awkward it can be with a man around the house all day.'[11]

With Dan ever present, Rita's opportunities for neighbourly chats with Mrs Feeney are limited, and the tension is palpable as Dan constantly interrupts the women. While Rita and her family are the main subject of *Tolka Row*, Mrs Feeney's own family problem is a matter of concerned discussion between the two women. She has eight children under the age of thirteen, is still of child-bearing age, and without access to any form of birth control may yet have many more. Mrs Feeney pops in and out of the Nolans' house regularly, usually just hopping over the railing dividing the two properties. She is inextricably linked to the laundry generated by her large family throughout the play, opening the action as she heads to the back of her house with a bucket of wet clothes for hanging out on the clothesline. At that time newspapers and magazines heavily advertised washing machines: 'You, too, can be free from washing day drudgery,' promised an advertisement for the Hoover Electric Washing Machine, with the comforting assurance that it 'will do your full family wash, however large.'[12] However, Mrs Feeney is clearly doing all the laundry by hand, as did many working-class and middle-class women in 1951, as a Hoover washing machine then cost £25, about a month's wages.[13] An electric washing machine is beyond the financial resources of Mrs Feeney, who declares that 'I never took me hands out of the soap suds this day,' when she appears at the opening of the second act with her arms full of laundry again.[14]

Across Laverty's three plays – *Liffey Lane*, *Tolka Row*, and *A Tree in the Crescent* – appearance and cleanliness are central, chiming with the contemporary advertising of electrical appliances. In addition to promoting washing machines, periodicals targeted women with advertisements for a range of electrical household tools that offered to ease their domestic burden. Small electrical items were popular, in the first instance because they were a lot cheaper than electric cookers and washing machines. Caitriona Clear points out that throughout the 1950s the electric iron vied for first place with the electric kettle, sometimes displacing it, and

[11] Laverty, *Tolka Row*, Act 1, scene 7.
[12] *Irish Times*, 10 January 1951.
[13] Clear, *Women of the House*, 147.
[14] Laverty, *Tolka Row*, Act 2, scene 1.

suggests that 'the fact that irons were sometimes more popular than electric kettles indicates that appearance of clothes was considered of paramount importance.'[15] Mrs Feeney's actions support this claim as she owns an iron and spends hours laundering and cleaning the house. Early in the first act Mrs Feeney calls to Mrs Nolan with 'her arms full of washing,' looking to borrow her neighbour's iron as her own is not working.[16] Mrs Feeney's regular visits to Mrs Nolan to borrow domestic items suggest that she could not afford them herself, and that she was seeking some respite from the demands of her domestic chores and her young family in the form of a friendly chat with her neighbour. On this occasion Mrs Nolan sends her father out into the garden for some sunshine so that the women can have a chat without his interruption. The conversation turns to Eileen's wedding as they admire a framed photograph of the bride, unaware that she would shortly arrive home crying over her broken marriage:

> MRS. FEENEY: There's no doubt you gave her a smashin' send-off. Such a day! I thought I'd never get Oliver Feeney up the stairs and into bed. He was footless. It must have cost you a queer penny.
>
> MRS. NOLAN: If it cost twice as much I wasn't going to give the Moores the laugh over her. I said it to Jack. I said, 'Our little girl is going to leave this house with her head high.' You'd find you'll do the same, Mrs. Feeney, when your time comes.
>
> MRS. FEENEY: Me eight times, you mean. And unless it's the mercy of God, maybe as many times more.
>
> MRS. NOLAN: Ah, maybe not. Sure isn't Pauline two-and-a-half now? Please God, that's the end of it.
>
> MRS. FEENEY: I do be keeping my fingers crossed. I never got that long before. And then they'll tell you that breast-feeding keeps you safe. But I warned Oliver Feeney. Start me off again, I said to him, and you'll be sorry you didn't keep easy. He's a shocking hard man to manage.
>
> MRS. NOLAN: Well, that's love for you.[17]

As the mother of eight daughters, Mrs Feeney is justified in her concern about paying for their future weddings. However, her more serious worry

---

15 Clear, *Women of the House*, 151.
16 Laverty, *Tolka Row*, Act 1, scene 7.
17 Laverty, *Tolka Row*, Act 1, scene 10.

is that she may yet have more children due to her lack of control over her sex-life and her fertility. That she is the only character whose Christian name is not given suggests that she does not have an identity beyond that of a wife and mother. Her youngest daughter is two-and-a-half years old, and she is enjoying the longest break she has yet experienced between pregnancies. She does not hold faith with the then commonly held belief that breast-feeding prevents pregnancy, and she is just hoping (to God) not to have any more children. But hoping is really all she can do, and her own attempts at preventing a further pregnancy, as explained to Mrs Nolan, prove ineffectual: 'Often and often I do deliberately pick a row with that man coming on for bed-time so as to have a good excuse for keeping myself to myself. Would you blame me if I shot him dead?'[18] Tellingly, this frustration is expressed upon her realisation later in the play that she is pregnant with her ninth child. Mrs Feeney is not unrepresentative: statistics attest to large families, and a student doctor at the Coombe maternity hospital in Dublin in the 1950s recalls 'dealing as a matter of routine with mothers of ten children.'[19] So it is not surprising that the women want information about birth control – and this includes Mrs Nolan, even though her child-rearing days are behind her:

MRS. FEENEY: It's my belief we're all far too obliging.
MRS. NOLAN: But what's a woman to do if she doesn't want to break up her marriage?
MRS. FEENEY: Not to mention getting the face ate off her in Confession. The Guard's wife down the road, Mrs. Farrell, she's terrible well up.
MRS. NOLAN: She was going on for a nurse, wasn't she? Before she got married?
MRS. FEENEY: So I believe. Well, she gave me a lend of a book all about this rhythm business. Oh, there's nothing agen religion in it – nothing at all. Only it tells you when.
MRS. NOLAN: I heard about that, and I was often wondering about it. Is it any use?
MRS. FEENEY: It's a cod. In my house, anyway. As I said to Mrs. Farrell when I was giving the book back to her, 'Maybe it works for you, Mrs. Farrell,' says I, 'your husband being in the Guards' Band and all. But my Oliver would never get the hang of rhythm. He has no ear at all for music.'

[18] Laverty, *Tolka Row*, Act 3, scene 4.
[19] Ferriter, *Occasions of Sin*, 300.

MRS. NOLAN: *(Laughing)* You're a caution!
MRS. FEENEY: Rhythm? Stop.[20]

Information about the rhythm method is available to them in the form of a book, unnamed, lent to Mrs Feeney by Mrs Farrell. The fact that Mrs Farrell's husband is a Garda raises the possibility that the book has been seized under the Censorship of Publication Act.[21] When introduced in 1929, the Act's 'main purpose was to restrict access to information about contraception.'[22] It was a crime to print, publish, distribute, or sell 'any book or periodical publication which advocates or might reasonably be supposed to advocate the unnatural prevention of conception.'[23] The book lent to Mrs Feeney is quite possibly one of two books written by Halliday Sutherland. The first, *Laws of Life*, banned in 1942, contained an explanation of the rhythm method. According to Mary E. Daly, the banning of the book, 'despite the fact that it carried a *permissu superiorum* from the archbishop of Westminster indicating that the book was not inaccurate in its references to Catholic doctrine, is one of the most notorious chapters in the history of the Irish Censorship Board.'[24] Halliday would later claim that the banning was not actually prompted by the chapter on birth control but 'because I had written in the cold language of physiology an account of the functions of sex ... In Éire too many people, including clerics, regard ignorance as synonymous with innocence.'[25] Sutherland's other book, *Control of Life*, was published in 1944, and it devoted two chapters to natural family planning. It was approved by the Westminster Diocesan Board of Censorship, and it escaped censorship in Ireland. Daly suggests that it was not banned due to government embarrassment about the previous controversy. So, when Mrs Feeney reassures Mrs Nolan, 'Oh, there's nothing agen religion in it – nothing at all. Only it tells you when,' the attitude of the Catholic Church, particularly in Ireland, to the rhythm method and to the safe period was not that straightforward.[26]

The absolute centrality of the Church in these women's lives is clear. Many would have had no other option other than to ask for advice from

---

20 Laverty, *Tolka Row*, Act 1, scene 12.
21 A Garda is a member of the Irish police force.
22 Daly, *The Slow Failure*, 88.
23 Daly, *The Slow Failure*, 88.
24 Daly, *The Slow Failure*, 92–93.
25 Daly, *The Slow Failure*, 93.
26 Laverty, *Tolka Row*, Act 1, scene 12.

a priest regarding their concerns about their large families, and risked, as Mrs Feeney puts it, 'getting the face ate off her in Confession.' Irish women had little or no access to factual information about sex and reproduction but many publications were available that disseminated Catholic doctrine on these subjects in clear terms. Publications such as the popular *Sacred Heart Messenger*, published by the Irish Jesuits, and the pamphlets of the Catholic Truth Society of Ireland (CTSI) were widely distributed.[27] The CTSI pamphlets, of which one and a quarter million were printed in 1951 alone, were clear in their message about marriage and birth control – of course, sex *outside* of marriage was unconscionable.[28] *They're Married*, first published in 1950, claims that attempting to avoid pregnancy 'takes the noblest natural power that God has shared with man, the power of creation, and turns it into a means of mere sensual pleasure. It lowers wives to the level of harlots and knocks down the barriers raised for youth by the fear of the consequences of sin.'[29] Mrs Nolan, far from being a harlot, describes her attitude to marital sex in terms that are far removed from 'sensual pleasure.' She compares marriage, by which she means marital sex, to cooking, and so reduces it to yet another domestic duty that must be undertaken whether she likes it or not:

> Well, this is the way I look at it. Whether we like it or not we have our duty. It's for all the world like cooking. There's days you wouldn't care if you never seen the sight of food. Just the same, you can't consider your own feelings – the dinner has to go on the table. And even if your stomach was turning, wouldn't you let on to be eating a bit and enjoying it so as not to spoil it on another. Marriage is the identical same.[30]

Publications like the CTSI leaflets made clear that those attempting birth control are committing a grave sin. Under a heading, 'The Clamour of Artificial Birth Control,' *Man, Woman, and God* declares that in such circumstances, 'the marriage becomes a source of disgrace, a spiritual thing become immoral, carnal, beauty become ugliness. God meant

---

[27] The Catholic Truth Society of Ireland was founded in 1899 to publish and distribute a range of religious material to the Irish people, and was the origin of Veritas Publications.

[28] Mac Cárthaigh, ed., *Vintage Values*, 6.

[29] Lord, *They're Married*, 22. My thanks go to Brian McMahon of Brand New Retro (brandnewretro.ie) for supplying this pamphlet.

[30] Laverty, *Tolka Row*, Act 1, 12.

married love to be aid to salvation. Many use it as a singularly potent means to damnation.'[31] Similarly, according to *Blest Union*, '[i]t is the old story of attempting to eat the cake and still have it, to enjoy the pleasure of parenthood without its responsibilities. It is mortally sinful for the parent or parents who consent to it.'[32] Lest there be any doubt on the subject of sinfulness and damnation, *Blest Union* cites Pope Pius XI's papal encyclical of 1930, *Casti Conubii*: 'Any use whatsoever of matrimony exercised in such a way that the act is deliberately frustrated in its natural power to generate life is an offence against the law of God and of nature, and those who indulge in such are branded with the guilt of a grave sin.'[33] So Mrs Feeney's belief of the rhythm method that 'there's nothing agen religion in it,' shared no doubt by many in the audience, was problematic for those trying to adhere to Catholic doctrine. Lack of access to sex education, including information about birth control, whether within or without the doctrine of the Church, was at the heart of the problem, so it is easy to imagine many Irish women having conversations similar to that taking place between Rita Nolan and Mrs Feeney.

Women's magazines offered another possible source of information about sex education and marriage: as Caitriona Clear observes, '[t]wo Irish women's magazines in the 1950s and 1960s encouraged women from different Irish worlds to articulate their problems, opinions and desires in a public forum and to communicate with each other.' *Woman's Life*, published fortnightly, ran from 1936 until 1959; *Woman's Way* started only in 1963. Clear explains that *Woman's Life*'s position regarding religion was complex due to censorship, and that 'this might partly explain the scarcity of articles on pregnancy and childbirth, and the fact that sex and unmarried pregnancy never featured on the problem pages, except perhaps as "reply only."'[34] Readers of *Woman's Life* were advised, '[i]f you have a personal problem perhaps Mrs Wyse, Delia Dixon or our Medical Adviser can assist you.'[35] Mrs Wyse answered personal problems and Delia Dixon supplied beauty advice, but according to Clear, one journalist replied to all queries and for some period of time Maura Laverty fulfilled this role, thus hearing at first hand the problems of the women

---

[31] McCown, *Man, Woman, and God*, 18. My thanks to Lir Mac Cárthaigh of Veritas Publications for enabling my access to the Veritas archive of CTSI pamphlets.

[32] McGee, *Blest Union*, 14.

[33] McGee, *Blest Union*, 14.

[34] Clear, *Women's Voices in Ireland*, 1–2.

[35] *Woman's Life*, 1 July 1950.

of Ireland.[36] A study of *Woman's Life* from the early 1950s shows regular queries about basic sex education and gynaecological problems, and it is clear that the correspondents were ignorant of the most basic facts of life. In response to nearly all requests for sex education, a pamphlet like *Sex and Innocence* was recommended.[37] Subtitled *A Handbook for Parents and Educators*, this pamphlet is representative of all publications recommended by *Woman's Life*, and it offered the reader only obtuse information expressed in religious terms. Much of the recommended reading material was published by religious organisations such as the CTSI. Women undoubtedly wrote to the magazine for information that they could not request anywhere else, but were referred only to those religious publications that were available to them anyway. Women seeking sex education, even at a basic level, were caught in a circle of silence and control maintained by the Catholic Church and the official censorship of the state. According to Clear, British women's magazines on sale in Ireland did not offer their readers any more information, for British periodicals 'were omitting advertisements for books or birth control devices in order to safeguard sales in Ireland.'[38]

This dearth of basic information and discussion about sex and reproduction in the public domain serves to make the women's on-stage conversation all the more remarkable. They are, of course, very careful that Dan is out of earshot, and their conversation is private and almost conspiratorial, overheard only by the audience. The women have an intimate chat about very personal aspects of their married lives. Mrs Feeney is struggling with her domestic workload and with meeting her husband's sexual expectations: 'Love? I'm after having me fill of love *(Holds out bundle of washing)* There's love for you! Eh, will you tell me this? Do men never get tired? Wouldn't you think after fifteen years hard going. God knows, all I ask is me night's rest.'[39] She believes that women are too compliant, but there is little she can do as Catholic doctrine does not allow her to avoid marital sex, even if she so wanted.

---

[36] For a detailed study see Clear, *Women's Voices*. Maura Laverty was agony aunt for *Woman's Way* when it was established in 1963 before Angela MacNamara took over six months later. *Women's Way* was the first to have a full letters page. While the magazine published articles supporting contraception and allowed free discussion of it in the letters page, the magazine's agony aunt was unequivocally opposed to birth control.

[37] O'Hea, *Sex and Innocence*.

[38] Daly, *The Slow Failure*, 89.

[39] Laverty, *Tolka Row*, Act 1, scene 10.

Critics and Audience

Tolka Row was very well received by the critics. However, most called in no uncertain terms for the scene between Mrs Nolan and Mrs Feeney to be completely cut, describing it as unnecessary. As the *Irish Independent* wrote, Mrs Feeney's 'confidences to Mrs Nolan … are embarrassing and unnecessary. … the play can do with cutting, particularly in the first act.'[40] The *Evening Herald* wrote: 'Some of the prattle – notably the quite unnecessary confidences of a neighbour, Mrs Feeney – betrays the crude humour occasionally purveyed by comedians in women's dress; these passages are unworthy of the play and could – and should – be omitted.'[41] Additionally, the London-based *Stage* claimed: 'It is a great pity that an enjoyable play should be marred by the distasteful dialogue of Mrs Feeney in her intimate conversations with her neighbour. It is not amusing, and quite unnecessary to the play,'[42] while, along similar lines, *Irish Tatler & Sketch* proclaimed: 'Angela Howlett, as Mrs Feeney, acted well in the rather too confiding part of a neighbour whose speeches could be improved by pruning.'[43]

While the critics strongly believed that this conversation, confiding and intimate as it is, had no place on the stage, their robust response implies that such discussion should also have no place in wider society, as indeed it did not. There is no evidence to suggest that demands were made for *Tolka Row* to be closed, but the critics' reaction is certainly suggestive of the fate that befell the Pike Theatre's production of *The Rose Tattoo* in 1957.[44] Critics may have desisted from such a demand due to the play's success in attracting a new audience to the theatre: the reviews of *Tolka Row* highlight their fear that cinema was growing at the expense of the stage. In the *Irish Press*, Niall Carroll explained how Edwards and mac Liammóir 'were alive to their responsibilities' of promoting theatre by sending a circular to the heads of large Dublin firms asking them to persuade younger employees to see 'the play as a trial to break off the dreadful film habit.'[45] The *Irish Times* reported that hand-bills had been

---

[40] *Irish Independent*, 9 October 1951.
[41] *Evening Herald*, 9 October 1951.
[42] *Stage* (London), 11 October 1951.
[43] *Irish Tatler & Sketch*, November 1951.
[44] Alan Simpson, director of Dublin's Pike Theatre, was arrested on 23 May 1957 during a performance of Tennessee Williams's play, *The Rose Tattoo*, on the grounds that parts of the play were considered objectionable.
[45] *Irish Press*, 5 November 1951.

supplied for display on staff notice-boards, '[a]nd it worked; the play is attracting an entirely new type of audience – Dublin teen-agers, who are discovering that the theatre is not necessarily high-brow.'[46]

Watching *Tolka Row*, Dublin teenagers were seeing aspects of their own lives portrayed by the Nolan's youngest child, Peggy. Older women would have recognised and shared Mrs Nolan's and Mrs Feeney's domestic and family problems. They saw 'the laughter and the heartaches of ordinary Dublin people whom they felt they could recognise.'[47] Humour is central to the play's success, not least in the discussion about the rhythm method. However, Anthony Cronin, critic for *The Bell*, while not calling for the scene to be cut, questions Laverty's use of humour: 'Nothing in these people's lives remained unsoiled, and it was only necessary to mention certain subjects for the audience to roar with laughter, the need to be at all witty about them could be dispensed with.'[48] Unlike Cronin, the audience clearly relished Laverty's use of humour. He raises the question of class when claiming that the play was written 'for the amusement of a middle-class audience,' adding that '[n]othing gives an audience such a virtuous feeling of superiority as sentiment they can laugh at later from the heights of Olympian understanding.'[49] Cronin's suggestion of an audience consisting of the middle class only does not stand up to scrutiny. The opening night audience, undoubtedly including critics such as Cronin, may have been predominantly middle class, but Edwards and mac Liammóir's marketing strategy for *Tolka Row* clearly gained new audiences ranging in age and social class.

Laverty wrote *Tolka Row* at a time when the Commission on Emigration and Other Population Problems (1954) was ongoing. Chapter Five of the commission report, titled 'Births, Fertility and Family Size,' faithfully reiterated Catholic social teaching.[50] Mary E. Daly recounts that '[f]amily size was a very sensitive topic' and suggests that 'marital fertility may well have been the most contentious topic that the commission confronted, or failed to confront.'[51] Laverty's friendship with Dr Robert Collis, paediatrician and social activist, would certainly have informed her social conscience on the subject of family size.[52] Collis, a member of

[46] *Irish Times*, 10 November 1951.
[47] *Evening Herald*, 3 November 1951.
[48] *The Bell*, November 1951.
[49] *The Bell*, November 1951.
[50] Daly, *The Slow Failure*, 123.
[51] Daly, *The Slow Failure*, 128.
[52] Robert Collis wrote *Marrowbone Lane*, a play set in Dublin's tenements and first produced at the Gate Theatre in 1939. Fitz-Simon reports that the play inspired

the Commission, warned of the danger of 'the large, unhappy, unhealthy family where the mother is a drudge.'[53] The Irish Censorship Board banned the (British) Royal Commission on Population in October 1949, on the grounds that it 'advocated the unnatural prevention of conception or the procurement of abortions or miscarriages.'[54] Although the ban was revoked a few months later following widespread criticism, Daly suggests that it would have served as a warning of the dangers involved in discussing family size or contraception in Ireland. Perhaps an even more contentious issue of the day was the failure of the Minister of Health, Noel Browne (a Clann na Poblachta TD in the coalition government) to have his proposed Mother and Child Scheme introduced, prompting his resignation. One of the grounds upon which the Church objected to the scheme was that it would empower doctors to discuss family planning with women, something that Archbishop John Charles McQuaid believed was the sole preserve of the Church.[55] The rhythm method discussion in *Tolka Row* can only be seen as Laverty's direct intervention in these affairs, and her timing was telling. On 29 October 1951, three weeks after the opening of *Tolka Row*, Pope Pius XII endorsed the use of the rhythm method for married Catholics, in certain restrictive circumstances. However, this change in papal teaching was not welcomed in Ireland and was not disseminated by the CTSI until 1957: in fact, information on the rhythm method would not become generally available in Ireland until the 1970s.

Conclusion

The success of both *Liffey Lane* and *Tolka Row* led Hilton Edwards to declare 1951 to be one of the best seasons they had ever had, and *Tolka Row* provided mac Liammóir with one of his most acclaimed roles.[56] Fitz-Simon has noted how *Tolka Row* was the Gate's 'great reliable' in the five years following its first production, 'when financial difficulties

the formation of the Marrowbone Lane Fund, the object of which was 'to feed the starving children of Dublin.' Fitz-Simon, *The Boys*, 126.

[53] Clear, *Women of the House*, 59.

[54] Daly, *The Slow Failure*, 129.

[55] The Mother and Child Scheme was a divisive healthcare programme introduced by Noel Browne, which received major opposition from the Catholic Church and the medical profession. The programme planned to introduce free ante- and post-natal care for mothers and to extend free healthcare to all children under the age of sixteen.

[56] Fitz-Simon, *The Boys*, 173.

became overpowering, as was frequent, or when other productions failed and a quick replacement had to be found.'[57] In light of this commercial success, Edward's initial bold move in encouraging Laverty to write for the stage is easily underestimated. To present the domestic life of urban working-class women was a radical undertaking. Laverty depicts women who have little or no agency over their lives, confined as they were by the prevailing social and religious constraints of Irish life in the 1950s. Yet to enable such women to discuss birth control and marital breakdown at a time when public discourse on such subjects was taboo was emancipatory for the audience: Mrs Nolan and Mrs Feeney discussing marital fertility empowered them to do likewise. Mac Liammóir revived his role of Dan in a BBC television adaptation filmed in London in January 1959. With a planned running time of only ninety minutes, the play clearly had to be cut.[58] Yet it is telling that Mrs Nolan and Mrs Feeney's conversation is cut along with most of Mrs Feeney's lines, including her despair when sharing her news about her ninth pregnancy. This editing out of Mrs Feeney and her fertility woes weakens the sexual politics of the play and reduces its social emancipatory power. An examination of the television script suggests that other sections could have been cut instead. Clearly, the subject matter was considered unsuitable for an English television audience. That this was so is testament to the success with which Hilton Edwards and Micheál mac Liammóir confronted a conservative society by questioning repressive ideas about gender and sexuality.

Bibliography

The Bell. November 1951, 63.
Clare, David. 'Reflections on Classic Gate Plays by Mary Manning, Christine Longford and Maura Laverty.' *Irish Archives: Journal of the Irish Society for Archives* 25 (2018): 28–34.
Clear, Caitriona. *Women of the House: Women's Household Work in Ireland 1922–1961*. Dublin: Irish Academic Press, 2000.
Clear, Caitriona. *Women's Voices in Ireland: Women's Magazines in the 1950s and 60s*. London: Bloomsbury Academic, 2016.
Daly, Mary E. *The Slow Failure: Population Decline and Independent Ireland, 1920–1973*. Madison, University of Wisconsin Press, 2006.
Evening Herald. 9 October 1951, 3.
Evening Herald. 3 November 1951, 5.

[57] Fitz-Simon, *The Boys*, 172.
[58] Maura Laverty Papers, National Library of Ireland, MS50,678/105.

Ferriter, Diarmaid. *Occasions of Sin*. London: Profile Books, 2009.

Fitz-Simon, Christopher. *The Boys: A Biography of Micheál MacLíammóir and Hilton Edwards*. Dublin: Gill & Macmillan, 1994.

Irish Independent. 9 October 1951, 8.

Irish Press. 5 November 1951, 4.

Irish Tatler & Sketch. November 1951, 44.

Irish Times. 10 January 1951, 3.

Irish Times. 10 November 1951, 5.

Laverty, Maura. *Tolka Row*. Unpublished play script. National Library of Ireland, Maura Laverty Papers, MS50,678/105.

Lord, Daniel A., S.J. *They're Married*. Dublin: Catholic Truth Society of Ireland, 1950.

Mac Cárthaigh, Lir, ed. *Vintage Values*. Dublin: Veritas Publications, 2013.

Maura Laverty Papers. National Library of Ireland, MS50,678/105.

McCown, James H., S.J. *Man, Woman, and God*. Dublin: Catholic Truth Society of Ireland, 1950.

McGee, Brendan. *Blest Union*. Dublin: Catholic Truth Society of Ireland, 1953.

O'Hea, Jerome, S.J. *Sex and Innocence*. Cork: Mercier Press, 1949.

O'Leary, Liam and Brendan Stafford. *Our Country*. Irish Civic Films, 1948.

RTÉ. 'Washing Machines Liberated Women?' https://www.rte.ie/news/2009/0311/115017-washingmachine/.

Stage (London). 11 October 1951.

Woman's Life. 1 July 1950, 40.

PART II
Emancipating Communities

◆ 4 ◆

'Let's Be Gay, While We May'

Artistic Platforms and the Construction of Queer Communities in Mary Manning's *Youth's the Season—?*

Grace Vroomen

'Abnormals' is how one audience member of *Youth's the Season—?*'s 1937 London production described the play's characters – a sentiment that was largely shared across the official English reviews. Both the London production and the earlier Dublin production (in 1931) were criticised for the sharp tonal shift towards the end of the play, which prompted the *News Chronicle* to describe *Youth's the Season—?* as '*Hamlet* tacked on to a Farce.'[1] At the time, the play's focus on non-conforming characters and its experimental treatment of genre were perceived as unconvincing and confused, but they have since begun to be recognised as radically innovative for their time and indicative of Manning's theatrical talent and revolutionary mission statement. Both during her time as editor of the Gate Theatre's magazine *Motley* and later in life, Manning was vocal about moving away from 'an Abbey kitchen interior'[2] and staging and exploring more complex and diverse Irish identities, which were changing in tandem with the rapidly urbanising landscape.[3] Authenticity, in this case, could not be realised via the more conventional theatre practice of realism, but rather via expressionist drama, which, according to Manning, more accurately reflected the 'confused and mainly experimental'[4] mind of the Free State.[5]

---

[1] Quoted in Leeney, 'Not-So-Gay-Young-Things,' 165.
[2] Manning, 'Dublin has also its Gate Theatre.'
[3] Van den Beuken, 'MacLiammóir's Minstrel and Johnston's Morality,' 3.
[4] Manning, 'Dublin has also its Gate Theatre.'
[5] Van den Beuken, 'MacLiammóir's Minstrel and Johnston's Morality,' 3.

This is precisely what she sets out to do with *Youth's the Season–?* (1931). The play focuses on a group of adolescents from the old Ascendancy, and the play, initially, masquerades as a comedy of manner that is intent on satirising these pampered youths who 'lounged or who posed melodramatically over lampshades, who admired their hair in mirrors, and who drank too much gin.'[6] They appear simultaneously desperate for a purpose in life and unmotivated to pursue it, and José Lanters concludes that Manning uses this restlessness to comment on the displacement of the 'anachronistic' and 'inauthentic' ascendancy, which had become obsolete in the new Free State.[7]

But, as Cathy Leeney argues, it is also through this coded representation that Manning resists traditional representations of Irishness and instead explores the heterogeneity of national identities through 'class difference, diversity of religion, and gender transgression.'[8] At its core, *Youth's the Season–?* is a play about queerness. Fintan Walsh establishes that the definition of queerness extends beyond LGBTQ+ subjects and cultures, and encompasses everything that challenges 'presumptions of stability and certainty' and boldly aspires to alternative modes of 'being, doing, feeling and knowing.'[9] Queerness was seen as particularly problematic during the Irish Free State, which was, among other things, coloured by conservatism and a return to rigid and uncompromising gender roles.[10] The play's conflict centres around the Free State's rejection of Desmond, Terence, and Toots's experiences due to their sexual and gender non-conformity. Despite the play's initial deceivingly comical tone, the play goes to great lengths to showcase the isolation and othering that these characters experience due to their queerness. The expressionist staging of the second act, set on Desmond's twenty-first birthday party, disrupts the façade of a realist comedy of manners and reveals the severe anxiety and inner turmoil that dictate the queer characters' lives. The violent conclusion of the play, epitomised by Terence's suicide, mercilessly exposes and cements the hopelessness of the queer characters' situation, leading Leeney to observe that queer people's exclusion from society results in severe depression and even 'self-immolating violence.'[11] The play thus confronts its audience with the painful reality that the queer characters face and implores it to empathise with their situation.

---

[6] Leeney, 'Not-So-Gay-Young-Things,' 160.
[7] Lanters, 'Queer Creatures, Queer Place,' 59.
[8] Leeney, 'Not-So-Gay-Young-Things,' 160.
[9] Walsh, *Queer Performances and Contemporary Ireland*, 2.
[10] Valiulis, 'The Politics of Gender in the Irish Free State, 1922–1937,' 569.
[11] Leeney, 'Not-So-Gay-Young-Things,' 165.

Interestingly, reviews of *Youth's the Season–?* showcase that Dublin audiences were more willing to commiserate with Manning's queer characters than London audiences. Leeney attributes this to two factors: first, the English production largely stripped the play from its Irish context and its commentary on the Ascendancy, which put even more emphasis on the characters' sexual and gender non-conformity; the English production, moreover, did not include Micheál mac Liammóir as Desmond and, as such, its reception did not benefit from his already established reputation in Ireland as a virtually openly homosexual man. While reinventing himself as an Irishman, mac Liammóir had succeeded in establishing himself as a prominent cultural and sexual figure. Eibhear Walshe argues that it was precisely this Irishness that shielded him from being associated with what was perceived as the immoral threat of homosexuality and, as such, he was able to live as a 'openly homosexual figure.'[12] Leeney adds that mac Liammóir's image was also deeply grounded in theatricality, and it was his reputation as an '*artistic* Irishman' that allowed Dublin audiences to 'laugh comfortably' at his explicitly queer and camp performance in *Youth's the Season–?*.[13] In this way, mac Liammóir and the Gate Theatre had created a safe and widely acceptable space for queer artists to perform in where queer characters could be represented in an (almost) explicit manner. The shocked and appalled reception of the queer characters by London audiences highlights what an extraordinary feat the Gate had accomplished. The inclusion of mac Liammóir and the play's reception showcase the strong connection between art and queerness at the Gate, and how it successfully used its stage to give a voice to queer characters and artists.

No less importantly, these themes of emancipation and inclusion also feature prominently in the plot of *Youth's the Season–?*. Manning's play establishes an intrinsic link between queerness and art, and highlights the importance of performance and artistic expression as a mode of creating communities and fostering understanding. Liora Bresler has argued that through recounting and performing narratives, artists can effectively share their experiences and enrich their audience's 'emotional as well as cognitive repertoire.'[14] This serves to foster what she identifies as 'empathic understanding,' which signifies a deep interpersonal connection that blurs the lines between the artist's experiences and those of the audience.[15]

---

[12] Walshe, 'Sodom and Begorrah, or Game to the Last,' 150–2.
[13] Leeney, 'Not-So-Gay-Young-Things,' 164–65. Emphasis in the original.
[14] Bresler, 'Embodied Narrative Inquiry,' 11.
[15] Bresler, 'Embodied Narrative Inquiry,' 8.

Artistic tools, such as paint brushes and musical instruments, may facilitate
the performance of these embodied narratives and, as such, their presence
on stage possesses symbolic value.

Another important aspect of Bresler's theory is tri-directional
communication. Through performance, a 'dialogical space for the creation
of meaning'[16] is opened up, which allows experiences and ideas to be
'appreciated, absorbed, and internalized'[17] between the artist, the audience,
and the artwork. In other words, performance is an invaluable way of
fostering understanding and human connection, and, consequently, a
sense of community, since it blurs the lines between the performer, their
performed narrative, and the audience. In spite of the great potential
that performance holds, it must be noted that establishing connections
in this way is not always successful. The audience first and foremost has
to be willing to open itself up to the experiences of the artist. And even
when the audience chooses to engage with the artist, interaction remains
open-ended and, as such, the audience is free to reject the validity of the
artist's experiences.[18]

The artists who feature as characters in *Youth's the Season–?* are
confronted with precisely this form of rejection and misunderstanding,
which ultimately prevents them from establishing and utilising a successful
artistic platform. This chapter will discuss Terence, Toots, and Desmond
respectively and highlight the connection between their queerness and
their identity as artists. It will, moreover, employ Bresler's theory on how
narratives create interpersonal connections as a lens to study the function
of performance in *Youth's the Season–?*. These insights into Manning's
representation of art and queerness, as well as the weight that she gave to
artistic communities such as the Gate Theatre, illustrate how playhouses
can both literally and figuratively provide an emancipatory stage for queer
artists as well as queer characters.

Terence

Terence, whose storyline is the main catalyst behind the sharp tonal shift
during the second act, serves to illustrate some of the ways in which
Manning creates intersections between art and queerness. He is introduced
by the play's notes as 'a shambling literary loafer'[19] while his companion

---

[16] Bresler, 'Embodied Narrative Inquiry,' 11.
[17] Bresler, 'Embodied Narrative Inquiry,' 11.
[18] Bresler, 'Embodied Narrative Inquiry,' 9.
[19] Manning, *Youth's the Season–?*, 330.

Egosmith is 'the model for the perfect young city man.'[20] The usage of the word 'perfect,' in particular, marks Terence as marginalised and queer, denoting everything that is non-conforming in the context of the play, whereas Egosmith comes to represent the centre and, consequently, conformity. Throughout the play, Terence is haunted by Egosmith, who functions both as his 'Doppelganger'[21] and his social consciousness, as Lanters observes: 'Rather than being Terence's real, inner self ... Egosmith dramatizes the reality principle that acts as his "bodyguard" and governs his functioning in society.'[22]

It is noteworthy that the juxtaposition of the two characters is characterised by Terence's identity as a 'literary' man, which establishes literature and, by extension, art as something that belongs to the margins and is inherently queer and 'other.' While there was a plethora of artists at the time, the Free State's heavy censorship displays a general distrust of the craft and wariness of its potential to challenge the state's conservative outlook and rigid societal norms. In contrast to art, business and commerce were regarded as safe and acceptable occupations. This opposition between the art world and the business world recurs frequently in the play and, in particular, in relation to Desmond, as will be discussed later. Egosmith embodies Terence's insecurities surrounding what a 'perfect' and conforming man should be, and actively tries to prevent Terence from being his authentic, non-conforming self:

EGOSMITH *coughs genteelly.*
TERENCE [*turns and sees him in the shadows.*] Oh, you –
    [*he laughs*] for the moment – d'you know, Horace old man
    – I thought I saw myself, and behold, I was a very ordinary
    fellow.[23]

As Terence's social bodyguard, Egosmith aims to influence Terence's conduct and tries to prevent him from making any social transgressions. Egosmith's cough is a reaction to Terence proclaiming publicly that he never loved Connie, Desmond's sister, because he cannot even love himself.[24] The cough can be understood as a warning that Terence is making a scene and revealing more about himself than is socially acceptable. It can also be

---

[20] Manning, *Youth's the Season–?*, 330.
[21] Manning, *Youth's the Season–?*, 395.
[22] Lanters, 'Queer Creatures, Queer Place,' 57.
[23] Manning, *Youth's the Season–?*, 352.
[24] Manning, *Youth's the Season–?*, 352.

understood as a painful reminder that if Terence had been 'ordinary'[25] like Egosmith, he could have returned Connie's love. For the continuation of the discussion, Egosmith hovers over Terence, 'rubbing his hands nervously,'[26] and ensures that Terence does not let the conversation escalate again or reveal anything personal. In other words, he tries to control Terence so that he does not commit any social transgressions.

Egosmith, moreover, controls and limits the way Terence expresses himself through art. When Toots asks Terence about his upcoming novel in the first act, Egosmith becomes visibly nervous, and he studies the other characters 'restlessly,'[27] to gauge their reaction. This implies that Egosmith regards creating art as something that should not be discussed and, as such, a form of social transgression. Terence confirms this unspoken suggestion by saying that writing novels has an intoxicating effect and he compares it to '[d]ancing, playing bridge [and] making love.'[28] He then states that he needs this feeling of intoxication to survive, but that he cannot hold onto it:

> ... to remain permanently intoxicated it is necessary to be
> everlastingly writing novels – or better still, thinking about
> writing novels. Of course I've tried more commonplace
> methods – for example, playing with the thought of
> suicide ...
> [EGOSMITH   *starts,   turns   around   and   looks   at   him*[.]][29]

This passage resonates in several ways. Terence's preference for *thinking* about writing novels rather than actually writing them ostensibly marks him as one of the pampered youths that the play, in its guise as a comedy of manners, sets out to satirise: he is someone who likes to think of himself as an important artist, but who is too untalented or too unmotivated to actually create a work of art.

However, the biting tone of Terence's words and Egosmith's quick interference also suggest a sense of internalised hatred and a deep insecurity surrounding his own talent and work. It underscores the importance of creating and thinking about art for Terence's happiness, but it also shows that something is preventing him from doing so. As soon as he mentions

25 Manning, *Youth's the Season–?*, 352.
26 Manning, *Youth's the Season–?*, 352.
27 Manning, *Youth's the Season–?*, 331.
28 Manning, *Youth's the Season–?*, 331.
29 Manning, *Youth's the Season–?*, 331.

the extent of his unhappiness, Egosmith cuts him off and prevents Terence from earnestly reaching out to the other characters. Terence then continues, while looking at Egosmith: 'I've no faith, no capacity of work, no purpose, and to be born without continuity of purpose is to be born under sentence of death. I am foredoomed to failure[.]'[30] Egosmith, then, has installed these thoughts in Terence's head and, consequently, is preventing him from thinking about and writing novels. Instead, Terence has fallen so deep under Egosmith's conformist spell that he has already given up on himself and his creative capacity.

During the second act, Terence opens up to Toots, and they seem to recognise each other as outsiders. Terence confides in Toots that he does not have 'one drop of artist's blood'[31] in his veins, and that he finds himself unable to write. When she asks him why he believes this, he answers that he is 'mentally constipated,' because there's 'too much Proust [and] Joyce' in his head.[32] This showcases that Terence is so anxious about living up to the established literary canon that he cannot bring himself to write at all. This again confirms Terence's fear of falling short: he believes that he cannot measure up to the standard set by the canonised artists, just as he believes that he cannot measure up to Egosmith's representation of the perfect man. He explains that he is only telling Toots this because he recognises that she is an outsider as well and, as such, will be able to understand and empathise with his perceived queerness. She is accorded this role because she has previously been involved in a serious romantic relationship and is now no longer perceived as a suitable marriage candidate. Toots immediately grasps that Terence is referring to her status as 'a woman with a past,' and briefly explains the situation to Egosmith: 'I want you to understand this: I didn't give him up without a struggle,'[33] confirming that she and Terence already understand each other and their respective situations.

This is related to how the fragmented dialogue and the more symbolic set design of this act employs a more expressionist staging, which Leeney interprets as destabilising the established identities and revealing them to be a 'performance.'[34] This break with realism strips away the masks and exposes the characters' 'fears, desires and obsessions,'[35] and explains why Toots and Terence are more susceptible to each other's feelings and

---

[30] Manning, *Youth's the Season—?*, 331–32.
[31] Manning, *Youth's the Season—?*, 366.
[32] Manning, *Youth's the Season—?*, 366.
[33] Manning, *Youth's the Season—?*, 366.
[34] Leeney, 'Not-So-Gay-Young-Things,' 163.
[35] Lanters, 'Queer Creatures, Queer Place,' 57.

are, ultimately, able to recognise each other as outsiders. The fragmented staging thus has a purposefully disorienting effect, which is heightened by the usage of dance and music. These elements combine to reflect and underscore the overall intoxicated state of the guests: as mentioned before by Terence, intoxication and self-expression are closely connected. The overtly performative nature of the scene, which depends on the staging as well as the supposedly intoxicated state of the characters, thereby facilitates the tri-directional connection (as outlined by Liora Bresler) between Terence, Toots, and the music. This connection is underscored when Terence and Toots spontaneously quote an excerpt from *Saint Teresa*, a novel that chronicles the life of Saint Teresa of Ávila, which Terence recommended to Toots:

> TERENCE: [*holding her hand with mock earnestness*]. Teresa
> Cepeda D'Avilia y Ahumada. Look on this Vanity and
> repent. ... Get out of this – before it's too late.
> TOOTS: I hear you, Brother, I hear you – and I'm moved to
> obey your words.[36]

Saint Teresa's icon is a heart pierced by an arrow. This symbol mirrors Toots's heartbreak as well as the impossibility of Terence's pursuing a romantic queer relationship. The passage both embodies and highlights their understanding of each other's pain and experiences, and signifies a clear empathic understanding. Terence recognises Toots's exclusion and urges her to leave Dublin, so that she may find love and happiness again somewhere else.[37]

Terence's words also have a darker meaning. The next time Terence is seen on stage he commits suicide by shooting himself through the heart, and it may be suggested that he is advising Toots to do the same. The shot through his heart mimics Saint Teresa's iconography, which is derived from her most famous vision. In this vision, a cherub pierced her heart with a flaming spear, which filled her with incredible pain and, simultaneously, the profound love of God. This transcendence of the physical state through pain is, among other things, one of the experiences that led to Saint Teresa's canonisation. She used a traumatic experience to get out of both literal and figurative confinements of this world. Terence's words and his reference to Saint Teresa resonate with Toots, confirming their mutual understanding, and she repeats that she 'hears' Terence and calls

---

[36] Manning, *Youth's the Season–?*, 370–71.
[37] Manning, *Youth's the Season–?*, 404.

him 'Brother.'[38] This term, in particular, confirms the deep connection that they experience in this moment. Through reading the same novel and their impromptu performance, Toots and Desmond are able to share their experiences and create a deeper understanding for each other, thus creating a temporary sense of family and community.

In the final scene, Terence frees himself of Egosmith and takes his life in his own hands in one final authentic act of self-expression. Unlike the other characters, Toots appears to understand the harmful relationship between Egosmith and Terence: 'Egosmith is Terence. Terence is Egosmith; the two in one, Dr. Jekyll and Mr. Hyde; and it's war to the death between them. I wonder which will win? [*Pause.*] Perhaps even now the battle is over.'[39] This intertextual reference is particularly apt considering the prevalence of readings that interpret the struggle between Dr Jekyll and Mr Hyde as the product of suppressed sexual desires and, in particular, those desires that deviate from what is seen as 'normal.'[40] Toots's insight confirms once more the lasting understanding that she and Terence established in the previous scene. Her premonition is validated when Terence crashes into the Millington residence and demands to speak to Desmond and Toots alone. He reasons that Toots will understand his situation and his wish to keep his promise to Desmond, namely to end his life if he ever met himself 'face to face.'[41] Terence acknowledges Toots and Desmond as fellow marginalised people, who recognise his pain and understand his motivation. This is supported by the fact that Terence called Desmond 'brother'[42] when he made this promise during the first act. Terence explains that, after his talk with Toots at the party, something snapped inside his brain and he realised that Egosmith had left him and he was 'free.'[43] However, he feels that Egosmith is already creeping up on him again and he can only commit suicide to achieve freedom: 'If only I could get away from those footsteps. Up and down, up and down ... You can hear them now. Listen ... I can no longer endure the intolerable agony of living.'[44]

Toots tries to stop Terence, but he tells her that it is no use and presses her one more time to 'get out of this.'[45] She reassures him hesitantly that

[38] Manning, *Youth's the Season–?*, 371.
[39] Manning, *Youth's the Season–?*, 395.
[40] Hall, *Queer Theories*, 115–16.
[41] Manning, *Youth's the Season–?*, 401.
[42] Manning, *Youth's the Season–?*, 332.
[43] Manning, *Youth's the Season–?*, 402.
[44] Manning, *Youth's the Season–?*, 402.
[45] Manning, *Youth's the Season–?*, 402.

she 'thinks' that she will go.[46] Terence then turns to Desmond and asks him the same question, but Desmond replies that he will not go and that he has 'resigned' himself. Terence answers that he has 'nothing to resign from' and that Desmond will never achieve anything: 'you must first cast out of yourself the illusion of non-conformity, and be a human being; just a nice, goddam, little human being.'[47] In this way, Terence urges Toots and Desmond to focus less on whether they conform or are perceived as queer, and instead to express their authentic selves. In other words, he disputes the dichotomy between conforming and non-conforming, between queer and straight, and instead underscores the individual qualities of every 'little human being.'[48] Desmond and Toots try to calm Terence, not fully able or willing to understand their friend's plan, but Terence is intent on keeping his promise to Desmond:

> Now I hope you don't mind – I'm bumping myself off here, because I think this house needs to be shaken to its bourgeois foundations. I swear that if anyone attempt to stop me I will take them with me. Terrible is he who has nothing to lose! [*His voice grows louder.* TOOTS *realises his intention too late, and rushes towards him.*] Santa Teresa, pray for this sinner now, and in the hour of his death![49]

After being controlled by Egosmith for the entire play, Terence uses his autonomy to perform one final act of self-expression. In this way, his last words and his subsequent suicide can also be seen as his last performance, albeit one that fails to successfully establish empathic understanding between the three characters. Terence hopes that his sacrifice will ensure the future happiness of Toots and Desmond, and will motivate them to divert from the conventions set by the 'bourgeois foundation' and instead become their authentic selves. This fits into the theatrical tradition of suicide as the ultimate heroic sacrifice and an act of self-perseverance, exemplified most prominently by Senecan tragic heroes.[50] Considering Terence's literary background, it may be assumed that he is aware of this tradition and tried to emulate it. This performative nature is reflected, in

---

[46] Manning, *Youth's the Season–?*, 402.
[47] Manning, *Youth's the Season–?*, 403.
[48] Manning, *Youth's the Season–?*, 403.
[49] Manning, *Youth's the Season–?*, 403–4.
[50] Braden, 'Senecan Tragedy and Renaissance,' 292.

particular, by his reference to *Saint Teresa*, which he and Toots partially performed during the previous act.

However, if the goal of his performance is to shake the Millington household to its 'bourgeois foundation,'[51] Terence is only partially successful in creating a tri-directional connection between himself, his performance, and his audience. Desmond is unwilling or unable to understand Terence's performance and states that he will go and work in his father's office the next day.[52] Toots, on the other hand, continues to understand Terence's pain and his reasoning, and becomes frantic when she realises what this means for her: 'I can't unlock the door! Help me Desmond! Somebody! Let me out!'[53] While she may lack the agency to follow Terence's advice, she does fully understand his message and is desperate to follow it, thereby highlighting the strong empathic connections that has been growing throughout the play between herself and Terence through several performances. Although the play's ending is tragic, it implies that community is possible even in the darkest moments, through art, and it poses the question what could have happened if Toots and Terence had stuck together.

Toots

While Terence and Toots forge an empathic understanding for each other based on their mutual queerness, Toots's status as a queer woman is similarly linked to her identity as an artist. Toots's queerness and subsequent social exclusion stem from her status as a 'woman with a past.' Toots is introduced as the girl-next-door and Desmond's dear childhood friend,[54] but it quickly becomes clear that they are not as close as they appear. While reminiscing on their childhood, Desmond brings up Toots's tragic love affair and argues that she cannot really have loved her ex-fiancé because she is not 'quite broken in'[55] yet. This reference to Toots's romantic history, first of all, establishes her as a 'woman with a past,' which, according to Leeney, can be linked to 'coded representations of homosexuality.'[56] Desmond, moreover, underscores the severity of Toots's situation and he assures her that there is a 'great big He-man,

---

[51] Manning, *Youth's the Season–?*, 403.
[52] Manning, *Youth's the Season–?*, 404.
[53] Manning, *Youth's the Season–?*, 404.
[54] Manning, *Youth's the Season–?*, 327.
[55] Manning, *Youth's the Season–?*, 327.
[56] Leeney, 'Not-So-Gay-Young-Things,' 161.

with a heavy golden moustache' out there, who is waiting to take her into his arms.[57] This reveals that Desmond does not understand the damage that Toots's romantic history has done to her status and that, as a result, it is unlikely that she will receive another proposal. It also showcases that Desmond does not recognise that Toots's future is as bleak as his own: he fails to acknowledge her position as a fellow outsider. This is in contrast with Terence, who did comprehend Toots's social exclusion and, subsequently, tried to connect with her.

Toots, in turn, argues that Desmond does not 'know what love is' and that she was, in fact, 'frightfully in love.'[58] The lack of understanding between the two characters seems to be mirrored by Toots singing 'And oh, how it hurts!' to the tune of *Three Blind Mice* just before Desmond mentions her affair.[59] Like the mice, Toots and Desmond are blind to each other's suffering. The farmer's wife, who mercilessly chases the mice in the song, can be seen as a reference to the centrality of peasants in Revival literature and ideologies. This is also precisely the homogeneous representation of Irishness that Manning diverted from in *Youth's the Season–?*. This idea is strengthened by the juxtaposition between the farmer's wife and the hopeless and helpless blind mice, which represent the queer characters. It showcases how people on the margins are hopelessly and helplessly excluded from society by the centre, which, by extension, applies to Toots's experience as a queer character.

As argued by Bresler, performance can be used to overcome social exclusion by sharing queer narratives and, subsequently, fostering a better understanding for queer experiences. Musical instruments, paint brushes, and other artistic tools facilitate these performances and, as such, their presence possesses symbolic value. Toots's link to art stems from her association with music and, in particular, the piano. Of all characters, Toots most frequently interacts with the piano: most notably, Toots seats herself at the piano[60] and, on another occasion, she proposes to play something for Desmond.[61] It is also implied that she accompanies herself on the piano when she sings *Three Blind Mice*, which links her artistic expression to her experience on the margin. Since Victorian times, the piano has been strongly associated with femininity and a woman's role

---

[57] Manning, *Youth's the Season–?*, 328.
[58] Manning, *Youth's the Season–?*, 328.
[59] Manning, *Youth's the Season–?*, 327.
[60] Manning, *Youth's the Season–?*, 327.
[61] Manning, *Youth's the Season–?*, 380.

in the home.[62] As Mary Burgan has observed, it came to symbolise one of the 'few legitimate channels for self-expression'[63] that were available to women or, at the very least, to more affluent women.

In light of this, it is significant that the piano in *Youth's the Season–?* is never heard during the play, with the possible exception of *Three Blind Mice* during the beginning of the first act. Whenever Toots plays or attempts to play something, she is quickly told to stop. It is noteworthy that the majority of the time, it is Desmond who tells her not to touch the piano. Toots's artistic expression challenges Desmond to consider a heterogeneous definition of queerness and to envision it as a spectrum that extends beyond the scope of his own experience. Desmond is unable or unwilling to accept this alternative mode of considering queerness and, as such, he rejects Toots's narrative and disrupts the creation of tri-directional connection. This suggests that while empathic understanding between Toots and Desmond is available and achievable, like the connection she established with Terence, it cannot be realised until Desmond recognises other expressions of queerness. In this way, the play addresses the juxtaposition not only between queer people and non-queer people, but also among queer people. It showcases that it is possible to establish queer artistic communities in Ireland, but that the characters cannot achieve this as long as they fail to acknowledge the validity of the other queer experiences and narratives.

The silent piano, moreover, symbolises the (gradual) silencing of female voices and, in particular, of Toots, as the action progresses. This mirrors her disenfranchisement due to her perceived queerness. The absence of the piano's sound in the play is countered by the mention of the female concert pianist, who is described as a 'piano thumper'[64] by Gerald, Deirdre's fiancé. By mocking and infantilising an acclaimed female pianist in this way, it becomes clear that even when self-expression is available to women, it is rarely taken seriously – to which Toots's experience further testifies.[65]

Toots's isolation and disenfranchisement are ultimately underscored during the final act. As mentioned before, the play leaves Toots helplessly banging on the door while she begs Desmond to 'let her out.' It showcases her lack of agency, and highlights that as a woman, and in particular a queer one, she is at the mercy of the men around her. Once again, the piano serves to illustrate as much, since both Desmond and Gerald violently interact with the instrument during the final act: the latter, in his 'impotent

---

[62] Burgan, 'Heroines at the Piano,' 52.
[63] Burgan, 'Heroines at the Piano,' 51.
[64] Manning, *Youth's the Season–?*, 344.
[65] Burgan, 'Heroines at the Piano,' 63.

fury,' 'very deliberately' smashes the books off the piano,[66] while the former 'stalks over to the piano' and 'plays a crashing chord.'[67] It is interesting that both acts of violence are aimed at women, Deirdre and her mother respectively, and are described as premeditated. This confirms the connection between women and the piano in the play and showcases how men can violently impede women's modes of self-expression as a form of unjustified punishment, manifested most prominently through Toots's lack of agency.

Desmond

While Desmond contributes to Toots's artistic silence and, consequently, her disenfranchisement, his own art is similarly prevented from being showcased. As mentioned before, Desmond is explicitly coded as queer, which was highlighted by mac Liammóir's portrayal in the Dublin production. This perceived queerness, moreover, is intrinsically linked to his identity as an artist. *Youth's the Season–?* opens in the drawing room of Desmond's family home where he and his sister, Deirdre, are both working on their respective projects. Desmond is described as 'sitting on the ground with a drawing-board balanced on his knees. The floor around him is strewn with paints and brushes,'[68] while the serious Deirdre is described as pouring over her writing table and working on her degree in 'Natural Science.'[69] This juxtaposition between the chaotic tableau of Desmond's painting supplies and Deirdre's neat desk is highlighted by the characters' physical description: Deirdre is 'mannishly dressed in sage green tweeds,' while Desmond looks 'frail and appealing,'[70] which can be understood as code for effeminate. Science, thus, is coded as masculine, while art is coded as feminine. In this way, both characters perform a type of gender transgression in their appearance and profession.

The link between Desmond's transgression and his artistic expression is reaffirmed in this scene by Toots. When she sees the lampshades that Desmond is working on, she exclaims: 'Greek! How phallic!'[71] Pursuing art and living a queer lifestyle are thus conflated as acts of social transgression, which is confirmed by the fact that Mr Millington, Desmond's father, strongly disapproves of his son's career. Desmond explains to Toots that

[66] Manning, *Youth's the Season–?*, 347.

[67] Manning, *Youth's the Season–?*, 390.

[68] Manning, *Youth's the Season–?*, 323.

[69] Manning, *Youth's the Season–?*, 323.

[70] Manning, *Youth's the Season–?*, 323.

[71] Manning, *Youth's the Season–?*, 324.

when he initially asked his father to send him to art school, his father replied: 'My God, I should have trashed the art out of you long ago!'[72] The play suggests that art is seen as possibly dangerous in the Free State and something that opens up too many possibilities for social deviance. This is particularly salient in light of the strict censorship of plays and art that was in effect when *Youth's the Season–?* was produced. By showcasing the pain and distress that Desmond and the other queer characters experience, the play illustrates the need for authentic and artistic self-expression.

Indeed, Desmond is convinced that he can never find happiness or community outside of artistic circles. As such, Desmond wishes to move to London to pursue a career as a designer. His father, however, insists that Desmond joins him in the office instead. This threat of having a conventional career instead of pursuing art hangs over Desmond's head throughout the play and comes to symbolise the dichotomy between conformism and transgression for the sake of individualism. As mentioned before, this strive for alternative ways of being and expressing individuality is one of Walsh's core characteristics of queerness and queer performance. In spite of Mr Millington's physical absence on the stage, he has a strong influence over his family and, consequently, the action of the play; Desmond's happy ending, for example, hinges solely on whether or not his father will support his decision to move to London.

Mr Millington looms over the action of the play as an unseen, but thoroughly felt, conservative force. In this way, he symbolises conventional societal norms and the workings of patriarchy, which are likewise invisible but potent. Mr Millington's office becomes a symbol of conformism as well: 'The umbrella – the symbolic umbrella. That's what I want to escape ... Father's office, the bowler hat, and the umbrella.'[73] Mr Millington and Desmond are both convinced that art and office life, just like social transgression and conformism, cannot be combined and pursuing one means irrevocably rejecting the other. It is unsurprising, then, that Mr Millington rejects Desmond's plea in the final act and orders him to go into the office right away. Desmond is distraught at this and calls his father's verdict 'a death-warrant.'[74] Toots tries to comfort him by proposing that he could always pursue art in his spare time, but Desmond disagrees:

Thanks, there are enough amateurs here already. No, you don't understand – How could you? You're normal. It's the loneliness

---

[72] Manning, *Youth's the Season–?*, 343.
[73] Manning, *Youth's the Season–?*, 326.
[74] Manning, *Youth's the Season–?*, 394.

that's driving me mad. I can't deceive myself, you know. I'm a
very sensitive person. I know I'm unpopular. I know exactly what
people say about me here – it all goes round in a vicious circle.
But I can't help it – I haven't the guts. I'm a coward, I'm soft.[75]

This reflection reveals that going to London was a way for Desmond not
only to pursue his artistic career, but also to join what he believed would
be a more welcoming artistic community. It moreover suggests that art is
about something more than the act of creating: it is about reaching an
audience and forging connections. Desmond believes that he will never
be able to do this in Dublin due to his unpopularity, which he attributes
to his perceived queerness. Even though Toots is considered queer as
well, due to her reputation as 'a woman with a past,' Desmond does not
recognise this and accuses her of being 'normal'[76] and, as such, unable
to have any empathic understanding for his predicament. It showcases
that Desmond has convinced himself that everyone, even his friends and
allies, are excluding him from their own communities: 'Circles! circles!
Everyone revolving in their own narrow little circle.'[77] This reinforces
the idea that without the artistic community in London, Desmond will
live his life in isolation. *Youth's the Season–?* thus suggests that there is
a hostile attitude towards queer artists in Ireland, while simultaneously
problematising this idea by showing that both Toots and Terence have
reached out to Desmond without success. Through performance, then,
community and understanding could also be established in Ireland, but
only when the full spectrum of queer narratives is acknowledged and
recognised.

Desmond's identity as an artist and his subsequent isolation are further
underscored when he experiences a brief moment of identification with a
musician who is playing outside of his window. His musings on Dublin's
amateur artists are interrupted by music: 'The Lord helps them who help
themselves and quite right too … [*He stands at the window looking out.
The wavering sound of a cornet playing 'Let Me Like a Soldier Fall' comes
from the street below.*] There's the cornet man playing in the rain – God
help him!'[78] This image of the artist all alone out in the rain serves to
externalise Desmond's feelings of being excluded and isolated, which is
underscored by the fact that Desmond and the man are separated by a

[75] Manning, *Youth's the Season–?*, 394–95.
[76] Manning, *Youth's the Season–?*, 394.
[77] Manning, *Youth's the Season–?*, 392.
[78] Manning, *Youth's the Season–?*, 395.

window and that the audience cannot see the musician at all: physical distance here symbolises emotional distance. The song, moreover, becomes significant: *Let Me Like a Soldier Fall* describes a man's wish to die a heroic death and be honoured for his bravery. The image of the soldier and his 'ancient chivalry,'[79] to which the narrator aspires, is an embodiment of traditional views on masculinity. The song thus mirrors Desmond's lament that he cannot adhere to conventional gender roles and, as a result, is excluded from social circles. In this way, the cornet man, Desmond, and the song forge a tri-directional understanding as described by Bresler. It shows that there are artistic communities out there that could provide the acceptance and understanding that Desmond craves, but that they are out of his reach.

After listening to the cornet man's song, Desmond resigns himself to working in an office and he believes that, as a result, he will be robbed of his queerness and his artistic expression. It is noteworthy that while Desmond first believed that it was impossible for him to live a conventional life, he now believes it is inevitable:

> Twenty-one years have I looked out on this square, and I see us all here, struggling to escape from our environment, fighting against it, refusing to conform; and Life, like a big sausage-machine, descends upon the raw material, grinds it up, moulds us into the required shape, and throws us out again as nice, pink, conventional little sausages – [80]

While Desmond previously maintained he could not be helped or changed, 'the machine' will turn him 'into the required pattern, and I shall become as normal as Phillip Pryce, as normal as Egosmith – [*the cornet breaks uncertainly into 'The Scenes That Are Brightest.' It grows perceptibly darker.*]'[81] Pryce and Egosmith function throughout the play as the embodiments of perfectly conventional men and are continuously juxtaposed to Desmond and, even more so, to Terence. *The Scenes That Are Brightest* warns that some things 'may charm awhile'[82] but can ultimately turn out to be deceptive and have a 'tearful cost.'[83] While Desmond may think of Pryce and Egosmith as perfectly masculine and happy, then,

---

[79] Fitzball and Wallace, 'Let Me Like a Soldier Fall.'
[80] Manning, *Youth's the Season–?*, 395.
[81] Manning, *Youth's the Season–?*, 395.
[82] Wallace and Bunn, 'Scenes That Are Brightest.'
[83] Wallace and Bunn, 'Scenes That Are Brightest.'

something more insidious is going on: the lighting in the scene growing 'perceptibly darker'[84] and Toots identifies Egosmith as Terence's 'Mr. Hyde.'[85] This darkness thus comes to embody the gradual repression of Desmond's queerness and his authentic self. This is also suggested by the last scene of the play, when Desmond has fully given up on his queer and artistic life and resigned himself to the office: 'Tomorrow, Terence – Tomorrow I'm going out to buy a bowler hat, and an umbrella – '[86] He has fully accepted his 'death in life.'[87] Even though Desmond is still alive, he has met a similar fate as Terence.

Conclusion

Youth's the Season–?, then, draws strong connections between artists and people that are perceived as queer, either from gender or sexual perspectives. Manning's play lays bare the painful consequences of depriving these queer artists of a platform for artistic self-expression and the opportunity to create and join artistic communities. It questions what Toots, Desmond and Terence might have achieved if they had been able to go to an art school, or were encouraged to create art that challenged society, or, even, when they had truly recognised each other's pain. At its very core, *Youth's the Season–?* argues for new artistic platforms that promote diverse voices and experimental work, and a general societal acceptance of those people that were isolated and pushed to the margins. In this sense, Manning's play is infused with the same ideas that she wanted the Dublin Gate Theatre to build its legacy on:

> If we have done nothing else we have emerged from the Celtic twilight and dragged into the light of day young writers and actors who might otherwise have withered away in obscurity. Ireland is passing through a transition period at the moment and the drama, which naturally reflects the minds of the people, is confused and mainly experimental; but it is taking shape out of the chaos and developing a character, a form of its own, national and international, collective and yet intensely individualistic.[88]

---

84 Manning, *Youth's the Season–?*, 395.
85 Manning, *Youth's the Season–?*, 395.
86 Manning, *Youth's the Season–?*, 404.
87 Manning, *Youth's the Season–?*, 344.
88 Manning, 'Dublin has also its Gate Theatre.'

Youth's the Season–? highlights the absolute necessity of giving a voice to the new generation of artists, strengthened by a sense of emancipatory collectivism and community without ever having to compromise that which makes them queer. As such, it is a perfect example of what the Gate was to Manning and so many other artists.

Bibliography

Braden, Gordon. 'Senecan Tragedy and Renaissance.' *Illinois Classical Studies* 9, no. 2 (1984): 277–92.

Bresler, Liora. 'Embodied Narrative Inquiry.' *Research Studies in Music Education* (2006): 1–34.

Burgan, Mary. 'Heroines at the Piano.' *Victorian Studies* 30, no.1 (1986): 51–76.

Fitzball, Edward and William Vincent Wallace. 'Let Me Like a Soldier Fall.' In *Maritana, A Grand Opera in Three Acts*, 17. London: W.S. Johnson, 1845.

Hall, Donald E. *Queer Theories*. New York: Palgrave Macmillan, 2003.

Lanters, José. 'Queer Creatures, Queer Place: Otherness and Normativity in Irish Drama from Synge to Friel.' In *Irish Theatre in Transition*, edited by Donald E. Morse, 55–67. Basingstoke: Palgrave Macmillan, 2014.

Leeney, Cathy. 'Not-So-Gay-Young-Things.' In *Irish Theatre in England*, edited by Richard Cave and Ben Levitas, 157–67. Dublin: Carysfort Press, 2007.

Manning, Mary. 'Dublin has also its Gate Theatre.' *Boston Evening Transcript*, 17 January 1935.

Manning, Mary. *Youth's the Season–?*. In *Plays of Changing Ireland*, edited by Curtis Canfield, 322–404. London: Macmillan and Co., 1933.

Valiulis, Maryann Gialanella. 'The Politics of Gender in the Irish Free State, 1922–1937.' *Women's History Review* 20, no. 4 (2011): 569–78.

Van den Beuken, Ruud. 'MacLiammóir's Minstrel and Johnston's Morality.' *Irish Studies Review* 23, no. 1 (2015): 1–14.

Wallace, William Vincent and Alfred Bunn. 'Scenes That Are Brightest.' In *Maritana, A Grand Opera in Three Acts*, 26. London: W.S. Johnson, 1845.

Walsh, Fintan. *Queer Performances and Contemporary Ireland*. Basingstoke: Palgrave Macmillan, 2016.

Walshe, Eibhear. 'Sodom and Begorrah, or Game to the Last: Inventing Micheál MacLiammóir.' In *Sex, Nation and Dissent in Irish Writing*, edited by Eibhear Walshe, 150–69. Cork: Cork University Press, 1997.

Images and Imperatives

Robert Collis's *Marrowbone Lane* (1939) at the Gate as Theatre for Social Change

Ian R. Walsh

In the summer of 1939 the Edwards–mac Liammóir Company at the Gate Theatre produced *Marrowbone Lane*, a new play that was remarkable not only in how it ran counter to their previous productions in its style and subject matter, but also because its production led to real social reform in the care of the poor, sick, and disabled in Ireland. Dr Robert Collis, an outspoken paediatrician, wrote this domestic drama of impoverished Dublin tenement life out of his frustration at seeing mothers and children presenting at hospitals with severe illness caused by their dire living conditions. Clair Wills writes, '[i]n 1939–1940 there were 23,250 registered unemployed in Dublin and 13,598 on benefit' and '[t]here were over 110,000 people living in crowded one-room tenements.'[1] The play achieved its aim of highlighting this awful situation in order to move people to take action. It stimulated the creation of the Marrowbone Lane fund for the poor that contributed, *inter alia*, to the Fairy Hill Home established in Howth, Co. Dublin, for the treatment of children with tuberculosis from Dublin's tenements, and to the formation of the National Association for Cerebral Palsy, known today as Enable Ireland. Wills also adds that it 'was the catalyst for the formation of the Irish Housewives' Association.'[2]

In scholarship, examination of the social impact that the theatre can make has been theorised and given rise to a distinctive area of research known as applied theatre. For Tim Prentki and Sheila Preston, the term describes a 'broad set of theatrical practices and creative processes that take

---

[1] Wills, *That Neutral Island*, 259.
[2] Wills, *That Neutral Island*, 261.

participants and audiences beyond the scope of conventional mainstream theatre into the realm of a theatre that is responsive to ordinary people and their stories, local settings and priorities.'[3] For those engaged in applied theatre there is often an 'overt political desire to use the processes of theatre in the service of social and community change.'[4] Although applied theatre more often takes the form of community-based performance projects, Dani Snyder-Young and James Thompson have also sought to 'include profes- sional theatre projects with overtly political goals as a form of applied theatre.'[5] It is thus the intention of this chapter to consider *Marrowbone Lane* as a piece of applied theatre that aimed for social change by examining how the dramaturgy of the play was constructed and produced in order to provoke audiences to action.

The artist and writer Christy Brown, one of the children to benefit from the National Association of Cerebral Palsy and a lifelong friend of Collis, wrote of him in a poem after his death:

> You strode rather than stepped through life
> Crushing many a demure bloom in your career
> Yet with the blunt sensitivity of one
> Trading not in images but imperatives.[6]

These not altogether flattering lines characterise Collis as a man of action ('strode rather than stepped'), but also as insensitive and demanding ('Crushing many a demure bloom'). Indeed, the line 'Trading not in images but imperatives' casts him as a pragmatist and not an artist. So too, has his drama been characterised as worthy agit-prop and not commendable theatre.

For Christopher Fitz-Simon (who is one of the few theatre historians to remember the play at all), *Marrowbone Lane* is simply a 'social tract in dialogue, rather than a piece of theatre.'[7] This viewpoint was also articulated in 1939 by Gabriel Fallon, the doyen of Irish theatre critics of that era, who criticised the play in *Irish Monthly* as marking 'the victory of sociologist over the artist,' although admitting that 'there was in all the circumstances of its reception a suggestion that the theatre is ready to welcome in no uncertain fashion a contemporary spate of "sociological

---

[3] Prentki and Preston, 'Applied Theatre: An Introduction,' 8.

[4] Prentki and Preston, 'Applied Theatre: An Introduction,' 8.

[5] Snyder-Young, *Theatre of Good Intentions*, 4.

[6] Quoted in Jordan, *Christy Brown's Women*, 131.

[7] Fitz-Simon, *The Boys*, 125.

drama."[8] However, the newspaper reviews after the opening night were much more complimentary, all considering the play as an important achievement in both its presentation and its political message. In the *Evening Herald*, David Sears wrote:

> This is the kind of play that gives significance to our national drama, for it might have been written in the very life-blood of our people. More vividly than all the speeches we have listened to for the past ten years it brings home to the audience the magnitude of our housing problem and the futility of the efforts that are being made to deal with it.[9]

There was no doubt in the author's mind either that what began as a protest piece to raise awareness became, for him, a transcendent piece of art. He writes in his introduction to the published play: 'Actually, as I have told, it started out in an attempt to show up the slums and ended in a story about the people in the slums, people whom I seemed to know and who became almost part of me as I wrote.'[10]

Indeed, the play had to be convincing drama in order for it to effect the social change that it did. It had to trade in a complex interplay of both images and imperatives to achieve its aims. James Thompson argues that an applied theatre 'is limited if it concentrates solely on effects – identifiable social outcomes, messages or impacts – and forgets the radical potential of the freedom to enjoy beautiful radiant things.'[11] He proposes a 'shift of focus from effects to affects,'[12] moving the ephemeral, unarticulated by-products of participation – 'such as joy, fun, pleasure or beauty'[13] – from the margins to the centre of applied theatre praxis. Collis's play was not simply a cold drama made up of social imperatives ('a social-tract in dialogue'), nor was it an unthinking theatre piece full of aesthetic images. It is argued here that the play instead functions to produce an experience of 'visceral empathy' in audiences as well as fostering in them an attitude of 'critical analysis.'[14] Dani Snyder-Young identifies these two modes of audience reception as fundamental to the ambitions of a theatre that

[8] Fallon, 'Those Dwellers in Marrowbone Lane,' 841.
[9] D.S., 'Marrowbone Lane.'
[10] Collis, *Marrowbone Lane*, 11.
[11] Thompson, *Performance Affects*, 6.
[12] Thompson, *Performance Affects*, 7.
[13] Thompson, *Performance Affects*, 7.
[14] Snyder-Young, *Theatre of Good Intentions*, 94.

aspires to social change. While these two modes may seem contradictory, Snyder-Young understands that audiences can experience both visceral empathy and critical distance at different points in a production, and that the most effective theatre for social change usually employs both modes of address.[15] Before I begin my analysis of how *Marrowbone Lane* addressed these modes of reception in its dramaturgy and in its production, I first wish to give some background on Robert Collis and the origins of the production of *Marrowbone Lane*.

Robert Collis and the Origins of *Marrowbone Lane*

William Robert Fitzgerald Collis, known professionally as Robert Collis, son of a solicitor and scion of a prominent medical family, was born and spent his early years in Dublin. He received his secondary education and medical training in England, France, and the United States, and played in Ireland's national rugby team. While working in King's College Hospital in London, he was inspired by Sir George Frederic Still to specialise in paediatrics, and he returned to Dublin to initiate substantial improvements in the provision of services for the health of children. He also 'became involved in campaigns to improve living conditions in the inner city and, at the end of the Second World War, he was among the first physicians to enter and work in the concentration camp in Belsen.'[16] He brought home survivor children from Belsen and resettled them in Wicklow, adopting two of them himself. When in Belsen, he met his second wife, a Dutch nurse called Han Hogerzeil. Later, he played an important role in the creation and administration of medical schools in Nigeria as it became an independent state, and finally returned to Co. Wicklow for his retirement. In addition to *Marrowbone Lane*, he also wrote another play entitled *The Barrel Organ* (1942), two autobiographies, *The Silver Fleece* (1936) and *To be a Pilgrim* (1975), and two books on the liberation of Belsen as well as two other writings on his experiences in Nigeria. In 1975 he died, shortly after falling off his horse during a hunt.

In 1936, *The Silver Fleece* brought plaudits from literary Dublin and subsequent introductions to several of its leading members. In this wider social circle, Collis met a Jesuit priest, Father Joseph Canavan (1886–1950), who asked him to help rouse public opinion about the living conditions in poorer areas of Dublin, which Collis had already visited as a student. A committee named the Citizens' Housing Council, comprising prominent

---

[15] Snyder-Young, *Theatre of Good Intentions*, 94.
[16] Breathnach and Moynihan, 'Robert Collis, Early Champion of Paediatrics,' 31.

people from a variety of religious and political backgrounds, was formed to report and agitate about the state of the city's slums, and Collis wrote an influential letter to the *Irish Press* in 1936. These activities in turn led the writer Frank O'Connor to ask Collis to pen a play about the problem and submit this to the Abbey. The Abbey Theatre declined *Marrowbone Lane*, but Collis then submitted it to the Gate, which agreed to produce it.

The play, at surface glance, would seem to be more typical of plays staged at the Abbey – that is to say, it follows in subject matter most closely O'Casey's Dublin trilogy. It is a three-act tragedy set in the Dublin tenements, which aims for the most part at a realism of character and situation. For the reviewer L.C. in the *Irish Press*, *Marrowbone Lane* was an 'Abbey Play' that had found its way to the Gate. The first of its kind to be produced at that theatre, it signals a success in a highly specialised province 'that is foreign to the Gate.'[17]

The play tells of Mary (performed to great aplomb by Shelagh Richards in the first production), a Mayo girl who marries Jim Kane, a Dublin labourer. The first act shows newly-wed Mary in shock at the living conditions of the Dublin tenement as she is dropped off at her new lodgings by her old friend Martin – a GAA (Gaelic Athletic Association) star from Mayo played by a middle-aged mac Liammóir. Despite the fact that her new home offers no running water or lavatory and that she will have to share her living space with Jim's mischievous sister Maggie and his hardened mother, Mary decides to stay. She is convinced by Jim's claim that lodging in the tenement will be a temporary measure. Martin feels sorry for Mary as he goes to leave her, and gives her five pounds. Mary adds this money to a sum she received for her wedding, stuffing it under her mattress so it is hidden away from her husband and his family. Jim is soon revealed to be unemployed while a lengthy union dispute is ongoing, and he has no income. He spends most of his time not with Mary but with his friend Joe, a union leader who espouses socialist views about a workers' republic. Joe is also a gambler and encourages Jim to join him in this pursuit. Resemblances to O'Casey's Captain Boyle, Joxer, and the Covey are hard not to discern here.

By the start of Act 2, many months have passed, and we now find Mary with a little baby. Frustrated with her living conditions, she visits the Housing Board to qualify for social housing and encourages the Canon to advocate on her behalf. The unfeeling workers on the Housing Board tell Mary she has no chance of getting a house unless she has eight children or she can prove she is gravely ill with consumption. Mary returns upset, and

---

[17] L.C., 'Marrowbone Lane at the Gate.'

ends up falling down the stairs in the tenement due to a broken banister. She is maimed for life through this accident and told she will have no more children. Martin comes to visit Mary as he is up in Dublin to play in the All-Ireland final. Mary shows Martin where she keeps her money and Maggie, Jim's sister, witnesses this unseen. Maggie, who fancies Joe, tells him of Mary's fortune lying under the mattress, and he steals the money to pay off a gambling debt. Maggie and Jim's mother witness Joe taking the money, but they cannot report him as we learn he paid for the family's survival during the previous year when Jim was gravely ill. Mary's baby then falls sick with pneumonia. She wishes to use the money to urgently get a dispensary doctor. When she goes to get her savings, she soon learns they have been stolen by Joe.

In Act 3, in a succession of short scenes, we see Mary journey with a kindly neighbour Mrs Mullins from hospital to hospital, trying to get her sick baby admitted. The baby is denied treatment or a bed by medical staff who are sympathetic but powerless to help, due to the overcrowded conditions in the hospitals and the lack of staff. Admitting defeat, the two women must then beg for tram fare home outside a cinema, where the privileged give them no charity. At the end of these scenes, the stage is plunged into a blackout with a chorus of voices chanting 'Hurry! Hurry! Hurry! Hurry!'[18] Eventually Mary and Mrs Mullins return to the tenement and it is there that the baby dies. Just as the family begins to mourn the infant's passing, a letter arrives informing them they have qualified for a new house. On hearing this news Mary ends the play screaming out against the injustice of it all and damning Free State Ireland. Jim tries to comfort her telling of how their circumstances and future will be alright now, to which she replies:

My God! – 'All right – all right!' That's what you've always said, Jim Kane, ever since you brought me into this place. 'It's all right.' It was 'all right' when they told us we couldn't have a house unless we had eight children or were dyin' of consumption, and now they're after murderin' the only baby we can ever have, it's all right. (*More hysterically*) I'm glad he's dead. (*Takes a step towards the others*) I'm glad I can't have any more children to be born in this city to die in sickness and pain. (*She crosses the room, looking wild, almost mad; the others back away from her. As she reaches the cot she stops, pauses for a moment, cries out, and sinks on her knees beside it in uncontrollable tears*) Oh, Mother of God! Brendan, my

18 Collis, *Marrowbone Lane*, 71.

baby! *Jim Kane is left standing in middle of stage. The letter falls from his hand and flutters to the floor. Curtain.*[19]

It seemed odd at the time that the Gate would produce such a play when they were, in the words of Hilton Edwards, more 'inclined to overstress the visual, the abstract, the international and the less naturalistic attitude to the stage.'[20] Indeed, in 1938, a year before producing *Marrowbone Lane*, mac Liammóir delivered a public lecture in celebration of the achievements of the Abbey Theatre on the tradition of problem plays in Ireland. He spoke of how Irish plays (meaning plays staged at the Abbey) thrived on the naturalistic presentation of social problems, and it was this topicality of the drama in its vibrancy and urgency that was of interest to audiences. He also lamented that 'the great tragedy of what is popularly known as the problem play lies in the fact that its problems belong so essentially to its own day, that it becomes tedious and pointless to the succeeding generation, and a mere corpse after that to all eternity.'[21] The lecture thus damns with faint praise the Abbey playwriting tradition as one of some merit but without lasting artistic appeal. Edwards, in his book on stagecraft *The Mantle of Harlequin*, articulates the same view, writing: 'Plays of national significance, or of purely local appeal carry a passport to success that makes them not quite legitimate examples of theatre fare.'[22] So why then would the Gate produce *Marrowbone Lane*, which could be considered by mac Liammóir's own criteria as a quintessential Irish problem play? No doubt 'the Boys' saw the financial opportunity that the success of the play could provide, given the public profile that Collis was enjoying at the time. This was an opportunity not to be missed, particularly since they were still suffering from the loss of the financial backing of the Longfords and were in need of a 'passport to success.'

However, Collis's script, when submitted to Edwards and mac Liammóir, underwent revisions, so that the final presentation was no longer a typical Abbey problem play but one that could only belong to the Gate. This is most evident in the final act, with its quick transitions from different spaces through a strategic use of dropped backcloths and the sound of the unseen chorus chanting 'hurry!' Such scenes were a signature of Edwards's expressionistic staging methods, which aimed to maintain an intensity of feeling and unity of design, but also functioned to create critical distance

[19] Collis, *Marrowbone Lane*, 95.
[20] Edwards, *The Mantle of Harlequin*, 36.
[21] Mac Liammóir, 'Problem Plays,' 214.
[22] Edwards, *The Mantle of Harlequin*, 41.

in the audience.[23] This movement from naturalism to expressionistic effects at the end of the play seems logical in its progression. The fragmentation of the realistic presentation charts the collapse of societal structures to support its most vulnerable citizens, while also mapping Mary's emotional breakdown as her plight becomes increasingly desperate, and urgent when her baby falls ill.

Visceral Empathy

Collis's play presents characters who fall victim to their circumstances, and whose behaviours are all environmentally determined. None of the characters are malicious, intentionally cruel, or Machiavellian. The implied villains in the piece are the people who allow these conditions to exist. In this respect, the play points the finger at Irish society and appeals for change. For the reviewer L.C. in the *Irish Press*, 'O'Casey accepts the slum as inevitable, Collis portrays it as something that should be fought.'[24] Gabriel Fallon in *Irish Monthly*, on the other hand, scorned the play for its sociological outlook and in particular its absence of religion:

> The dwellers there were robbed of their rights of 'character', cheated of their wholeness as men and women, and relegated to the rank of puppets by the absence of religion. It is a strange thing, perhaps the result of the victory of sociologist over the artist that not once in the whole passage of this play was there the slightest indication that the lives of these people, even the best of them were animated by anything beyond the hope of an amelioration of their material surroundings.[25]

For Fallon, the lack of any mention of religion undermines the realism of the play. This is a fair point, but also perhaps explains why the drama worked so well as a theatrical piece for social change. In excluding religion, the suffering experienced by the characters is witnessed as disconnected from determinism and divine inevitability. As such, redemption can only be found through societal or political change.

In this way, the catharsis experienced by the audience in engaging in this tragedy is one that does not simply purge emotions but instead creates the conditions for what Snyder-Young has termed 'visceral empathy'

---

[23] See Walsh, 'Hilton Edwards as Director,' 29–45.
[24] L.C., 'Marrowbone Lane at the Gate.'
[25] Fallon, 'Those Dwellers in Marrowbone Lane,' 844.

from the audience. In explaining this term, Snyder-Young refers to Martha Nussbaum's understanding of Aristotelian catharsis, which reminds us that the fear and pity that produce catharsis are not only an empathetic response but also deeply personal: 'what we pity when it happens to another, we fear lest it should happen to ourselves.'[26] Catharsis in this sense becomes visceral empathy as a device that moves an audience *beyond sympathy*, towards a fear that the events that they have witnessed are something that could happen to them as well. The power of Collis's play is in how he managed to create such empathy for his characters in the relatively affluent audience of the Gate, moving them to see themselves in these impoverished and desperate people on the stage. This personal identification with the characters creates the impetus then to address the issues causing the suffering just witnessed. It should also not be forgotten that empathy for a character on stage is not the work of the playwright alone but is also largely attributable to the skill of the actor. The reviewer in the *Irish Press* described Shelagh Richards's portrayal of Mary as 'her greatest' part and admired how she created such empathy for her character, writing that '[s]he felt the part and it was impossible not to feel with her. For the first time, it seemed to me, that she was deeply moved by the tragedy of a character.'[27]

Marrowbone Lane follows classical Aristotelian tragic structures aimed at producing visceral empathy for the audience. Mary is a hero with a fatal flaw, which is her trust. She trusts Jim when marrying him, thinking that he will provide a home for her. She is naively confident that she will get a house from the Housing Board. She is convinced she will have money for her baby if anything happens to it. Her blind trust leads to tragedy and the reversal of her fortunes. Mary ends the play like Oedipus, physically damaged and exiled from her role as a mother – a role enshrined as the primary role for women in De Valera's 1937 Constitution of Ireland. Melissa Sihra points out in the introduction to *Women in Irish Drama* that 'mother' and 'woman' are used interchangeably in Article 41 of the constitution.[28] Indeed, Mary quotes the constitution in an early scene in *Marrowbone Lane* where she quips: '"the woman's place is in the home", I suppose – well then, give us the homes.'[29] Mary's fate, unlike a classical hero, is determined not by the gods but by the social conditions in which she finds herself. It is her confidence in people and the state to care for her and their failure in these duties that mark her tragedy. The cause of

---

[26] Nussbaum, 'Aristotle on emotions and rational persuasion,' 309.
[27] L.C., 'Marrowbone Lane at the Gate.'
[28] Sihra, *Women in Irish Drama*, 2.
[29] Collis, *Marrowbone Lane*, 33.

the suffering here does not rest with the individual hero and their hubris but with the society in which she lives. This shift allows for the possibility that such a tragedy could be avoided if the ills of the society were to be addressed.

Critical Distance

It has already been outlined that while the play may adhere to a tragic dramaturgical structure, it does not follow the neoclassical unities of time, place, and action. In particular, the play undermines the unity of place in changing locations from the tenement to the offices of the Housing Board and then in the third act moving rapidly from outside the hospital, to inside the hospital, to the doorstep of the cinema, and finally back inside the tenement. For the scenes that take place outside the room of the tenement (beginning in Act 3, scene 2), the stage directions read: 'These three scenes to be treated as one. Drop cloth with large dark building projected from back with numerous amber lit windows.'[30] In these scenes, the repeated image is one of a large building that contrasts with the small, vulnerable human figures of the lame Mary and old Mrs Mullins, trying to gain admittance.

These three scenes function as a type of Brechtian social *gestus*, which David Barnett describes as entailing 'the aesthetic gestural presentation of the socio-economic and ideological construction of human identity and interaction.'[31] For Elin Diamond, this can take on the form of '[a] moment in performance that makes visible the contradictory interactions of text, theatre apparatus, and contemporary social struggle.'[32] The recurring images in the three successive exterior scenes that take place in the third act of *Marrowbone Lane* serve not only to further the plot but also as gestic moments that make visible how the large institutions in Ireland hold no welcome for the most vulnerable – a starving, maimed mother and her gravely ill child. First, it is the hospital that will not admit Mary and her child, symbolising how care is not on offer to her. However, when the building is transformed into a cinema on stage, it additionally highlights how a world of desires, pleasure, and joy are also denied to her. The ideological position of the state is revealed and the social struggle of the poor made shamefully apparent in these gestic *tableaux*. Biblical allusion is also apparent here, with a mother Mary and her infant looking for refuge.

[30] Collis, *Marrowbone Lane*, 79.
[31] Barnett, *Brecht in Practice*, 94.
[32] Diamond, 'Brechtian Theory/Feminist Theory,' 84.

However, in this instance, the mother is not given sanctuary anywhere and humankind is not redeemed by the birth of new life, but damned through the death of Mary's child.

The movement of locations in these rapid scene changes in the third act would also have destabilised the realism of the presentation. The urgency created by the dropped backcloths and the subsequent blackouts filled with the phantom voices shouting 'Hurry!' would also have intensified emotions in the audience and empathy for Mary's plight. The momentum of these scenes would have allowed for the audience to feel like Mary at the end of the drama – raw with emotion – but the theatricality of the scenes would have also allowed for them to be distanced enough from the action to use their felt emotion to fuel a critique of the social conditions of the play.

Conclusion

In staging *Marrowbone Lane*, the Gate Theatre proved to have produced work that led to real impactful social change. There are few plays in theatre history that have inspired such material transformations in people's lives as in this case. The benefit performance of the revival of the play along with a radio appeal in 1941 helped raise £1,700 for the Marrowbone Lane Samaritan Fund.[33] This money was donated to the Fairy Hill Home for children with tuberculosis to extend the facilities to 'include a modern kitchen, sanitary annexes, open-air wards, isolation wards, staff quarters, a laundry and bathrooms, bringing the capacity to twenty beds. It also enabled the hospital to extend its remit to include the admission of active cases of primary tuberculosis.'[34] The home went on to treat hundreds of patients throughout the 1940s and 1950s, eventually closing in 1961 after tuberculosis in children was no longer a major complaint in Ireland.

In 1948 money from the Marrowbone Lane fund was used by Collis to set up an assessment and treatment clinic for children with disabilities and this eventually led to the establishment of the National Association of Cerebral Palsy Ireland, which later became Enable Ireland. Today, Enable Ireland provides services for '8,500 children and adults with physical, sensory and intellectual disabilities in 15 counties across Ireland.'[35] After seeing the 1941 revival of *Marrowbone Lane*, an Irish housewife, Hilda Tweedy, wrote letters to numerous friends asking, '[w]hat is your dream of Ireland? What does the story of Marrowbone Lane mean to you? Are you

---

[33] Carthy, *The treatment of tuberculosis in Ireland from the 1890s to the 1970s*, 303.
[34] Carthy, *The treatment of tuberculosis in Ireland from the 1890s to the 1970s*, 304.
[35] 'Enable Ireland,' https://www.enableireland.ie.

satisfied that you are doing all in your power to build the kind of world you wish your children to live in?'[36] Tweedy then organised a petition calling for government rationing of all essential foods in order to control prices and to suppress the black market. This government petition came to be known as the 'Housewives petition' and led to the establishment of the Irish Housewives Association in 1942. The IHA would go on in subsequent decades to become a major voice in Ireland advocating for social welfare provision, public health, and women's rights.

What is fascinating about the production of *Marrowbone Lane* in light of all the subsequent social transformations that it inspired is that it was produced by a commercial theatre that did not view itself as ideologically driven. Edwards stated that the Gate was 'not a national theatre' but 'simply a theatre.'[37] However, after examining the dramaturgical design of the play in production in terms of what it aimed to affect, it is found that Edwards and mac Liammóir's great knowledge and experience of theatre-craft greatly aided the impact of Collis's play. The Gate Theatre is rightly remembered for its innovations in stagecraft, its professionalism, and its international outlook. It should not be forgotten that these very attributes made it also a theatre that was often socially and politically efficacious, as is made apparent in remembering the achievement of *Marrowbone Lane* as exemplary theatre for social change.

Bibliography

Barnett, David. *Brecht in Practice: Theatre, Theory and Performance*. London: Bloomsbury Academic, 2015.

Breathnach, Caoimhghin S. and Moynihan John B. 'Robert Collis, Early Champion of paediatrics.' *Ulster Medical Journal* 86, no. 1 (2017): 31–35.

Carthy, Alan Francis. *The treatment of tuberculosis in Ireland from the 1890s to the 1970s: A case study in medical care in Leinster*. Unpublished PhD Thesis, Department of History NUI Maynooth, 2015.

Collis, Robert. *Marrowbone Lane: A play in three acts*. Dublin: Runa Press, 1943.

D.S. 'Marrowbone Lane.' *Evening Herald*, 11 October 1939. 7.

Diamond, Elin. 'Brechtian Theory/Feminist Theory: Towards a Gestic Feminist Criticism.' *The Drama Review* 32, no. 1 (1988): 82–94.

Edwards, Hilton. *The Mantle of Harlequin*. Dublin: Progress House, 1958.

'Enable Ireland.' https://www.enableireland.ie.

---

[36] Tiernan and Canavan, 'Hilda Tweedy – The Original Desperate Housewife,' 7.
[37] Edwards, *The Mantle of Harlequin*, 3.

Fallon, Gabriel. 'Those Dwellers in Marrowbone Lane.' *The Irish Monthly* 67, no. 798 (December 1939): 841–45.

Fitz-Simon, Christopher. *The Boys: A biography of Micheál MacLíammóir and Hilton Edwards*. Dublin: New Island, 2002.

Jordan, Anthony J. *Christy Brown's Women – A Biography*. Dublin: Westport Books, 1998.

L.C. 'Marrowbone Lane at the Gate.' *Irish Press*, 11 October 1939. 6.

Mac Liammóir, Micheál. 'Problem Plays.' In *The Irish Theatre*, edited by Lennox Robinson, 201–27. London: Macmillan, 1939.

Nussbaum, Martha Craven. 'Aristotle on emotions and rational persuasion.' In *Essays on Aristotle's Rhetoric*, edited by A. Rorty, 303–23. Berkeley: University of California Press, 1996.

Prentki, Tim and Sheila Preston. 'Applied Theatre: An Introduction.' In *The Applied Theatre Reader*, edited by Tim Prentki and Sheila Preston, 7–16. London, New York: Routledge, 2009.

Sihra, Melissa. *Women in Irish Drama*. Basingstoke: Palgrave Macmillan, 2007.

Snyder-Young, Dani. *Theatre of Good Intentions: Challenges and Hopes for Theatre and Social Change*. Basingstoke: Palgrave Macmillan, 2013.

Thompson, James. *Performance Affects: Applied Theatre and the End of the Effect*. Basingstoke: Palgrave Macmillan, 2009.

Tiernan, Sonja and Tony Canavan. 'Hilda Tweedy – The Original Desperate Housewife.' *History Ireland* 19, no. 6 (2011): 6–7.

Walsh, Ian R. 'Hilton Edwards as Director: Shade of Modernity.' In *The Gate Theatre Dublin: Inspiration and Craft*, edited by David Clare, Des Lally, and Patrick Lonergan, 29–45. London: Peter Lang, 2018.

Wills, Clair. *That Neutral Island: A Cultural History of Ireland During the Second World War*. London: Faber & Faber, 2007.

+ 6 +

Authenticity and Social Change on the Gate Stage in the 1970s
'Communicating with the People'

Barry Houlihan

In a 2018 *Irish Times* article titled 'The Irish Working-Class and Their Place in the Literary Canon,' writer Dermot Bolger suggested that

> Many playwrights since [Sean O'Casey] faced the dilemma that even when their actors on stage portrayed the realities of working-class life (in plays as diverse as Billy Roche's *A Handful of Stars* and Christina Reid's *Tea in a China Cup*), the majority of audiences in most mainstream theatres still predominantly hailed from areas like Wrathmines [*sic*]. And they were inclined to view such characters through a sentimental prism of nostalgia, more as colourful characters (in the sense of oddities) rather than as people who share the same everyday dilemmas as them.[1]

Bolger thereby outlines a prescient point regarding the important role that theatre, and art in general, can play in examining the structures and arrangements of social order. The treatment of working-class characters in the theatre in particular tends to take place through the prism of romanticised affection, with little attempt to empathise with the challenges that so often pervade such conditions.

Bertolt Brecht discussed this point in detail in his essay 'The Popular and the Realistic.' In this essay, Brecht defines 'the popular' as that which is 'intelligible to the broad masses, taking over their own forms of expression and enriching them/adopting and consolidating their standpoint,'[2] and, in

---

[1] Bolger, 'The Irish Working-Class.'
[2] Brecht, 'The Popular and the Realistic,' 108.

doing so, offers a powerful artistic rebuke to the voyeuristic misappropriation of class. Brecht instead argues for a repositioning of popular drama (a folk- or people-driven popular form) in ways that are authentic to the people it depicts and represents, focusing on those 'who are not only fully involved in the process of development, but are actually taking it over, forcing it, deciding it. ... We have in mind a fighting people and also a fighting conception of "popularity."'[3]

With these points in mind, this chapter investigates the production and presentation of plays at the Gate Theatre that reflected marginalised and working-class communities, as well as the social and political contexts of working-class characters, settings, and their reception by audiences at the Gate during the 1960s and 1970s. In examining such emancipatory plays, it is also necessary to deepen our understanding of the creative and directorial processes at the Gate Theatre at this time, and examine new directors' work at the theatre. This chapter will therefore also recover the work of women directors at the Gate Theatre during the period.[4] Chloe Gibson, for example, worked with Edwards–mac Liammóir Productions at the Gate Theatre and also in an independent capacity through her own company, Chloe Gibson Productions. Through evidence provided by actors with whom she worked, and as outlined in this chapter, Gibson was recognised as having utilised innovative creative and directorial practices to present the stories of working-class and marginalised communities at the Gate Theatre.

Central to these investigations is the premise of authenticity in terms of both form and social representation within the medium of theatre versus that of television in Ireland during this period, which absorbed much of Hilton Edwards's energies in his later years. Edwards was Telefís Éireann's first director of drama and considered the medium of television as a vehicle to reach new Irish audiences directly in their homes.[5] Working in television also provided both Edwards and mac Liammóir with the enriching experience of collaboration with new artists and producers, such

[3] Brecht, 'The Popular and the Realistic,' 108.
[4] For more on the history and experience of women artists at the Gate Theatre see Meaney, O'Dowd, and Whelan, *Reading the Irish Woman*, 196–217.
[5] In the National Library of Ireland, within the Edwards–mac Liammóir papers (MS 45, 871), there is a hardback file marked 'Hilton Edwards, 4 Harcourt Terrace, Dublin, 4 May 1961.' Within the file is a detailed Plan of Organisation and Directives for the Drama Department, Radio Éireann – Irish Television, 34–37, Clarendon Street, Dublin 2. This file includes memoranda, circulars, plans, notes, mainly typescript, for various operations within RTÉ in the early years of television in Ireland.

as Adrian Vale,[6] producer at RTÉ and long-time associate of Edwards, and the playwright and critic Carolyn Swift, among many others. Television also disseminated works that originally began as productions at the Gate Theatre an extension into the new medium of television, such as *Tolka Row* by Maura Laverty.[7]

During these decades, there was a proliferation of independent theatre companies and theatre makers in Ireland who were influenced by international styles, as well as by developments in other popular media forms, such as television. Figures such as Hilton Edwards, Lelia Doolan, Chloe Gibson, Carolyn Swift, and Alan Simpson, to name a few, had careers in the theatre as well as important and formative roles in the development of television in Ireland from its inception in 1961.[8] Some of these figures found a home at the Gate Theatre, where they could develop their work and practice. Chloe Gibson, for example, first served as Head of Drama at Raidió Teilifís Éireann (RTÉ) from 1965 until 1971, and directed Telefís Éireann's opening night broadcast on New Year's Eve 1961. Gibson then went on to direct five shows at the Gate Theatre during the 1970s, and is an important, if not also overlooked, figure in the study of direction at the Gate. Gibson experimented in the presentation, style, and form of her directing, often focusing on working-class and socialist themes in both new contemporary works and revivals of classics.[9]

The founding ethos of the Gate Theatre was to provide European and international work, enriched with modernist thinking, in contrast to the new Irish writing of the Abbey Theatre (which broadly addressed issues of nation, Gaelic Ireland, and 'Irishness'). Class relations in

---

[6] Adrian Vale (1928–2000) was the RTÉ's television drama script-editor in the 1960s and 1970s. Vale was invited to Ireland by Hilton Edwards to work in RTÉ Drama Department, which he did for seventeen years, working on numerous plays. For more information on Adrian Vale see 'Hilton Edwards Invited Him.'

[7] *Tolka Row* was first broadcast on 3 January 1964 and aired weekly for five series until it ended on 31 May 1968. It was first produced as a play by Dublin Gate Theatre Productions in October 1951, directed by Hilton Edwards.

[8] For more detail on the social and political context and impact of the beginning of Telefís Éireann in Ireland, see Savage, 'Film and Broadcast Media' and Morash, *A History of the Media*.

[9] Plays directed at the Gate Theatre by Chloe Gibson include *The Signalman's Apprentice* by Brian Phelan (1 June 1971); *Arms and the Man* by G.B. Shaw (1 September 1971); *Fanny's First Play* by G.B. Shaw (1 April 1972); *The Late Edwina Black* by William Dinner and William Morum (1 May 1972); and *The Antoinetta* by John and Maurice Good (1 June 1972).

Ireland were nevertheless an ever-present trope at the Gate.[10] Reflecting on and considering Ireland's postcolonial status, questions such as the political radicalism of women in the Free State and the conditions of slum tenements in inner-city Dublin, as well as the changing standing of the middle classes in Irish society, were interrogated by playwrights at the Gate. More specifically, Brian Phelan's 1971 play *The Signalman's Apprentice* (1971), which was directed by Chloe Gibson, is an important example of a play that brought attention to working-class experience in the form of Brecht's notion of popular drama (as outlined above), drawing as it did on authentic experiences and representations of character. In doing so, Phelan's play also eschewed didactic realism and embraced experimental form, featuring elements of *grand guignol* and horror in its depiction of male working-class experiences.

Authenticity and Class: Form and Representation in Popular and Experimental Performance

Garde and Mumford define authenticity in contemporary European theatre as being underpinned by a number of primary performative concerns. These seek to destabilise the audience's experience of societal norms that otherwise would be presented through realist performance. Such dramaturgical structures allowed for new ways of encountering the unfamiliar and performing cultural differences on stage. As Garde and Mumford argue, the expectations of audiences 'are shaped by schemata which are in turn shaped by local (theatre) histories, collective and personal memories.'[11] In the presentation of working-class and socialist/political concerns of the 1970s, as Phelan does in *The Signalman's Apprentice*, Gibson's direction of the play follows this pattern of destabilisation of middle-class societal representation. It seeks to achieve this through the violent and surrealist depiction of the breaking of social *ennui* and disinterest in labour protests, and foregrounds the experimental dramatisation of working-class characters and settings. Garde and Mumford's thesis helps us to consider Phelan's objectives in outlining the history of contemporary socially reflective performance and 'theatre of the authentic' through what they call the counter-culture and theatricalisation of everyday life. This occurred in Europe in the 1960s and 1970s, and was characterised by an increased emphasis on collective theatre-making,

---

[10] For more on the examination of class, gender and identity at the Gate Theatre, see Leeney, 'Class, Land, and Irishness,' 161–80.

[11] Garde and Mumford, *Theatre of Real People*, 12.

self-representation, cultural diversity, and the blurring of boundaries between art and life.[12]

Following on from this description of the European experience of the 'theatre of the authentic,' it is necessary to consider and to contextualise Chloe Gibson's work as a director during this period at the Gate Theatre. It is also important, therefore, to reflect on the dramaturgical as well as directorial advances and experimentation in post-World War II Europe in relation to the Gate Theatre, thereby creating insights into the ways in which directing techniques were practised. For example, Henning Fülle, in his discussion of the 'radicality' with which texts, form, and practice was developed, observes how

> Alongside new forms of production praxis and dramaturgy, a number of authors also embark on new directions in theatre text beyond the drama: with Samuel Beckett as practitioner of the highest degree of radicality, but also with Eugène Ionesco and the French 'absurdists', Jean Genet and the British authors Harold Pinter, Edward Bond and Arnold Wesker; while in Eastern Europe, alongside Socialist Realism, above all in Poland, Jerzy Grotowski and Tadeusz Kantór develop forms of theatre work inspired by Artaud.[13]

Regarding the 1960s and 1970s, Fülle cites the emergence of Eugenio Barba, Robert Wilson, Ariane Mnouchkine, Luca Ronconi, and others who contributed to the focus of theatre (and theatre art) on authenticity in terms of contemporary social(ist) realism in European theatres, the trademarks of which include:

> exploratory theatre art for an audience of contemporaries that refers to their time and the Zeitgeist while tackling the demand to treat present-day perception and enable and mediate experiences for their audience ... each artist of postmodernity assumes the tasks of ushering the traditions of stagecraft into each respective NOW, processing stories of political and societal reality and developing the art of perception as a central technique for the evolution of civilisations, and as a vital coping mechanism for post-industrial cultures.[14]

---

[12] Garde and Mumford, *Theatre of Real People*, 29.
[13] Fülle, 'A Theatre for Postmodernity,' 281.
[14] Fülle, 'A Theatre for Postmodernity,' 281.

In the exploratory nature and objective of such theatre (or 'theatre art,' as
Fülle defines it), the unifying characteristics relate to form, visualisation,
and scenography rather than purely textual elements, since these function
as means of communicating to mass audiences. This multi-sensory appeal
and presentation take the form of pop-art and other forms of contemporary
avant-garde performance art, and indeed we see such devices employed by
Gibson in her direction of Phelan's play (and in her other work produced at
the Gate in this period). Phelan's stage direction also places much emphasis
on physical and bodily representation to convey repetition, boredom, and
psychological isolation. At the beginning of Act II, Scene 1 of *The Signalman's
Apprentice*, for instance, Phelan's stage directions describe the monotony of
daily acts such as oiling the model trains, laying out newspapers, moving
the furniture; movements that Phelan notes as all being 'ritual.'[15]

Influenced by the forms in European theatre production and direction
that Fülle outlines, Gibson and Phelan worked in a period that can be
loosely defined as the 'late Edwards–mac Liammóir era':[16] a time when
innovative engagements with form and production were explored in
new Irish venues as well as established venues such as the Gate Theatre.
Experimentation in popular forms of drama – as a mode of political
protest and resistance – was also growing in popularity in Ireland in
these decades. Susanne Colleary[17] and Elizabeth Howard[18] have reflected
on the highly significant contribution of community arts, independent
theatre, devised production, and amateur theatre. Patrick Lonergan observes

---

[15] Phelan, *The Signalman's Apprentice*, 49.

[16] In the context of this essay, I define the 'late Edwards–mac Liammóir era' as
coinciding with the refurbishment and reopening of the Gate Theatre in March
1971, until the death of Micheál mac Liammóir in 1978 and of Hilton Edwards
in 1982. The opening production of 'the new Gate' was *It's Later Than You Think
(or Being the Strange Case of Monsieur Ornifle)*, a translation by Lucienne Hill of
Jean Anouilh's *Ornifle*, as part of the 13th Dublin Theatre Festival. The play starred
Micheál mac Liammóir and was directed and lit by Hilton Edwards. Records in
the Gate Theatre Digital Archive at NUI Galway show that mac Liammóir and
Edwards were planning as early as March 1970 to open the new Gate Theatre
with a translation on Anouilh's *Cher Antoine*. Desmond Graham, rights manager
at Dr Jan Van Loewen Ltd Agency, London, stated that Hilton Edwards was 'one
of the few people who could do justice' to Anouilh. By 1970, Jean Anouilh was
awarded the Prix Mondial Cino Del Duca, one of the world's richest literary prizes,
which recognises 'a French or foreign author of whom the work constitutes, in
scientific or literary form, a message of modern humanism.' See 'Correspondence
concerning the Gate Theatre's production of *It's Later Than You Think*.'

[17] Colleary, 'Long Flame in the Hideous Gale,' 201–19.

[18] Howard, 'Performance in the Community,' 165–80.

how, as the decade of the 1960s was progressing, the Gate Theatre, too, was regenerating itself.[19] He further notes that at this point of cultural transmission and transition in relation to European influences on Irish theatre, '[the Gate] held the conviction that a truly national theatre should engage with non-Irish work, both as a way of developing the craft of Irish theatre artists and enriching the experience of Irish audiences.'[20] This craft of Irish theatre artists would find outlets, expression, and influences through the emergence of new media in Ireland during the 1960s and 1970s, and also through the emergence and nurturing of new relationships between artists at the Gate in this period.

Transitions: New Media, Influences, and Networks at the Gate

The onset of television in Ireland from 1961 gave rise to a new medium for Irish writers, artists, and dramatists. Hilton Edwards was among the first to engage with the medium at the fledgling Telefís Éireann. While openly admitting, though with tongue in cheek, that he knew nothing about the new medium, Edwards was still aware of its ability to directly speak to and reach a broad spectrum of audiences of all backgrounds, outside of those who would traditionally come to the Gate:

> I now enter a fascinating and quite terrifying new medium, fraught with technical complications ... the ace up television's sleeve is to penetrate the sacred circle of the family hearth ... another is that of catching people, as it were, on the wrong foot, letting us glimpse how they are, not how they wish us to believe them.[21]

These closing years of the Boys' tenure at the Gate Theatre would offer much by way of new work not previously seen on the Gate stage, perhaps emboldened by the Gate's recent refurbishment, as the Theatre reopened on 15 March 1971 to host the new season. This also coincided with the largest stage grant in the theatre's history, worth £30,000.[22]

---

[19] Lonergan, *Irish Drama and Theatre Since 1950*, 86.

[20] Lonergan, *Irish Drama and Theatre Since 1950*, 85.

[21] Quoted in Fitz-Simon, *The Boys*, 242.

[22] In May 1969, prior to a Government subsidy being arranged for the Gate Theatre, a fundraising committee was initiated, called the Edwards/mac Liammóir Playhouse Society. The group also utilised personal political contacts within the newly appointed Fianna Fáil-led Government, such as the new Minister for Finance, Charlie Haughey.

Actor David Byrne called this period from the Gate's refurbishment, from early 1971 through to Patrick Bedford's production of *Equus* in 1977, the Gate's 'Renaissance.' As Christopher Fitz-Simon states, 'The Gate Theatre was now "officially" recognised; but the irony was that its founders were now elderly and by recent own admission, were out of touch with trends in the international theatre.'[23] I would argue that the production of *The Signalman's Apprentice* (in June 1971) helped to reinvigorate the Gate as a contemporary theatre, and demonstrated how the Gate engaged anew with modern audiences and the influence of new media and globalising culture. In doing so, the Gate collaborated with new artists, writers and directors, such as Brian Phelan and Chloe Gibson, looked to settings outside of Ireland (as in this case, Liverpool) and to the examination of topics not readily associated with the Gate's repertoire, notably that of working-class communities. In looking further at this topic, it is useful to situate the Gate's production of Phelan's play within the wider tradition of Irish writing and the depiction of working-class communities.

Constructing Authenticity: Working-Class Experiences on the Gate Stage

Michael Pierse's monograph *Writing Ireland's Working Class: Dublin after O'Casey* (2010) defines working-class perspectives in literary representation as being consistently projected to the periphery of social experience. Such forms then naturally gravitate to alternative expressions through non-realist performance and expression. Pierse further suggests that as an alienated group within society, working-class people recognise their position of alienation in terms of material deprivation, including the physical positioning of their localities to under-serviced and over-populated planned urban suburbs on the periphery of middle-class existence.

The failure of realist forms of theatre to adequately express working-class themes, Pierse argues, is also symptomatic of bourgeois realism's failure to represent the realities underlying their experience.[24] Pierse cites Terry Eagleton's concerns that expressionism as a form feels the need to transcend the limits of the naturalistic aesthetic and assumes the ordinary bourgeois world to be solid and authentic – the refusal of reality.[25] Likewise, *The Signalman's Apprentice* is a play that eschews traditional realist form and embraces non-realist and experimental forms

23　Fitz-Simon, *The Boys*, 291–93.
24　Pierse, *Writing Ireland's Working Class*, 4.
25　Pierse, *Writing Ireland's Working Class*, 24.

of performance and direction, including those of *grand guignol*, horror, and grotesque in order to represent the experience of train workers in isolated train yards in 1970s London.[26]

In striving to define and stage an authentic representation of working-class railway workers in Dublin, Hilton Edwards wrote an acknowledgement in the play programme thanking the Station Master and staff of Connolly [Train] Station in Dublin where he and cast members visited a signal box to observe the men at work.[27] Similarly, Eamonn Morrissey, who played the young apprentice, Edward, in Phelan's play at the Gate, described in an interview what the rehearsal process for the play entailed: 'They [Edwards and mac Liammóir] really convince you that you ARE the characters.'[28] Morrissey would further clarify that:

> The play is extraordinarily relevant to the three of us as people. To Hilton and Micheal, the character I play is really *black*. They dislike the apprentice almost as much off-stage as they do on it. To me, he is relatively sympathetic. When we discuss the play after rehearsals, we find ourselves airing completely different views of the play and of life in general.[29]

In addition to this apparent resentment on the part of Edwards and mac Liammóir towards the young socialist character in the play, Morrissey also cites a generation gap evident in the processes and methodology of rehearsing, acting, and directing for this play. Morrissey explained that, as a director, 'Edwards likes to finalise all movements and speech as early as possible in the process, in Week 1 if possible, and repeat the process continually.'[30] However, Morrissey's experience of working with directors at the more experimental venues in Dublin, such as the Eblana, the Pike, or the Globe, where Alan Simpson, Roland Jaquarello, and Phyllis Ryan presided, offered a more fluid attitude towards ensemble devising. Morrissey describes the rehearsal process preferred by Gibson as being more progressive and inclusive of devising within the ensemble as a whole:

---

[26] Other works of the *grand guignol* style were produced at the 1971 Dublin Theatre Festival, such as *The Children of the Wolf* by John Peacocke, which was directed by Vincent Dowling and transferred to London after the Dublin Theatre Festival. 'An Irishman's Diary.'

[27] 'Programme for *The Signalman's Apprentice*.'

[28] 'What's on in the Arts.'

[29] 'What's on in the Arts.'

[30] 'What's on in the Arts.'

> From working with younger directors, I've come to enjoy trying
> things out, playing a scene different ways before deciding how to
> do it. Chloe Gibson has managed brilliantly to let us all work the
> way we're happiest without upsetting each other.[31]

This new and modern vision for contemporary Irish drama was a conflicted
space for the ageing directors of the Gate Theatre in the 1970s. Micheál mac
Liammóir told the *Boston Globe* in an interview that 'I don't understand
contemporary theatre ... I just don't get the new boys [Beckett, Pinter,
Ionescu]. I watch their work, say Yes in my head, but my heart yawns.'[32]
This sense of disconnection to dramatic modernity was not confined to
the Gate. When the Abbey Theatre, for example, reopened in its new
premises in 1966, director Roland Jaquarello described the main stage as
unwelcoming, featuring bad acoustics being remote and inaccessible.[33] This
resulted in an alienation between actors and audiences and precluded the
staging of marginalised communities, including working-class experiences,
that had been largely absent in a meaningful way at Ireland's major theatres
since Seán O'Casey imposed a ban on the professional production of his
plays in Ireland in the 1950s.

However, Brian Phelan's work continued the tradition of O'Casey
of challenging the dominant state–class hegemony in terms of character,
dramaturgy, and scenography. Phelan's body of work, spanning over forty
years, includes original work, adaptations and docudramas, which focus on
issues of Irish emigration and international politics, socialist and feminist
themes, and contemporary world events.

Brian Phelan and Chloe Gibson – Backgrounds and Journey to the Gate Theatre

Phelan was thirty-six years old when *The Signalman's Apprentice*, his first
play, was produced in his home city of Dublin at the Gate Theatre. Born
in 1935, his father worked as a builder and the family lived in Kilmainham
on the city's north side. Phelan was largely self-educated and has discussed
frankly his experiences regarding his lack of formal training or university
education, which he argues has set him apart from others working in the
theatre scene at the time. Phelan said in an interview: 'I feel so ignorant
sometimes and everything I do know is all jumbled up. I'd have loved

---

[31] 'What's on in the Arts.'
[32] Quoted in Fitz-Simon, *The Boys*, 285.
[33] Jaquarello, *Memoirs of Development*, 28.

Figure 1. Brian Phelan and Chloe Gibson on the set of
The Signalman's Apprentice, 1971, courtesy of the
Gate Theatre Digital Archive, Hardiman Library, NUI Galway.

to go to University – to have three years just to think and learn things.'[34]
Reflecting on Phelan's personal experiences of such disparities, James
Wickam, whose work focuses on socialist histories, has reflected more
generally on the relationship between education and class:

> If capitalism is a structure of economic domination then it is also
> one of cultural domination. In any capitalist country, working class
> children 'learn' in school that they are not suited to anything else
> but manual work – their values, lifestyle, their very language, are
> not proper.[35]

Phelan's family emigrated to Canada from Dublin in the 1950s, where he
worked low-paid jobs in theatre and television production. It was at this
time that Phelan started writing for both theatre and television, but drama

[34] 'Interview with Brian Phelan.'
[35] Wickham, 'The New Irish Working Class,' 82.

was his primary focus. In the late 1950s, Phelan returned to Dublin before moving to London, where he shared a flat with Donal Donnelly, the actor long associated with the Gate Theatre.

Phelan acted in some plays at the Mermaid Theatre in London, but was self-conscious and uncomfortable working as an actor.[36] He wrote a successful television play, *The Tormentors*, for ATV television in England, which starred James Mason and Stanley Baker, and which prompted Phelan to commit to writing full-time thereafter. Phelan also acted in television adaptations of plays such as Arnold Wesker's *The Kitchen*, which, after its 1959 stage premiere, became a landmark piece in addressing socialist and working-class labour concerns in the workplace of a large hotel kitchen. A committed socialist, Phelan stated that he was focused on writing his views into his plays but was wary of large producers who were changing the components of his work.[37]

Phelan traces elements and influences of Pirandello in his dramatic work, especially with regard to the presentation and representation of fantasy, identity, and the multiplicity of existence within contemporary society. Phelan also cites international writers and playwrights who had political and social issues at their core. Arthur Miller is one such stated key influence on Phelan. With a mix of European and American literary, theatrical, and political influences, Phelan is an important if also a minority figure within the Gate's history and within its examination of marginalised communities.

When *The Signalman's Apprentice* made its debut in June 1971,[38] as part of the first season programmed by Edwards and mac Liammóir after the reopening of the theatre in March 1971, it was directed by Chloe Gibson, who had an association with Hilton Edwards and the Gate Theatre that preceded this production. Along with Michael Hayes and Peter Collinson, who were more experienced directors of television drama in England, Gibson directed the first television productions for Hilton Edwards at the newly formed Telefís Éireann. By the time *The Signalman's Apprentice* was performed at the Gate in 1971, Chloe Gibson was Head of Drama at RTÉ. Gibson succeeded Hilton Edwards in that role in 1965 until she retired from Telefís Éireann in December 1971. In her role at the national

---

[36] 'Interview with Brian Phelan.'

[37] 'Interview with Brian Phelan.'

[38] The play received its world premiere at the Oxford Playhouse, Oxford, in 1971, where it received positive notices and reviews, in particular for its set, which was designed by Stephanos Lazaridis. The play was also noted as a 'chilling thriller.' For more on the original production of the play see Chapman, *Oxford Playhouse*.

broadcaster, Gibson directed mac Liammóir in the television adaptation of *The Importance of Being Oscar* and also directed Edwards in *King Herod Explains*, by Conor Cruise O'Brien, also for Telefís Éireann.

Gibson first came to Ireland at the invitation of Hilton Edwards after he saw her production of *Family Portrait* starring Fay Compton at the Strand Theatre in London. Gibson later directed television dramas for the BBC, including the serial *Pepys' Diary*. She was determined to contribute more time to theatre work in her retirement. Gibson became a director of the Dublin Arts Company for a time and also worked in association with the Amalgamated Artists at the Eblana Theatre during the 1970s, a group that produced many works by playwrights addressing socialist and working-class themes while employing avant-garde forms.[39]

The Signalman's Apprentice and *Finding the Authentic*

Brian Phelan's play is set in a signal box of a railway station in contemporary Fulham, London, occupied by two elderly railway employees, Alfred and Albert, who have been made redundant but, by virtue of an apparent administrative error, are still in receipt of payment and registered as employees of the railway company. The apprentice of the play's title is a young man named Edward who was sent to the train yard by 'Head Office' to serve his apprenticeship. The play sets out an exploration of the adherence to tradition, craftsmanship, and employment regulation, but also of the power dynamics of relationships and dominance in society. Christopher Fitz-Simon notes that there was initially an absence of rapport and atmosphere at rehearsals of the play, with mac Liammóir commenting that 'it's very boring – all these working-class characters repeat themselves.' It was reported there was a shaky opening night performance, in particular from mac Liammóir, who was not in full health at the time, and when he missed his lines would simply interject 'cor blimey' ad nauseam in a thick Cockney accent, jokingly mimicking the colloquial language of the characters he was inhabiting within the production.

By the end of the first act, Edward has uncovered the lie that is perpetrated by Alfred and Albert regarding their ongoing false employment and their falsified receipt of income. Edward, who comes from a working-class Liverpool background, cannot tolerate the entitled position of Alfred

---

[39] Theatre groups such as the Amalgamated Artists staged works regularly at the Eblana Theatre, Dublin, during the 1970s that address political and working-class themes and also experimental theatre productions. The company was managed by A.J. Murphy.

and Albert: they are in permanent employment, but only enjoy this privilege due to an administrative error. In essence, they perform no actual work or labour in return for the full payment they receive. Edward's response to this inequity is captured by Kane Archer, who, reviewing the play for the *Irish Times*, describes him as

> the destructive kind that must take all but still remains unsatisfied. First, destroying the relationship that had existed between the two men and contemptuous of their honest pride, as after all, dishonesty is at the heart of their existence. Edward brings violence and disaster to all three. When his work is finished, only ruin remains.[40]

Conflict within the play resides upon the premise of pitting youth against authority and power, and tradition and craft in opposition to experimentation. Eamon Morrissey, playing the young and brash Edward, challenges the values, assumptions, and place of the ageing chief and his assistant, played by Edwards and mac Liammóir, with the elderly couple threatened by the aspirations of the younger Edward to move beyond the class of his birth. As Alfred comments to Albert: 'You were born for the high livin', I can see that.'[41]

In order to pass the daily routine and monotony of non-labour, and therefore essentially unfulfilling the production of labour within a capitalist context, Albert builds an intricate model railway that operates in place of their present and outward actual labour. Edward disrupts the linear and chronological sense of both time and place through his suspicion of Albert and Alfred's fraudulent employment status, and seeks to extort the elderly men of their pensions through threats to smash the model railway. Edward partially succeeds at this in the second act before ultimately Edward dies during a struggle. Edward attempts to strangle Alfred first before receiving a violent blow from Albert, and he is killed in a graphic and grotesque manner on stage during the third act, marking the climax of the play.

Edward, then, fulfils the embodiment of the 'Angry Young Man,' popularised by John Osborne and Arnold Wesker and others who sought to destabilise the state's capitalist and market-driven economic orientation. Phelan's play can thus be read as a critique of then British Prime Minister Edward Heath's economic policies following his Conservative Party election success of 1970. The Industrial Relations Act 1971, for example, sought to stymie the influence of trade unions by reliance on the courts. Hugely

---

[40] 'The Signalman's Apprentice Opens at the Gate.'
[41] Phelan, *The Signalman's Apprentice*, 51.

Figure 2. Set design by Robert Heade for
The Signalman's Apprentice, 1971, courtesy of the
Gate Theatre Digital Archive, Hardiman Library, NUI Galway.

unpopular with trade union membership in Britain, the Act became a symbol for authority and power seizing control over labour and strike rights of workers.[42] As outlined by Albert in the play, the increased presence of authority within workplace and industrial relations ensured prominence of production over worker rights: 'It's to do with modernization. Yes. We are scheduled for modernization.'[43]

The play received very positive reviews at the Gate and there is substantial evidence within correspondence files present within the Gate Theatre Digital Archive at NUI Galway that it was also very well attended. The play later ran for a year and a half in Paris and had fifteen productions in Germany, signifying its broad appeal and illustrating that it brought the Gate Theatre of the 1970s into dialogue with contemporary European drama. Phelan's play was also the last time that Edwards and mac Liammóir played together on the Gate or indeed any stage. The previous occasion had come almost a decade earlier, in 1963, when they acted together in Patrick Paterson's *The Roses are Real* at the Gaiety Theatre.

A number of administrative records from the production of *The Signalman's Apprentice* are in the Gate Theatre Digital Archive, though artistic and creative records are missing. The play was initially sent to Edwards and mac Liammóir by the actor Donal Donnelly for consideration.

---

[42] For more on this see article by Phillips, 'The 1972 Miners' Strike,' 187–207.
[43] Phelan, *The Signalman's Apprentice*, 23.

Reader-report comments by mac Liammóir on the play include him describing Phelan's drama as 'A near master piece of horror – a brilliant play written with great authority and an uncanny knowledge of Cockney mentality and speech.'[44] Mac Liammóir continued in his report to say that:

> Edward's manner towards the other two men changes immediately and with a frankness that would I feel, be foreign to his nature and certainly less dramatically effective than if he made the revelation insidiously and in the manner of a tactful dentist who starts his drill in the most deceptively painless manner until the victim in the chair becomes slowly conscious that a diabolical instrument is indeed at work.[45]

This point addresses mac Liammóir's concern for authenticity in performance, confirming him to be an actor who would approach the role in a manner that could work consciously within the framework of psychological tension rather than by a sudden or 'uncharacteristic' turn of mood and tone. This can be interpreted as an indicator that mac Liammóir was supportive of a naturalistic dramaturgy for the play, and put less emphasis on the experimental performance style that Phelan preferred and had constructed within the play. Moreover, mac Liammóir added criticism of its ending:

> I am sad about the tragic Guignol-esque ending of the play: The wretched Alfred with two murders on his hands utterly alone and penniless in a grim deserted setting. I would have preferred a wryly comic turning of the tables with Alfred the boss and Albert the smiling obedient figure ... not for my own personal taste but with a genuine desire for the plays [sic] wider popularity. As it is, the final situation is too appalling to accept.[46]

Mac Liammóir also expressed concerns regarding the focus on highly technical specifics of train mechanics and operating systems for the model railway that would be used in the play. Further concerns raised were regarding the logistics of smashing the model train on stage every night

---

44 'Correspondence concerning the Gate Theatre's production of *The Signalman's Apprentice*,' 1.

45 'Correspondence concerning the Gate Theatre's production of *The Signalman's Apprentice*,' 2.

46 'Correspondence concerning the Gate Theatre's production of *The Signalman's Apprentice*,' 2.

as well as the impact of violence on objects within the playing area. The confinement caused by the restrictive physical space of the set reflected the experience of social, class, or economic confinement by the characters in the play and, in turn, by working-class communities in reality. Violence, especially by young men acting out and against their physical environment, was often used in plays that reflected working-class experiences, such as *Hatchett* by Heno Magee in 1972.[47]

Conclusion

A number of playwrights working in Ireland during the 1970s, such as Heno Magee, Lee Dunne, Peter Sheridan, and James McKenna, as well as groups such as the Amalgamated Artists, wrote and produced plays that addressed working-class social issues, characters and settings. These plays were produced at the Peacock Theatre, the experimental space at the Abbey Theatre, or other theatre spaces, such as project Arts Centre, the Eblana, or other independently run spaces in Dublin.

While the Gate did not have a defined policy for developing work of working-class themes, Edwards and mac Liammóir did add to these important examinations of Irish social conditions and class debates of the time with productions such as Robert Collis's *Marrowbone Lane* (1939) and *Tolka Row* by Maura Laverty (1951). Indeed, by the 1970s, more experimental and diverse work (in terms of theme and production) became more commonplace, and, as described above, Phelan's *The Signalman's Apprentice* (1971), as directed by Chloe Gibson, is a reminder of attempts by the Gate to authentically examine social conditions of working-class communities. Such productions are emblematic of the spaces in Irish theatre in which working-class writers can present their stories and those of other marginalised groups in Irish society at this time, counteracting cultural blind spots in the repertoire of Irish drama.

At the same time, various questions arise from studying these plays and themes: where, for example, are the working-class women? These plays are

---

[47] *Hatchett* was first presented in the Peacock stage, Abbey Theatre, Dublin, in May 1972. Written by Heno Magee, the play was set in a working-class area of Dublin. Brendan 'Hatchet' Bailey is a man caged by the animalism of his environment. Conditioned by his thug of a mother, the conditioning being reinforced by the violence of his friends, Hatchet is a man whose heritage and whose environment condemn him to thuggery in place of thought. Despite the opportunities to escape that are offered, Hatchet is bound to be the victim of the violent cage in which he has been reared. See 'Hatchet.'

largely dominated by male characters, their experiences, and their common resort to physical violence (often against women), which often functions as a dramaturgical expression of their personal concerns and issues. A deeper examination of the gendered experience of class disparity would be an important subsequent result. Another example of such blind spots within many major arts venues towards authentic exploration of marginalised communities can be seen when Hilton Edwards passed on the opportunity to premiere Thomas Kilroy's *The Death and Resurrection of Mr Roche* in 1968.[48] In a letter from Kilroy's archive at NUI Galway, Edwards simply dismisses the violence of the play even though he acknowledges its truthful and accurate 'photographic verity' in its depiction of a homophobic attack upon the titular character of the play.[49]

However, as this chapter has demonstrated, the Gate Theatre did espouse a modernising agenda through collaboration and partnership with independent producing companies, innovative new directors and playwrights, and in line with contemporary European trends. There were efforts made, through collaboration with writers such as Brian Phelan, to reflect new themes, attract new audiences, and engage with contemporary production and direction practices internationally. As Chloe Gibson directed many other works at the Gate Theatre throughout the 1970s, she worked to diversify the directing practices of the Gate as well as by working with new writers and by modernising classical works from the Gate's repertoire. With the newly available volumes of unexplored material in the Gate Digital Archive at NUIG (National University of Ireland Galway), there is much to examine in relation to the representation of working-class communities at the Gate.

Bibliography

'An Irishman's Diary.' *Irish Times*, 19 March 1971. 11.
Bolger, Dermot. 'The Irish Working-Class and Their Place in the Literary Canon.' *Irish Times*, 31 March 2018. https://www.irishtimes.com/culture/books/the-irish-working-class-and-their-place-in-the-literary-canon-1.3439712.
Brecht, Bertolt. 'The Popular and the Realistic.' In *Brecht on Theatre*, edited by John Willett, 107–14. London: Methuen Drama, 2001.

---

[48] The play had already been rejected by the Abbey Theatre in a letter to Thomas Kilroy from Tomás Mac Anna, informing Kilroy that the play, in the opinion of the Managing Director, Ernest Blythe, was 'not our line of territory.' See 'Letter from Tomás Mac Anna to Thomas Kilroy.'

[49] See 'Letter from Hilton Edwards to Thomas Kilroy.'

Chapman, Don. *Oxford Playhouse: High and Low Drama in a University City.* Hertfordshire: Hertfordshire University Press, 2008.

Colleary, Susanne. 'Long Flame in the Hideous Gale: The Politics of Irish Popular Performance 1950–2000.' In *The Palgrave Handbook of Contemporary Irish Performance*, edited by Eamonn Jordan and Eric Weitz, 201–19. London: Palgrave Macmillan, 2018.

'Correspondence concerning the Gate Theatre's production of *It's Later Than You Think*.' 1971. Gate Theatre Digital Archive at National University of Ireland, Galway, GADM_00002174.

'Correspondence concerning the Gate Theatre's production of *The Signalman's Apprentice*.' Includes reader's report on the script, 1970–71. Gate Theatre Digital Archive at National University of Ireland, Galway, GADM_00002156.

Fitz-Simon, Christopher. The Boys: A Biography of Micheál MacLíammóir and Hilton Edwards. London: Nick Hern, 1994.

Fülle, Henning. 'A Theatre for Postmodernity in Western European Theatrescapes.' In *Independent Theatre in Contemporary Europe Structures – Aesthetics – Cultural Policy*, edited by Manfred Brauneck and ITI Germany, 275–320. Bielefeld: Transcript, 2017.

Garde, Ulrike and Meg Mumford. *Theatre of Real People: Diverse Encounters at Berlin's Hebbel am Ufer and Beyond.* London: Bloomsbury Methuen Drama, 2016.

'Hatchet.' *PLAYOGRAPHYIreland*, www.irishplayography.com/play.aspx?playid=31347.

'Hilton Edwards, 4 Harcourt Terrace, Dublin, 4 May 1961.' Edwards–mac Liammóir Papers, MS 45, 871. National Library of Ireland, Dublin.

'Hilton Edwards Invited Him to Come to RTE.' *Irish Times*, 29 July 2000. https://www.irishtimes.com/culture/books/the-irish-working-class-and-their-place-in-the-literary-canon-1.3439712.

Howard, Elizabeth. 'Performance in the Community: Amateur Drama and Community Theatre.' In *The Palgrave Handbook of Contemporary Irish Performance*, edited by Eamonn Jordan and Eric Weitz, 165–80. London: Palgrave Macmillan, 2018.

'Interview with Brian Phelan.' *Irish Times*, 2 July 1971. 12.

Jaquarello, Roland. Memoirs of Development: My Time in Irish Theatre and Broadcasting. Dublin: Liffey Press, 2016.

Leeney, Cathy. 'Class, Land, and Irishness: Winners and Losers: Christine Longford (1900–1980).' In *The Gate Theatre Dublin: Inspiration and Craft*, edited by David Clare, Des Lally, and Patrick Lonergan, 161–80. Oxford: Peter Lang Press, 2018.

'Letter from Hilton Edwards to Thomas Kilroy, 1968.' Thomas Kilroy Archive, Hardiman Library, NUI Galway. P103/57.

'Letter from Tomás Mac Anna to Thomas Kilroy, 1968.' Thomas Kilroy Archive, Hardiman Library, NUI Galway. P103/57.

Lonergan, Patrick. *Irish Drama and Theatre since 1950*. London: Methuen Drama, 2019.

Meaney, Geraldine, Mary O'Dowd, and Bernadette Whelan. *Reading the Irish Woman: Studies in Cultural Encounter and Exchange, 1714–1960*. Liverpool: Liverpool University Press, 2013.

Morash, Chris. *A History of the Media in Ireland*. Cambridge: Cambridge University Press, 2009.

Phelan, Brian. *The Signalman's Apprentice*. London: Faber & Faber, 1972.

Phillips, Jim. 'The 1972 Miners' Strike: Popular Agency and Industrial Politics in Britain.' *Contemporary British History* 20, no. 2 (2006): 187–207.

Pierse, Michael. *Writing Ireland's Working Class: Dublin after O'Casey*. London: Palgrave Macmillan, 2011.

'Programme for *The Signalman's Apprentice*, 1 June 1971.' Gate Theatre Digital Archive at National University of Ireland, Galway, 1365_MPG_0001, 4.

Savage, Robert J. 'Film and Broadcast Media.' In *The Oxford Handbook of Modern Irish History*, edited by Alvin Jackson, 268–86. Oxford: Oxford University Press, 2014.

'The Signalman's Apprentice Opens at the Gate.' *Irish Times*, 30 June 1971. 10.

'What's on in the Arts.' *Irish Times*, 21 June 1971. 12.

Wickham, James. 'The New Irish Working Class.' *Saothar* 6 (1980): 81–88.

Part III
Staging Minority Languages

Micheál mac Liammóir, the Irish Language, and the Idea of Freedom

Radvan Markus

Micheál mac Liammóir is best known as an actor of international fame as well as one of the co-founders of the Gate Theatre in Dublin, along with his partner Hilton Edwards. The most visible part of his career, including his highly successful one-man show *The Importance of Being Oscar* (1960), took place in his native English language. However, he was actually a polyglot and claimed that he had 'never found life complete if it is lived with one language only.'[1] He developed a special attachment to Irish, which he learned in his late teens and which became an integral part of his self-definition. Apart from being the first producer of the Galway Irish-language theatre An Taibhdhearc (1928–29) and later directing plays for the Dublin An Comhar Drámaíochta (1930–34), he was also a prolific writer in the language, authoring several plays, a number of short stories and prose poems, and a substantial corpus of travel writing as well as numerous essays. His first text in Irish, a letter to the Gaelic League newspaper *An Claidheamh Soluis*, was published in November 1917, a mere two years after he had started learning the language.[2] The last text, the prose poem 'Dul Faoi na Gréine' ('The Setting of the Sun') appeared in 1975, just three years before his death.[3] Mac Liammóir's creative engagement with Irish thus spans the whole of his artistic career. This chapter concentrates

This work was supported by the European Regional Development Fund-Project 'Creativity and Adaptability as Conditions of the Success of Europe in an Interrelated World' (No. CZ.02.1.01/0.0/0.0/16_019/0000734).

[1] Mac Liammóir, *All for Hecuba*, 199.

[2] Mac Liammóir, 'Aistriúchán agus Litridheacht,' 14–15. Information about mac Liammóir's Irish-language training can be found in Madden, *The Making of an Artist*, 15; Fitz-Simon, *The Boys*, 41.

[3] Mac Liammóir, 'Dul Faoi na Gréine.'

mainly on mac Liammóir's essays in order to examine his position within Irish-language discourse. In particular, it focuses on the ways in which mac Liammóir connected Irish with the idea of personal and artistic freedom, and on his effort to reconcile his cosmopolitan outlook with his commitment to the language's revival. In the same way as he helped shape the Gate's emancipatory mission, he also outlined an emancipatory programme for Irish-language literature.

The Irish Language as Sanctuary

To understand mac Liammóir's opinions, it is worth examining the reasons that led him to engage with the language in the first place. The typical image of an Irish-language revivalist is that of someone who promotes Irish for patriotic reasons. Micheál mac Liammóir does not fit this stereotype too easily. Apart from the information that he circulated about his Irish birth and ancestry, which is clearly a fabrication, mac Liammóir's statements about his motivation point mainly to artistic concerns. In his autobiographical text 'Fallaing Arlaicín' ('The Mantle of Harlequin'), published in the collection *Ceo Meala Lá Seaca* (*A Honeyed Mist, Frosty Day*, 1952), he prominently mentions the influence of W.B. Yeats's 1901 essay 'Ireland and the Arts.'[4] In the essay, Yeats imagines Ireland as a utopia in which the artist, without having to compromise his creative freedom, will find a warm reception with the majority of the population and not, as in other countries, with only a small elite. Mac Liammóir thus clearly saw his 'becoming Irish' as an artistic opportunity. And Yeats dropped another hint in his essay, which possibly inspired mac Liammóir's engagement with the Irish language: 'I might have found more of Ireland if I had written in Irish.'[5]

It is also important that this 'conversion' came at a point of crisis in mac Liammóir's life. Due to his voice breaking, he was no longer able to perform in child roles, and had to think seriously about his future career. He also became aware of his homosexuality at that time – regardless whether we choose to believe the romantic story in his stylised autobiography *Enter a Goldfish* or the much more prosaic history that Christopher Fitz-Simon recounts in *The Boys*.[6]

Another of mac Liammóir's biographers, Micheál Ó hAodha, points out that the transformation of Alfred Wilmore to Micheál mac Liammóir

---

4 Mac Liammóir, *Ceo Meala Lá Seaca*, 28. Ó hAodha, *The Importance of Being Micheál*, 23–24.
5 Yeats, 'Ireland and the Arts,' 329.
6 Mac Liammóir, *Enter a Goldfish*, 94. Fitz-Simon, *The Boys*, 38–39.

was not a unique phenomenon during the period, and mentions examples of other Englishmen, not all of them of Irish ancestry, who also believed in Ireland as a 'land apart, a place where [they] could recreate [themselves].'[7] A broader framework, and one that takes also the linguistic element into account, was recently established by Barry McCrea in his monograph *Languages of the Night* (2015). The book examines the reasons why a number of European authors of the modernist period used minority languages as artistic means. According to McCrea, many of them were in search of a 'utopian' language in which the subject would be united with itself as well as with its environment. Major languages were not able to fulfil this hope as they were too closely connected with the conventions of mainstream society that the authors often felt at odds with. McCrea also links this desire with queerness, focusing on the cases of the Italian poet Pier Paolo Pasolini and the Irish writer Brendan Behan. Ultimately, he implies that the adoption of an endangered language as a means of expression might provide a sanctuary and an oasis of freedom for individuals, who, due to their sexual orientation or other reasons, share 'a general sense of not being at home in the world.'[8] One can argue that in mac Liammóir's case, this abstract notion of sanctuary found a concrete realisation in his relationship with Máire O'Keefe, his fellow student at Slade School. Being of partial Irish ancestry, O'Keefe did much to instigate his interest in Irish culture. At the same time, as Tom Madden states, she 'had complete acceptance of MacLiammóir's homosexuality.'[9]

Interestingly, the theme of how language can provide sanctuary still resonates in Irish-language literature. In Dave Duggan's dystopic novel *Makaronik* (2018), the term *tearmann* (sanctuary) is frequently used in relation to Irish and other natural languages, which are opposed to Empirish, the impersonal language of the omnipotent 'Empire.'[10] And on a more humorous note, a conservative character in Micheál Ó Conghaile's play *Go dTaga do Ríocht* (*Your Kingdom Come*, 2008) complains: 'This is the thing about Irish, it attracts all sorts. [...] All sorts of nutters, crackpots and outcasts that have problems of their own and don't know what to do with themselves.'[11] Interestingly, the targeted character in the play is, in fact, a homosexual.

[7] Ó hAodha, *The Importance of Being Micheál*, 27.
[8] MacCrea, *Languages of the Night*, 69.
[9] Madden, *The Making of an Artist*, 48.
[10] Duggan, *Makaronik*, 62.
[11] 'Sin é an rud faoin nGaeilge, meallan sí chuile chineál. [...] Chuile chineál nutters, crackpots is outcasts a bhfuil problems dá gcuid fhéin acu is nach bhfuil fhios

The Autonomy of Art

If mac Liammóir's motivation is perceived through this lens, it was inevitable for him to clash with the conservative strand of the language movement. As Philip O'Leary has shown, there was a vociferous group within the movement that emphasised Irish tradition, including medieval tales and living folklore, as the only true basis of the revived literature. Their focus was, in O'Leary's words, '*siar* in the dual sense of the Irish word, back to a real, imagined, or invented past [...] and to the West, where it [the Irish tradition] had maintained itself most tenaciously.'[12] In addition, numerous conservative voices among these 'nativists' linked the language to a narrow notion of Irishness that had more in common with the Catholic Church and Victorian morality than with any genuine manifestation of the tradition. They imagined that Irish could serve as a protective wall against foreign influences and placed severe limits on what was permissible in the nascent modern literature.[13]

Admittedly, mac Liammóir's work displays some 'nativist' traits. His creative output was partly informed by a romanticising attitude inherited from W.B. Yeats. His first play, *Diarmuid agus Gráinne* (1928), is based on an early Irish text replete with fantastic motifs; the later plays, *Where Stars Walk* (1940) and *Ill Met by Moonlight* (1946), contain supernatural elements inherited from Irish mythology and folklore, and the same can be said about his Irish-language short stories. He even wrote a whole essay, 'Lucht an Aeir' ('Creatures of the Air,' 1925), outlining his belief in supernatural beings.[14] However, most of his other essays are far removed from such mysticism and attack numerous nativist pieties with unrelenting frankness.

In direct contrast to the conservative wing among the revivalists, mac Liammóir was a firm defender of the autonomy of art from all ideologies, be they nationalist or otherwise. Already one of his early essays, 'An tSaoirse: Sglábhuíocht Aigne in Éirinn' ('Freedom: Slavery of Mind in Ireland'), published in the Gaelic League newspaper *Misneach* in December 1920, gave rise to a substantial controversy. At the beginning of the text, mac Liammóir mentions the ideals of political and economic freedom, highly topical in the context of the Irish War of Independence, which was

---

acu céard a dhéanfas siad leo fhéin.' Ó Conghaile, Murphy, and McDonagh, *Go dTaga do Ríocht, Boicíní Bhóthar Kilburn, Cripil Inis Meáin*, 92–93. All translations of Irish-language texts in the chapter are my own.

[12] O'Leary, *The Prose Literature of the Gaelic Revival, 1881–1921*, 15.

[13] O'Leary, *Prose Literature of the Gaelic Revival*, 14–16, 33–37.

[14] Mac Liammóir, *Ceo Meala*, 273–85.

raging at the time. However, for mac Liammóir, these ideals are merely the starting point. He asks the following rhetorical question: 'When the English are driven away, when everybody has a good salary for their work, and a clean and comfortable house, good food and low rents, will we be free? Or will we just move from one slavery to another – from English tyranny to the yoke of Irish prejudice?'[15] He continues by pleading for the freedom of literature and the arts, maintaining that they 'should be as free from the laws of Church and State as Ireland should be free of foolish English control.'[16]

To support his analogy with political freedom, he even summons the great nationalist leader, Charles Stewart Parnell, to his help, modifying his famous statement that 'No man has the right to fix the boundary to the march of a nation' to 'No man has the right to fix the boundary to the march of the arts.'[17] Mac Liammóir explicitly lists the forces that aim to curtail artistic freedom – 'our prejudice, *respectability* (strange that there is no Irish for this word that we are so enamoured with nowadays in Ireland), narrow-mindedness and false piety (that we borrowed from England for the occasion).'[18] In this way, he openly attacks the Gaelic conservatives, claiming provocatively that many of their ideas about the 'pure Gaelic soul' that they were so intent on defending were, in fact, derived from English sources. In this way, mac Liammóir anticipated Myles na gCopaleen's jibes two decades later.[19] To support his plea for the autonomy of art, mac Liammóir mentions the cases of numerous famous authors whose writings transgressed the narrow codes of puritan morality, such as Charles Baudelaire, Friedrich Nietzsche, and Walt Whitman, as well as the Irishmen W.B. Yeats and Oscar Wilde. The essay claims, rather provocatively, that

---

[15] 'Nuair bhéas na Sasanaigh glanta as an tír, nuair bhéas pádh maith ag dul do chuile dhuine as ucht a gcuid oibre [...] an mbéimid saor? Nó an mbéimid taréis, dul ó dhaoirse go daoirse eile – ó chuing thíorántachta Shasana go cuing chlaoinbhreithe Éireann?' Mac Liammóir, 'An tSaoirse: Sglábhuíocht Aigne in Éirinn,' 10.

[16] 'go mba chóir dóibh bheith saor, saor ar fad, chó saor ó dhlithe na hEaglaise is an Stáit is ba cheart do náisiún na hÉireann bheith saor ó smacht dícéillí Shasana.' Mac Liammóir, 'An tSaoirse,' 10.

[17] 'Ná cuireadh éinne teóra le gluaiseacht na hEaladhna.' Mac Liammóir, 'An tSaoirse,' 11.

[18] 'ar gclaoinbhreath is ár *respectability*, (aisteach an rud é nach bhfuil aon Ghaedhilg ar an bhfocal sin dá dtugamuid an oiread sin grádha sna laethanna seo in Éirinn), ár gcumhangas is ár mbréagcráibhtheacht (a fuaireamar ar iasacht ó Shasana don ócáid).' Mac Liammóir, 'An tSaoirse,' 10.

[19] See, e.g. Ó Conaire, *Myles na Gaeilge*, 74. I have discussed Brian O'Nolan's attitude to the language revival in Markus, 'The Prison of Language,' 32–34.

artistic freedom is more important than political freedom, and finishes with
the statement that 'from freedom and only from freedom shall come the
great revival that all of us have been expecting for ages.'[20]

The reactions were soon to come. In the following issue, an author
with the penname 'An Buachaillín Buidhe' ('The Little Yellow Boy')
published a lengthy article arguing that 'not many fathers or mothers of
families would agree' with the opinion that national culture should be
independent of the Church. He proclaimed: 'If Gaelic culture is our destiny,
it would be a sad story if it was not clean [in a moral sense].'[21] Other
passages reveal much of the obsessive mindset that would later lead to the
Censorship of Publications Act of 1929. In one of them, 'An Buachaillín
Buidhe' condemned an unnamed author, possibly George Moore, who
had 'abandoned the Catholic Church as he could find no freedom under
its control.'[22] The perceived obscenity of the writer led 'An Buachaillín
Buidhe' to express an opinion worthy of the Spanish Inquisition: 'If all
his works were put on a heap, and this clever, but dirty-minded author on
top of it, and the whole lot set on fire, the world would be the better for
it.'[23] 'An Buachaillín Buidhe''s judgements on the topic of painting also
revolve around the notion of 'indecency': 'This world is full of so many
truly beautiful, fine and good things apart from naked women, but the
likes of Rubens are so desirous of flesh, flesh, flesh, as a drunkard is of
beer.'[24] The identity of 'An Buachaillín Buidhe' is an interesting issue: it
was the penname typically used by the Protestant revivalist Ernest Joynt,
and Philip O'Leary mentions him as the author of the article in question.[25]
However, the sentiments revealed in the text are distinctively Catholic. Be
it as it may, in February 1921 mac Liammóir published a long reaction

---

[20] 'gurab as an tSaoirse, agus as an tSaoirse amháin, thiocfas an Oll-Aithbheóchaint
úd a bhfuilimid uile ag fanacht léi leis na ciantaibh.' Mac Liammóir, 'An tSaoirse,'
11.

[21] 'Is beag athair nó máthair chlainne a ghlacfas leis an mbarúil'; 'más rud é go
bhfuil cúltúir Ghaedhealach i ndán dúin ba olc an scéal gan í bheith go glan.'
'An Buachaillín Buidhe' [pseud.], 'Saoirse Aigne: Ní Daoirse é, ach Spadántacht.'

[22] 'thréig [...] an Eaglais Chatoiliceach as ucht nach raibh saoirse a sháith le fagháil
fá na smacht.' 'An Buachaillín Buidhe,' 'Saoirse Aigne.'

[23] 'Dá ndéanfaí carn mór dá oibreacha, agus ughdar cliste an aigne shalaigh ar a bharr,
agus dá gcurfaí trí theinidh iad ar fad, b'fhearrde an saoghal é.' 'An Buachaillín
Buidhe,' 'Saoirse Aigne.'

[24] 'Tá an domhan so lán líonta de rudaibh sár-áilne, breaghtha, maiseacha, seachas
mná lomnochta, ach tá leithéidí Rubens ann agus iad chomh dúlaidhe i bhfeóil,
feóil, feóil, agus tá pótaire i mbeóir.' 'An Buachaillín Buidhe,' 'Saoirse Aigne.'

[25] O'Leary, *Prose Literature of the Gaelic Revival*, 470.

to this diatribe, as well as to another lengthy critique of his essay that had appeared in the meantime.[26] In his response, mac Liammóir again vehemently defends the opinion, inspired by Oscar Wilde, that art should be judged according to its own standards, as opposed to the standards of politics, religion, or morality.[27]

Concern for the freedom of the arts also remained at the centre of mac Liammóir's thinking after this controversy. In 1923, he published the article 'Lucht Ealadhna agus an Tírghrá' ('Artists and Patriotism'), in which he uses the religious language of his opponents to further support his point about the independence of art, in this case from patriotism itself.[28] He describes the artist as *sagart áilneachta* (a 'priest of beauty'), who should resist the temptation of politics. Going even further, mac Liammóir argues that he must lay aside the very idea of the country: 'if an artist wants to add to the beauty of Ireland seriously, he has to forget Ireland first.'[29] In addition to this basic question of loyalty, mac Liammóir deplores the fact that Ireland lost many promising writers simply because, led by patriotic feelings, they attempted to do too much at once. The following quotation calls into mind writers that took part in the struggle for independence, such as Patrick Pearse (in combination with Éamon de Valera) in the passage: 'We don't have the least respect for a man who can't compose poetry, write constitutions, edit newspapers, shoot the English, play hurling, paint pictures, throw explosives, give orations that would squeeze tears out of green stones, lead armies, sing songs and escape from prison.'[30] The editor clearly saw a potential for controversy in the article as he added the disclaimer, 'the article expresses Micheál's own opinion.'[31] Moreover, almost thirty years later, mac Liammóir potently summarised his attitude

---

[26] 'Sagart Capúisíneach,' 'Saoirse Aigne: Tuairim Shagairt ar an Sgeul.'

[27] Mac Liammóir, 'Saoirse na hEaladhna: Cad is Pagántacht ann?'

[28] This is a marked development from his early article in *An Claidheamh Soluis*, where he defends the connection between the language revival and nationalist politics. See mac Liammóir, 'Poilitidheacht,' 10–11. Mac Liammóir clearly changed his opinion shortly after and remained consistent in his subsequent essays.

[29] 'Má's mian leis cabhrú le n-a bhfuil d'áilneacht ag baint le Éirinn i ndá ríribh caithfidh sé dearmad dhéanamh ar Éirinn sul má ghní sé rud ar bith eile.' Micheál mac Liammóir, 'Lucht Ealadhna agus an Tír-Grádh.'

[30] 'Níl meas madra againn, cuir i gcás, ar an bhfear nach dtig leis dánta sgcríobha, bunreachta chuma, páipéirí nuaíochta chur in eagar, Sasanaigh lámhach, iomáint, pioctúirí dhathú, pléasgáin chaitheamh, óráideacha bhainfeadh deóir as na clochaibh glasa thabhairt, airm stiúra, abhráin ghabháil, agus éalú ó phroisún.' Mac Liammóir, 'Lucht Ealadhna.'

[31] 'Tuairim Mhichíl féin atá san alt seo.' Mac Liammóir, 'Lucht Ealadhna.'

in the essay 'Éire agus an Ghaeilge san Am atá le Teacht' ('Ireland and the Irish language in the future,' 1951), in which he stated that 'the artist is an enemy of any power, political, religious or communal, that wants to bring him under control.'[32]

The same anxiety about freedom can be found in mac Liammóir's travel writing. In his description of Orson Welles's 1950 German tour, in which he took part as an actor, mac Liammóir includes two remarkable passages that explicitly reject both major European totalitarian systems of the twentieth century.[33] While preaching against the Nazis, he argues that the freedom of the individual is more valuable than the national idea, 'because what is the whole nation apart from a big collection of personalities?'[34] Mac Liammóir condemns Irish Nazi supporters and, in a bold move, equates the desire for freedom with Irishness: 'the Irish [...] constantly demand the freedom of thought, opinion and speech and could not put up for a week with the narrowness and tyranny of Hitler's philosophy.'[35] Characteristically, mac Liammóir also makes a connection between aesthetics and freedom that is palpable in many of his other essays. Not only is Nazi ideology oppressive, but it also gives rise to 'hideous big buildings and a handful of intellects even more hideous.'[36]

A similar attitude can be gleaned from mac Liammóir's description of the Soviet military cemetery and monument in Schönholzer Heide in Berlin. He spares no words describing the ugliness of the monument, labelling it also as *go hoirearc, go péacach, go costasach* ('grandiose, spectacular, expensive'), and *go millteach* ('enormous'). He also criticises the poor composition, the bad drawing and 'a revolting vulgar note in the subject matter.'[37] The main cause of this ugliness, in his opinion, is again the dependence of art on ideology: the place swarms with statues of 'noble heroic Communists stepping on the faces of ugly wicked non-Communists,' and 'the propaganda is so apparent and childish that

---

32 '[tá] an t-ealaíontóir ina namhaid do chumhacht ar bith, bíodh an chumhacht sin ina cumhacht pholaitíceach, dhiaganta, nó chumannach, ar mhian léi iad chur faoi smacht.' Mac Liammóir, *Ceo Meala*, 295.

33 For details about the tour, see Fitz-Simon, *The Boys*, 162–65.

34 'óir céard tá sa náisiún iomlán ach ollchruinniú pearsantachtaí?' Mac Liammóir, *Ceo Meala*, 190.

35 'bíonn na hÉireannaigh [...] ag síor-éileamh saoirse meoin is machnaimh is cainte, agus ní fhéadfaidís cur suas ar feadh seachtaine amháin le cúngas ná le tíoránacht fealsúnachta Hitler.' Mac Liammóir, *Ceo Meala*, 190.

36 'foirgneamh móra úrghránna, agus dornán intleacht ní b'úrghránna fós.' Mac Liammóir, *Ceo Meala*, 190.

37 'nóta déisteanach gráisciúil ar a leithéid d'ábhar.' Mac Liammóir, *Ceo Meala*, 220.

it makes one ashamed.'[38] To people in Ireland who might cherish illusions about circumstances in the Stalinist Soviet Union, he adds: 'Any artist with romantic feelings about Communism should see it: he would forever change his opinion.'[39]

Reconciling the Global and the Local

How, then, did mac Liammóir reconcile his markedly cosmopolitan outlook with his enduring commitment to the revival of the Irish language? This is a theme that resonates in various guises throughout his work. In a way, the choice of the opening play of the Gate Theatre, Ibsen's *Peer Gynt*, already thematised this crucial question. The play as a whole is an elaborate comment on the dichotomies of cultivating one's identity on the one hand and openness to the world on the other; of localism and globalism. Act IV even contains a direct satire of (Norwegian) language revival in the character of Huhu, an inmate of an Egyptian lunatic asylum. His goal is to reinstate the original language of Malabar, spoken in the jungle by the orangutans. He wants to return prestige to the primeval screeches and growls and purify the forest language of all foreign elements, such as words. This is clearly a parody of the effort of some revivalists to create a 'pristine' form of the language as well as their obsession with the past and the countryside as the true repositories of the national spirit. Huhu's attitude is clearly untenable (that is, outside the mental institution), yet the opposite pole, that of a global economy thriving on colonial exploitation, represented by Peer Gynt himself at the beginning of the same act, is not particularly enticing either. The play thus posits a pressing question whether some middle path between the two extremes is feasible.

The same search is palpable also in mac Liammóir's writing. A very good example is the aforementioned essay 'Éire agus an Ghaeilge san Am atá le Teacht,' written just a year after Orson Welles's German tour. In the text, mac Liammóir describes the contemporaneous mood in post-war Europe and compares it to the Irish situation: '[Europe] no longer believes in nationality and in what it involves, and our big noble story that we are now a true nation, or nearly one, again, does not impress anyone in the

---

[38] 'de Chumannaigh uaisle gaisciúla agus iad ag satailt ar aghaidh na Neamh-Chumannach gránna urchóideacha'; 'an propaganda chomh lom follasach leanbaí sin go gcuirfeadh sé náire ort.' Mac Liammóir, *Ceo Meala*, 220.

[39] 'Ealaíontóir ar bith a mbeadh dúil rómánsach aige sa gCumannacht ba chóir dhó í fheiceáil: Bheadh a mhalairt de bharúil aige go deo.' Mac Liammóir, *Ceo Meala*, 220.

world apart from ourselves.'[40] He also frankly admits that 'nationality is a miserable and unnecessary thing.'[41] However, he does not propose getting rid of nationality, as such a move would necessarily lead to the dominance of stronger cultures over weak ones. Instead, he argues,

> the best way to create harmony in this world, in my own understanding, is not to encourage the big things to destroy the weak, but to persuade them that all exist, that there is difference among them, but that none of them needs to think that it is better than any other, or worthier, or more spiritual. There is difference among them: that's all.[42]

Remarkably, the passage does not merely criticise the expansiveness of dominant cultures, but also throws a shadow of doubt on the Celticist idea of the Irish as an innately spiritual nation, used by W.B. Yeats and Lady Gregory in the manifesto of the Irish Literary Theatre. The true value of Irish culture, in mac Liammóir's view, does not lie in its superiority over others, but in its distinctiveness, which enables it to contribute to the pluriform harmony of world culture.

Mac Liammóir's rationale for the advocacy of language revival is precisely the effort to maintain this cultural difference. In many aspects, his essay is a latter-day adaptation of Douglas Hyde's seminal lecture 'The Necessity for de-Anglicising Ireland' from 1892. Like his predecessor, mac Liammóir contrasts the rampant political nationalism and anti-British feeling in Ireland with the widespread imitation of the nearest neighbour in cultural matters.[43] For mac Liammóir, just as for Hyde, language is the most important marker of cultural difference, and for this reason it should

---

[40] 'Ní chreideann sí sa náisiúntacht a thuilleadh ná ina mbaineann léi, agus an scéal mór uasal seo againne go bhfuilimid inár bhfíornáisiún, nó geall leis, arís, ní haon iontas é sin dar le héinne ar dhroim an domhain ach linn féin amháin.' The last three words clearly mock the political slogan 'Sinn Féin Amháin' [Ourselves Alone]. Mac Liammóir, *Ceo Meala*, 298.

[41] 'gur bocht neamhriachtanach an rud an náisiúntacht.' Mac Liammóir, *Ceo Meala*, 290.

[42] 'an bealach is fearr chun comhcheol dhéanamh as an saol seo, do réir mar thuigimse é, ní hé na rudaí is treise ghríosú chun na rudaí is laige scrios, ach chur ina luí orthu go bhfuil siad go léir ann, go bhfuil difríocht eatarthu, ach nach gá d'aon cheann orthu cheapadh go bhfuil sé níos fearr ná an ceann eile, ná níos fiúntaí, ná níos spioradálta. Tá difríocht eatarthu: sin an méid.' Mac Liammóir, *Ceo Meala*, 290.

[43] Mac Liammóir, *Ceo Meala*, 288–89.

be preserved. If it was lost, Ireland would be reduced, culturally, to a mere province within the anglophone world. As he argues in *Theatre in Ireland:* 'There could be worse fates than add our share to the fire of a tradition that includes Chaucer and Shakespeare and Keats. Yet the feeling persists that another fire is smouldering still among the half-forgotten ashes and must by this means or that be fed.'[44]

In contrast to the nativist views, a successful revival of Irish would not imply, in mac Liammóir's opinion, isolation of Ireland from the outside world. In fact, the opposite would be the case. Mac Liammóir believed that the decline of Irish led to an obsession with other, unduly exaggerated markers of national identity. This is precisely his explanation for the persistence of the stage Irishman in Irish plays, despite the initial effort of the Abbey to suppress the figure. Without the language, Irish people 'lack so much of the natural, undeliberate individualism that divides nation from nation, and [...] the simple fellow can visualize no other way of not being mistaken for an Englishman but by behaving in a manner that at least is not the classic Anglo-Saxon manner.'[45] The same reason, in his opinion, also lay behind what he saw as the parochialism of the Abbey Theatre. He often criticised its clinging to peasant themes combined with its refusal to stage foreign plays and its reluctance to apply other than naturalist modes of production.[46] If the Irish language were to be truly revived, Irish theatre and Irish life in general should become more confident and open to foreign influences. As he argued concerning Edward Martyn's relationship with the Irish language, 'his interest in it had its usual unexpected and not generally recognized effect of awakening a desire in his soul for two things: the expansion of Irish expression beyond the limits of peasant life, and the linking up of Ireland with European tendencies other than English.'[47]

In other words, mac Liammóir's vision was such that once the most important marker of Irishness, the language, were safe, writers would gain more freedom to devote themselves to any theme of their choice without unduly bothering about questions of national identity. A very similar opinion was presented by novelist Alan Titley in 1981: 'Anglophone Irish literature attempts to define us according to national traits, quirks of

---

[44] Mac Liammóir, *Theatre in Ireland*, 63.

[45] Mac Liammóir, *Theatre in Ireland*, 48.

[46] See, for instance, CWC, 'Evolution of the Drama.'

[47] Mac Liammóir, *Theatre in Ireland*, 18. The rationale behind mac Liammóir's defence of the Irish language is also discussed, in an abridged form, in Dean and Markus, 'Internationalist Dramaturgy at the Gate,' 31–32.

behaviour, local dialects, placenames, priests and púcas. In Irish-language literature, we are defined solely by our humanity.'[48] While the statement may be criticised as overly generalising, it is certainly valuable as an articulation of an ethos that Irish-language literature should strive for.

Irish-language Literature and the World

Much of mac Liammóir's effort within the revival movement was aimed at counteracting the threat of the attitude represented by Huhu in *Peer Gynt* – the danger that the revival will be solely past-oriented and self-contained. He was critical of Ireland's short-sightedness:

> The worst thing that England did to Ireland, in my opinion, is that it blinded Ireland's perception in the rest of the world. [...] The image of England is so perverted and so absurd in the mind of an Irish person, and his knowledge of other world countries is so small, that he uses the adjective 'English' to describe anything that is not Irish. [...] Each of us has heard somebody describe 'English dances' whereby he actually meant Viennese waltzes, Afro-American jazz, Brazilian rumbas and Polish mazurkas.[49]

In order to overcome this deficiency, mac Liammóir strove to make Irish-language culture as open to the world as possible. The publication of travel writing was certainly part of this effort, as it brought new, non-Irish (as well as non-English) experience into Irish-language literature. Thus, in the collection *Ceo Meala, Lá Seaca* we can find descriptions as diverse as those of dancers in Seville, a long trip to the American southwest, and a journey from Paris to the French seaside, as well as the above-mentioned

---

48 'Bíonn litríocht Bhéarla na tíre ag iarraidh sainmhíniú a thabhairt orainn de réir tréithe náisiúnta, gothaí iompair, canúna áitiúla, cáilíochtaí logánta, logainm-neacha, sagairt agus púcaí. Níl de shainmhíniú orainn i litríocht na Gaeilge ach an daonnacht.' Titley, 'Litríocht na Gaeilge, Litríocht an Bhéarla agus *Irish Literature*,' 121, quoted in Nic Eoin, *Trén bhFearann Breac*, 92.

49 'Sé an donas is mó dá bhfuil déanta ag Sasana ar Éirinn, do réir mo thuairimese, gur dhall sí léargas Éireann ar an gcuid eile den domhan mór. [...] Bíonn íomháigh Shasana chomh camtha is chomh háiféiseach sin in aigne an Éireannaigh, agus a laghad de léargas aige ar thíortha eile an domhain, go dtugann sé 'Sasanach' mar aidiacht ar rud ar bith nach bhfuil Éireannach. [...] Tá aithne ag gach éinne againn ar an té bhíos ag cur síos ar 'rincí Sasanacha,' agus a smaointe lán de bhálsaí Viennéasacha, jazz Aifriceánach, rumbaí Braisiléineacha, agus Mazúrkaí Pólainneacha [...].' Mac Liammóir, *Ceo Meala*, 290.

tour of Germany. These texts definitely merit reconsideration in the canon of Irish-language travel writing. The genre, established by Micheál Breathnach's *Seilg i Measc na nAlp* (*Hunting in the Alps*) in 1917 has recently gained more currency and popularity as Irish-language culture has increasingly opened up to the world. In Máirín Nic Eoin's words: 'The travelogue has replaced Gaeltacht autobiography as the foremost genre of life writing in recent decades, with all major continents now represented and new titles appearing regularly.'[50]

In addition to the travel memoirs, mac Liammóir also strove to broaden the horizons of his compatriots as regards European literature and other art forms. In this, he displayed a particular affinity to Russian culture. In 1927 he published a three-part essay 'Triúr Sgríbhneoirí i Nua-Litridheacht na Rúise' ('Three Modern Russian Writers') that posits the development of modern Russian literature as a model for Irish-language writing. The essay engages with the work of Pushkin, Turgenev, and Chekhov as representatives of three periods in the history of nineteenth-century Russian prose.[51] Mac Liammóir also wrote two articles on the ballet star Vaslav Nijinsky in 1950.[52] His interest in Nijinsky might have been sparked by the dancer's homosexuality – it is hardly a coincidence that the protagonist of mac Liammóir's play *Prelude in Kazbek Street* (1973) is a gay ballet dancer.

Mac Liammóir also believed in translation as a suitable means of developing Irish-language literature. This is the theme of his first published text in Irish, a letter to *An Claidheamh Soluis* from 1917, in which he argues against the translation from Irish to English, as this would diminish the readers' motivation to engage with the Irish original. Rather, he promotes the other direction, that is, the publication of Irish-language versions of masterpieces originally written in English (especially by Irish authors), but also in other European languages.[53] But it clearly had to be done in the correct way. In a review from 1921, he criticises the famous revival writer Peadar Ó Laoghaire for what he saw as an overly free and bowdlerised translation of *Don Quixote*, deploring the fact that despite the translator's effort, 'Cervantes is not yet available in Irish.'[54] Translation was also

[50] Nic Eoin, '"We are no Longer Gaels,"' 97.

[51] Mac Liammóir, 'Triúr Sgríbhneoirí i Nua-Litridheacht na Rúise,' part 1, 5; part 2, 2; part 3, 2–3. Reprinted in mac Liammóir, *Ceo Meala*, 243–62.

[52] Mac Liammóir, 'Mo Chuimhne ar Nijinsky'; 'Nijinsky – an tAisteoir ba mhó sa Domhan.'

[53] Mac Liammóir, 'Aistriúchán agus Litridheacht,' 14–15. A similar argument is repeated in 'An Litríocht Nua agus an Pobul.'

[54] 'Níl Cervantes le fáil i nGaedhilge go fóill.' Mac Liammóir, 'Don Quijote de la Mancha.'

a crucial part of the whole project of An Taibhdhearc. A list of mac Liammóir's productions in 1928 and 1929 confirms this: along with five original plays, An Taibhdhearc staged seven translations of dramatic works by authors of diverse nationalities. Two of them, *Prunella* by Housman and Granville-Barker, and *A Marriage Proposal* by Chekhov, were translated by mac Liammóir himself. In addition, he produced plays by Eça de Queirós, Foley, Molière, Lady Gregory, and Martínez Sierra.[55] As Pádraig Ó Siadhail has shown, the same emphasis on translations accompanied also mac Liammóir's subsequent engagement with An Comhar Drámaíochta.[56]

But it was not enough merely to allow the world to enrich Irish language literature; the literature itself needed to gain enough confidence so that it could contribute to the world on its own. In order to do so, it was necessary to be daring and tread off the beaten path. In the 1924 essay 'Misneach' ('Courage'), mac Liammóir argued that it is precisely courage that Irish-language literature needs the most, more than a literary standard, a suitable style, *uaisleacht meóin* ('nobility of mind') or *tír-ghrádh* ('patriotism'). Only 'courage of opinions, originality, and mental energy' can help the literature escape the peasant cliché it has fallen victim to, according to mac Liammóir.[57] This would give a necessary impetus to the revival itself – the language movement could hardly recruit many adherents if all the intellectual life of the country was taking place through the medium of English.[58]

Mac Liammóir outlined the possible contribution of Irish-language literature to world culture more specifically in the realm of drama. In his essay 'Drámaíocht Ghaeilge san Am atá le Teacht' ('Irish-language Drama in the Future,' 1940) he recommended theatre practitioners to escape from the straitjacket of realism and to try out the alternative modes of romanticism and expressionism. Above all, however, he proposed a wholly new mode called 'drama of the imagination,' inspired by the native traditions of storytelling and placename lore. He envisioned that this type of drama 'could, maybe, if applied in the right way, influence world drama just as Greek drama influenced Europe a long time ago.'[59]

---

[55] Bateman, Hoare, and Pilkington, *Na Drámaí a Léiríodh i dTaibhdhearc na Gaillimhe, 1928–2003*. The booklet does not have numbered pages.

[56] Ó Siadhail, *Stair Dhrámaíocht na Gaeilge*, 69.

[57] 'misneach na dtuairimí, na bunúsachta, is an fhuinnimh aigne.' Mac Liammóir, 'An Misneach Nua sa Litríocht,' 172.

[58] Mac Liammóir, 'An Misneach Nua,' 172.

[59] 'a d'fhágfadh a rian, b'fhéidir, ar dhrámaíocht an domhain iomláin dá bhfostófaí i gceart í, faoi mar a d'fhág drámaíocht na Gréige a rian ar an Eoraip fadó.' Mac

Micheál mac Liammóir and Pádraic Ó Conaire

Mac Liammóir's voice was distinctive in the Irish-language movement, but was neither unique nor isolated. A plea for a greater openness to foreign influences had already been made by Patrick Pearse in 1906:

> Irish literature, if it is to live and grow, must get into contact on the one hand with its own past and on the other, with the mind of contemporary Europe. It must draw the sap of its life from the soil of Ireland, but it must be open on every side to the free air of heaven.[60]

There are even more affinities between mac Liammóir's views and those of Pádraic Ó Conaire, arguably the best prose writer of the Irish-language revival. Ó Conaire was a personal friend of mac Liammóir's – according to the account in *All for Hecuba*, the two men met on a Howth train shortly after mac Liammóir had moved to Ireland.[61] Neither did the connection between them cease after Ó Conaire's untimely death in 1928. In 1931, mac Liammóir illustrated *The Woman at the Window*, a selection of Ó Conaire's short stories translated into English, and as late as 1973, he wrote a preface to a new edition of Ó Conaire's novel *Deoraíocht* (Exile, 1910). Significantly, he was one of the first critics to see the novel in a wider context of European culture, likening it to primitivist paintings of artists such as Henri Rousseau.[62] Arguably, Ó Conaire also influenced mac Liammóir's own writing – the play *The Mountains Look Different* (1948) is, in many ways, a reworking of Ó Conaire's short story 'Nóra Mharcais Bhig' (1907). Like the play, the story features a woman from the West of Ireland who immigrates to London, becomes a prostitute, and eventually returns home with the intention to lead an ordinary life, with a disastrous outcome.[63]

Ó Conaire's opinions were an important predecessor for mac Liammóir's. In his short essays 'An tSaoirse' ('Freedom') and 'Saoire Phearsanta' ('Personal Freedom'), both from 1918, Ó Conaire discussed the relationship between political, economic and personal freedom, placing the greatest

---

Liammóir, *Ceo Meala*, 237. The essay is extensively analysed in Dean and Markus, 'Internationalist Dramaturgy,' 33–36.

[60] Pearse, 'About Literature,' 6.

[61] Mac Liammóir, *All for Hecuba*, 59.

[62] Mac Liammóir, 'Réamhrá,' vii.

[63] Ó Conaire, 'Nóra Mharcais Bhig,' 84–97.

emphasis on the last of the three concepts – one can easily imagine that he gave inspiration to mac Liammóir's exploration of the same theme two years later.[64] Ó Conaire was also relentless in his promotion of modern European literature as a model for Irish-language prose, praising especially French and Russian authors. Of special interest in this respect is his essay 'Seanlitríocht na nGael agus Nualitríocht na hEorpa' ('Old Irish and Modern European Literature,' 1908) where he enumerates a range of European authors as possible sources of inspiration.[65] And, just like mac Liammóir, he deplored the constraints placed on Irish-language literature by narrow-minded revivalists, and urged authors to write in a courageous way. In the essay 'Scríbhneoirí agus a gCuid Oibre – an Easpa Misnigh atá orthu?' ('Writers and their Work – Do They Suffer from a Lack of Courage?', 1920) he pleaded: 'I beseech you, writers, to be bold and daring and not to fear the world. Reveal the truth that is known to you, even if it may enrage certain people.'[66]

Conclusion

Mac Liammóir never gained a high status as a creative writer in Irish – perhaps rightly so, as his more mature and accomplished output, such as the plays *Ill met by Moonlight* or the show *The Importance of Being Oscar*, were written in English. However, he can be regarded as an important voice within the progressive wing of the language movement. He developed ideas of W.B. Yeats, Patrick Pearse and Pádraic Ó Conaire, added his own emphases, and thus helped pave the way for the profound changes in the Irish-language movement from the 1940s onwards. His role is not often explicitly acknowledged, but it is clear that his ideas, especially about the theatre, resonated among later generations of Irish-language writers.[67] At a time when the Irish language was, often hypocritically, exploited as a constituent of a conservative state ideology, mac Liammóir showed that it could be as plausibly connected with the idea of freedom, both personal and artistic. In contrast to narrow nativist views, the language was always an emancipatory force for him, a path to new possibilities in life as well as in literature and drama. He also strove to reconcile his lifelong commitment to Irish with his markedly internationalist

---

[64] Denvir, ed., *Aistí Phádraig Uí Chonaire*, 98–103.
[65] Denvir, ed., *Aistí Phádraig Uí Chonaire*, 42–52.
[66] 'Impím oraibh, a scríbhneoirí, a bheith dána misniúil gan scáth gan eagla roimh an saol, ach an fhírinne is eol daoibh a nochtadh, cuma cén t-olc a chuirfeas an fhírinne ar dhaoine áirithe.' Denvir, *Aistí Phádraig Uí Chonaire*, 167.
[67] See Dean and Markus, 'Internationalist Dramaturgy,' 39–40.

outlook, palpable in his engagement with the Gate Theatre. The various ways in which he managed to do so are of great inspirational value even now, at a time when the world as such is striving to find a balance between localism and cosmopolitanism. While it is necessary to avoid the pitfalls of nationalism, the cultivation of cultural diversity is a prerequisite for transnational communication as well as for good art.

Bibliography

Bateman, Fiona, Kieran Hoare, and Lionel Pilkington. *Na Drámaí a Léiríodh i dTaibhdhearc na Gaillimhe, 1928–2003*. Galway: James Hardiman Library, NUIG, 2003.

'An Buachaillín Buidhe.' 'Saoirse Aigne: Ní Daoirse é, ach Spadántacht.' *Misneach*, 8 January 1921. 4.

CWC. 'Evolution of the Drama.' *Drogheda Independent*, 12 July 1929. 8.

Dean, Joan FitzPatrick and Radvan Markus. 'Internationalist Dramaturgy at the Gate.' In *Cultural Convergence: The Dublin Gate Theatre, 1928–1960*, edited by Ondřej Pilný, Ruud van den Beuken and Ian Walsh, 15–46. Basingstoke: Palgrave, 2021.

Denvir, Gearóid, ed. *Aistí Phádraig Uí Chonaire*. Indreabhán: Cló Chois Fharraige, 1978.

Duggan, Dave. *Makaronik*. An Spidéal: Cló Iar-Chonnacht, 2018.

Fitz-Simon, Christopher. *The Boys: A Double Biography of Micheál MacLíammóir and Hilton Edwards*. London: Nick Hern, 1994.

MacCrea, Barry. *Languages of the Night*. New Haven and London: Yale University Press, 2015.

Mac Liammóir, Micheál. 'Aistriúchán agus Litridheacht.' *An Claidheamh Soluis*, 10 November 1917. 14–15.

Mac Liammóir, Micheál. *All for Hecuba: an Irish Theatrical Autobiography*. Boston: Branden Press, 1947.

Mac Liammóir, Micheál. 'An Litríocht Nua agus an Pobul.' *An Sguab*, 29 November 1922. 29.

Mac Liammóir, Micheál. 'An Misneach Nua sa Litríocht.' *An Sguab*, 21 September 1924. 172–73.

Mac Liammóir, Micheál. 'An tSaoirse: Sglábhuíocht Aigne in Éirinn.' *Misneach*, 18 December 1920. 10–11.

Mac Liammóir, Micheál. *Ceo Meala Lá Seaca*. Dublin: Sairséal agus Dill, 1952.

Mac Liammóir, Micheál. 'Don Quijote de la Mancha.' *Misneach*, 12 November 1921. 6.

Mac Liammóir, Micheál. 'Dul Faoi na Gréine.' *Comhar* 34, no. 3 (March 1975): 12.

Mac Liammóir, Micheál. *Enter a Goldfish: Memoirs of an Irish Actor, Young and Old*. London: Thames and Hudson, 1977.

Mac Liammóir, Micheál. 'Lucht Ealadhna agus an Tír-Grádh.' *An Sguab*, 12 September 1923. 233.

Mac Liammóir, Micheál. 'Mo Chuimhne ar Nijinsky.' *Indiu*, 28 April 1950.

Mac Liammóir, Micheál. 'Nijinsky – an tAisteoir ba mhó sa Domhan.' *Indiu*, 5 May 1950.

Mac Liammóir, Micheál. 'Poilitidheacht.' *An Claidheamh Soluis*, 1 December 1917. 10–11.

Mac Liammóir, Micheál. 'Réamhrá.' In *Deoraíocht*. Pádraic Ó Conaire. Dublin: Helicon, 1980. iii–vii.

Mac Liammóir, Micheál. 'Saoirse na hEaladhna: Cad is Pagántacht ann?' *Misneach*, 5 February 1921. 5.

Mac Liammóir, Micheál. *Theatre in Ireland*. 2nd edn. Dublin: Three Castles, 1964.

Mac Liammóir, Micheál. 'Triúr Sgríbhneoirí i Nua-Litridheacht na Rúise,' part 1. *Fáinne an Lae* (March 1927): 5.

Mac Liammóir, Micheál. 'Triúr Sgríbhneoirí i Nua-Litridheacht na Rúise,' part 2. *Fáinne an Lae* (June 1927): 2.

Mac Liammóir, Micheál. 'Triúr Sgríbhneoirí i Nua-Litridheacht na Rúise,' part 3. *Fáinne an Lae* (July 1927): 2–3.

Madden, Tom. *The Making of an Artist*. Dublin: The Liffey Press, 2015.

Markus, Radvan. 'The Prison of Language: Brian O'Nolan, *An Béal Bocht*, and Language Determinism.' *The Paris Review* 4.1 (2018): 29–38.

Nic Eoin, Máirín. *Trén bhFearann Breac*. Dublin: Cois Life, 2005.

Nic Eoin, Máirín. '"We are no Longer Gaels": War and Conflict in Modern and Contemporary Irish-Language Poetry.' *Litteraria Pragensia* 28, no. 55 (July 2018): 96–116.

Ó Conaire, Breandán. *Myles na Gaeilge: Lámhleabhar ar shaothar Gaeilge Bhrian Ó Nualláin*. Dublin: An Chlóchomhar, 1986.

Ó Conaire, Pádraic. 'Nóra Mharcais Bhig.' In *Scothscéalta*, 84–97. Dublin: Sáirséal Ó Marcaigh, 1982.

Ó Conghaile, Micheál, Jimmy Murphy, and Martin McDonagh. *Go dTaga do Ríocht, Boicíní Bhóthar Kilburn, Cripil Inis Meáin*. Indreabhán: Cló Iar Chonnachta, 2009.

Ó hAodha, Micheál. *The Importance of Being Micheál*. Cooleen: Brandon Book Publishers, 1990.

Ó Siadhail, Pádraig. *Stair Dhrámaíocht na Gaeilge*. Indreabhán: Cló Iar-Chonnachta, 1993.

O'Leary, Philip. *The Prose Literature of the Gaelic Revival, 1881–1921: Ideology and Innovation*. University Park: The Pennsylvania State University Press, 1994.

Pearse, Patrick. 'About Literature.' *An Claidheamh Soluis*, 26 May 1906. 6–7.

'Sagart Capúisíneach.' 'Saoirse Aigne: Tuairim Shagairt ar an Sgeul.' *Misneach*, 29 January 1921. 4.

Yeats, William Butler. 'Ireland and the Arts.' In *Ideas of Good and Evil*, 223–32. London: A.H. Bullen, 1903.

The Use of Minority Languages at Dublin's Gate Theatre and Barcelona's Teatre Lliure

Feargal Whelan and David Clare

The Teatre Lliure must fulfil the function of democratizing the cultural space to which the audience can come to experience the sort of productions they would never see in a commercial theatre: new creations, those that have a very personal or idiosyncratic style, and internationally renowned shows. Regarding the role of the Lliure, not only is there room for this – it's necessary.[1]

The work and founding philosophy of the Teatre Lliure, established in Barcelona in 1976 in the wake of the Spanish dictator General Franco's death, has been very similar to that of Dublin's Gate Theatre. Both theatres are known as practitioners' theatres; both have struggled to understand whether embodying an alternative national theatre is necessarily undermined by accepting a state subsidy; both have benefited from the central involvement of female, LGBT, and migrant theatre-makers. Furthermore, both took Bertolt Brecht as a model at key points in their history; and both have used a combination of international plays and original, home-grown dramas to address changing political circumstances in the regions where they are based. An issue related to this last point is the main focus of this chapter.

The Irish language played a key role in the early Gate Theatre, and Catalan has been the language used at the Teatre Lliure since its founding. This essay will demonstrate that the cosmopolitan/transnational character of both theatres was not undermined but actually strengthened by their use of the local language. As Maddy Janssens and Chris Steyaert

---

[1] Rigola, 'Backpages 17.3,' 474.

have shown, embracing cosmopolitanism and deciding to use a local language are not contradictory impulses. These two scholars – drawing on sociolinguistics as well as critical theories around globalization and cosmopolitanism – demonstrate that when it comes to 'language issues in a global context,' 'universality and particularity' are inevitably 'intertwined.'[2] This is because 'we can only understand the global through the local and, simultaneously ... in our globalized world, there is no local which is not global.'[3] Janssens and Steyaert show the limitations of promoting 'one lingua franca as the [best] communication vehicle in a cosmopolitan world,' and alternatively of encouraging multilingualism while also unreflectively treating languages as 'discrete, hermetically sealed unit[s].'[4] Building on the work of Ulrich Beck and Natan Sznaizer, these scholars convincingly argue that true cosmopolitanism involves 'being part of the world and at the same time being part of a particular, locally and historically grounded place or situation.'[5]

The founders of both the Teatre Lliure and the Gate Theatre therefore exhibited true cosmopolitanism when they repeatedly translated works from the wider world into a local, minority language. Specifically, in addressing Catalan audiences with stories that might be relevant to them, the Teatre Lliure has always translated works from across Europe (and, indeed, the world) into Catalan – as opposed to focusing primarily on works written originally in Catalan or Spanish. Similarly, the Irish-language productions mounted by An Comhar Drámaíochta, the Irish-language company hosted in the Gate on Sunday nights between 1931 and 1942, came from a wide array of sources. For example, Gate co-founder Micheál mac Liammóir directed plays for An Comhar Drámaíochta during those years that were originally written by playwrights from France, Spain, Russia, the United Kingdom, and the United States. By examining key examples of international plays translated into the local minority language at both theatres, it will be shown that the Teatre Lliure and the Gate were in fact showing a great interest in *local* political affairs – not encouraging their patrons to escape into another socio-political reality.

[2] Janssens and Steyaert, 'Re-considering Language,' 624.
[3] Janssens and Steyaert, 'Re-considering Language,' 624; see also Appadurai, *Modernity at Large.*
[4] Janssens and Steyaert, 'Re-considering Language,' 626, 628.
[5] Janssens and Steyaert, 'Re-considering Language,' 628; see also Beck and Sznaider, 'Unpacking Cosmopolitanism for the Social Sciences,' 1–23.

Teatre Lliure

The growth of Catalan nationalism, culminating in the region's short-lived independence before the Spanish Civil War of 1936–39, bears a remarkable resemblance to the development of Irish nationalism in the late nineteenth and early twentieth centuries. Catalonia experienced an artistic renaissance (*la renaixença*) in the mid-nineteenth century, which had at its core the promotion of literature, most notably poetry, in the Catalan language. Despite a long and successful history, Catalan had declined as a literary language since the disintegration of Catalonia as a major territorial power in the Middle Ages and its subjugation in 1814 during the Napoleonic Peninsular War. The nineteenth-century impulse for national independence became inextricably linked with the rejuvenation of the language, setting the tone for a politicisation of Catalan which continued over the next century and a half, and granting it a central role following the foundation of an autonomous Catalan government, within the Spanish Republic, in 1932.[6]

With the military victory of the Spanish army, however, and the overthrow of the democratically elected Spanish and Catalan governments in 1939, Catalonia was assumed into a unitary Spanish state and a culturally homogeneous unit, theoretically at least, with a strong censure on separatist (i.e. solely Catalan) culture. Theatre in the Catalan language was not entirely outlawed but was confined to a largely inert and mostly light comedic programme, unwilling and unable to contain political comment. Rodolf Sirera has described Catalan theatre at this time as 'essentially commercial, populist, [and] melodramatic,' while also noting occasional and yet 'isolated attempts to recover a form of high comedy.'[7] By the late 1960s, plays that tackled political issues – albeit in a slightly obtuse manner (blending fantasy, symbolism, and realism) – were beginning to appear. Examples of such works are the plays of Josep María Benet i Jornet and Jordi Teixidor (both of whom emerged in the 1960s) and the aforementioned Sirera (who began getting produced in the late 1970s).[8] While the existence of such works contradicts the popular myth that Catalan language and culture was completely outlawed under the regime of General Franco, it must still be stressed that following his death, the Catalan language and theatre in Catalan became an integral part of the expression of nationalism and the desire to construct a new separate, independent state. That is to

---

[6] See Balfour and Quiroga, *The Reinvention of Spain*, 128–30.
[7] Sirera, 'Drama and Society,' 44.
[8] Gallén, 'Catalan Theatrical Life,' 28.

say, in the years following the death of the dictator in November 1975, a need to solidify a separate and unified vision became imperative for many Catalans, and the theatre – particularly a newly formed theatre working in the Catalan language such as Teatre Lliure – would perform a central role in that move towards greater linguistic, artistic, and regional autonomy. The impulse of this project is discernible through the eagerness of administrative bodies to heavily subsidise individual Catalan theatre projects through 'the new democratic political institutions at various levels: state, autonomous community (i.e. Catalonia), province (the Diputacions) and town council.'[9]

The desire to emphasise Catalan separateness through both political and cultural activities in the wake of Franco's death was similar to the need among many in Ireland, in the wake of independence in 1922, to stress the country's political and cultural distinctiveness from its old colonial master, England. There was a sense that even the playwrights of the early Abbey had betrayed a subconscious, 'literary Unionism' in their work.[10] The process of building a singular and refined/distilled Irish identity post-Independence is marked by the proliferation of public cultural events such as the public pageants, in which the Gate was centrally involved, the promotion of an Irish landscape painting style, in the manner of Paul Henry in particular, and development of a nativist sporting culture through the foundation of the Tailteann Games.[11] Culturally, the indigenous spirit that marked the post-Franco age in Catalonia is seen in the work of visual artist Antoní Tapiès, the singer Joan Manuel Serrat, and the revival of traditional dancing, while politically it was expressed by support for nationalist groups stressing Catalonia's historical uniqueness. Some of these political groups employed contemporary campaigning methods, such as the Convergence and Union (CiU) alliance of nationalist parties, and some were armed with contemporary weaponry, such as the Catalan Movement of Armed Liberation (MCAN). These broad manifestations of nationalism combined a mixture of tradition and legend with modern modes of expression, and it is in this context that the group Teatre Lliure emerged in Barcelona in 1976.[12]

The company was formed as a fifteen-member cooperative made up of actors, directors, and technicians nominally under the leadership of the designer/director/actor Fabià Puigserver. He was greatly assisted by

---

[9] Gallén, 'Catalan Theatrical Life,' 30. See also Balfour and Quiroga, *Reinvention*, 130.

[10] Deane, *Heroic Styles*, 10.

[11] See Cronin, 'Projecting the Nation through Sport and Culture'; Dean, *All Dressed Up*, 21; Kennedy, *Paul Henry*, 90.

[12] See Balfour and Quiroga, *Reinvention*, 128–32.

Carlota Soldevila, Lluís Pasqual, and Pere Planella. The group's vision was the creation of a theatre in Catalan, which would be *un hecho normal* (a normal thing), in order to normalise that which had not hitherto existed. Whether entirely true or not, there was a clear belief that the lack of a theatrical tradition in the region demanded that the audience, as much as the company, be created from scratch. As Pasqual noted, 'the most important thing about the Lliure was the parallel growth of the company, our theatrical work and the spectators. This happens very rarely in the history of the theatre.'[13] With this in mind, a decision was taken to base its repertoire on what the founders termed 'the solidity' of the international repertoire, both classical and contemporary.[14] All decisions and output relating to each production were to be arrived at in-house, including play choice, set design, set building, lighting, programme design, and auditorium design. Fundamental to the philosophy was the formation of a 'free' space, a versatile area that could be reconfigured to accommodate the needs of each individual performance, and it was also decided that the company would be a 'fluid' group of professionals, in which all members could and would perform all the tasks, both on and off stage, necessary for the mounting of each production.[15]

From the beginning, although the common language would be Catalan, it was thought that the project was best served by presenting performances of already existing works in translation, unlike the original intention of, for example, the Abbey Theatre, which had promoted newly written pieces by local playwrights from the outset. The vision of Lliure

---

[13] Pasqual, 'Backpages 17.3,' 471. This statement can be compared to the founders of the Gate suggesting in the four-page circular sent out at their founding that they would be introducing Irish audiences to 'new and progressive' plays from outside Ireland that would 'not otherwise ordinarily be within the reach of Dublin Theatrical circles.' Quoted in Hogan, Untitled, in *Enter Certain Players*, 13. This statement was disingenuous to the degree that – as Richard Pine has noted – 'the Dublin Drama League, Edward Martyn's "Theatre of Ireland" (where macLíammóir as a young man assisted with scene painting), and Casimir Markievicz's "Dublin Repertory Theatre" and "Independent Theatre,"' as well as 'the cabaret theatre of Madame Cogley,' had all previously presented the type of international fare that would be produced at the Gate. See Pine, 'Micheál macLíammóir,' 85. That said, given the limited lifespan of these earlier organisations, the Gate's avant-garde staging techniques and its absorption of another Irish company interested in such work (An Comhar Drámaíochta, as discussed later in this chapter), it is no exaggeration to suggest that the Gate did witness – like the Teatre Lliure – 'the parallel growth of the company, [their] theatrical work and the spectators.'

[14] 'Timeline.'

[15] 'Timeline.'

was of a theatre that looked outward and abroad, and the Gate, of course, had a similar vision upon its founding in Dublin in 1928, with its mix of new and existing plays but with a significant tilt towards international work.[16] As the Teatre Lliure's artistic director Àlex Rigola said in a 2007 interview: 'I think of Lliure as a Catalan and a European theatre,'[17] a sentiment echoed by co-founder Lluís Pasqual, who further suggests that the reason for such an internationalist focus derives from Catalonia's lack of a readymade theatre tradition. He elaborates:

> During the 1960s we had no teachers ... I found teachers in Poland in Hanuszkiewicz and Grotowsky and in Italy with the Piccolo theatre and Giorgio Strehler ... we have all been influenced by [Bertolt] Brecht.[18]

In this regard, it is illustrative that the leading founder of the company, Puigserver, had grown up in Poland, graduating with a degree in theatre design from the University of Warsaw.

The international plays chosen for translation and production at Teatre Lliure did not simply give Catalan theatre-makers and audiences the chance to develop their knowledge of drama and to experience the pleasure of engaging with stories from other nations. Puigserver and company also used scripts of foreign origin to speak to local political concerns. For this reason, and also because of the interests of Puigserver and Pasqual, Brecht stylistically underpinned the programme for the first few years of Lliure.[19] One early Brecht production came to define the company's ethos while also providing a platform for wider political comment and engagement.

In 1978, the theatre first presented its celebrated production of *La Vida del Rei Eduard II de Anglaterra*, a translation of Brecht's 1923 resetting of Christopher Marlowe's *The Troublesome Reign and Lamentable Death of Edward the Second, King of England* (1592). It is hard to imagine

---

[16] For example, over the Gate's first three seasons it produced six new Irish plays and twenty-one plays that had originally premiered abroad.

[17] Rigola, 'Backpages,' 474.

[18] Pasqual, 'Backpages,' 472.

[19] Brecht had dominated the Catalan stage since the 1960s and is visible through various performances. For a more detailed history of Brecht in performance in Catalonia from the 1960s onwards see Gallén, 'Catalan Theatrical Life,' 26. Asked why Brecht held such an influence, Lluís Pasqual opined that 'German theatre is constantly renewing itself and the dialogue it maintains with its audience is a mature and demanding dialogue.' See Pasqual, 'Backpages,' 472.

a more politically inflected play to demonstrate the intention of the company in relation to the conversation it intended to inspire within the Catalan community, or a better demonstration of the company's belief that theatre could best provide that forum. Marlowe's play foregrounded the homosexual relationship between the king and his partner Gaveston, and the playwright uses the latter's gruesome final execution, as a result of court intrigue orchestrated by the King's enemy Mortimer, to inspire meditation on the nature of kingship, court polity, and disjointed public discourse. The attraction to socialist Brecht of such a meditation is obvious, but the mixture of atavistic violence with personal animosity and administrative power seems to have resonated for Teatre Lliure in the volatile immediate post-Franco era. In the same year as the Lliure's first production of this play, a failed *coup d'état* was attempted; its protagonists eventually came even closer to success in February 1981. And the years immediately preceding that first production had witnessed street violence from separatist terrorist and Marxist groups as well as from nationalist and fascist organisations.[20]

As regards the play's themes around kingship and public discourse, in 1947, Franco had declared himself dictator and *caudillo* (protector) of all of Spain, allowing himself the power of an absolute monarch in all but name, instituting a regime that was culturally proscriptive and clientelist. Throughout Franco's reign, he suppressed and heavily controlled public discourse, and used the educational system and media to promote Spanish in order to marginalise minority languages in regions with distinct linguistic identities like Galicia, the Basque Country, and Catalonia. Given Catalonia's recent experience of the vagaries of absolute and ill-wielded power, the resonance for audiences in attendance at the play (during both its original run and subsequent revivals) could not be avoided. What is more, the relationship between Edward II and Gaveston in Brecht's play would also seem to have had a parallel in the relationship between Franco and his 'court favourite' Serrano Suñer.[21]

It was not merely the subject matter handled in Brecht's adaptation of Marlowe that attracted the theatre-makers at Teatre Lliure, but also the way in which the politically resonant material was presented. It was famously during rehearsals for this play that Brecht was afforded the moment of epiphany that revealed his method of 'epic theatre,' as he described it to Walter Benjamin.[22] In 1983, while discussing his various

---

[20] See Carr and Aizpura, *Spain: Dictatorship to Democracy*, 190–94.
[21] Smyth, *Diplomacy and Strategy of Survival*, 76.
[22] Benjamin, *Understanding Brecht*, 115.

productions of the play, Pasqual emphasised the centrality of the audience in each performance:

> En todo montaje, yo me planteo primero la relación del espectador con el espectáculo y después miro las posibilidades técnicas; no al revés ... un microcosmos muy universal, con los espectadores alrededor y muy cerca.

> (In each production, I place the relationship of the audience to the spectacle first and afterwards look at the technical possibilities, not the reverse. [It becomes] a universal microcosm, with the audience all the way around and very close [to the action]).[23]

Pasqual also made sure to draw attention to the nature of the piece as a disruptive anti-establishment performance, describing it as 'una especie de grito desesperado sobre la opción individual frente a todas las actitudes históricas' ('a type of desperate individual's howl against all historic posturing').[24] A review of the 1988 Spanish-language revival of Pasqual's production in Madrid noted that the resonances of miscarriages of justice and illegal punishment from the time of the play's premiere were still apparent although fading, revealing another aspect of the play that Pasqual and the Teatre Lliure hoped would speak to its audiences. The reviewer Eduardo Haro Tecglen in 1983 also made connections to current unjust convictions and punishments, and despairingly suggested that what now persisted was a sense of anguish, dirt and filth.[25]

Another prominent example of the Teatre Lliure using a play from abroad to speak to local issues is its critically acclaimed and hugely successful 1993 staging of Brian Friel's *Dancing at Lughnasa*. The play was translated into Catalan as *Dansa d'agost* (*An August Dance*) by Guillem-Jordi Graells, and the production was directed by Pere Planella. It is easy to understand why Catalan theatre-makers and audiences would warm to a play depicting women living in a hyper-Catholic and patriarchal society that is attempting to deal with the legacy of having had its local traditions and historic language suppressed by a neighbouring power. When Graells's translation of the play was revived at Barcelona's La Perla 29 in 2016, Catalan theatre critic Laura Serra wrote:

---

23 Torreiro, 'Centro Dramático Nacional.'
24 Torreiro, 'Centro Dramático Nacional.'
25 Tecglen, 'La llamada de Eduardo II.'

L'espectacle Dansa d'agost, que Pere Planella va dirigir a l'antic Teatre Lliure de Gràcia l'any 1993 amb actors de la casa, com Muntsa Alcañiz, Anna Lizaran, Emma Vilasarau i Josep Montanyès, va ser un fenomen teatral que va quedar gravat a la retina dels espectadors.

(The *Dancing at Lughnasa* show, directed by Pere Planella at the old Teatre Lliure de Gràcia in 1993, with house actors such as Muntsa Alcañiz, Anna Lizaran, Emma Vilasarau, and Josep Montanyès, was a theatrical phenomenon that engraved itself in the retinas of the spectators.)[26]

Serra went on to suggest that the popularity of the play's 'aroma ... nostàlgica' ('nostalgic scent') and the important parallels between Irish and Catalan history made the play's return to the Barcelona stage inevitable.[27]

In addition to plays by Brecht and Friel, over the years the Teatre Lliure has also mounted high-profile productions of works by (among others) William Shakespeare, Carlo Goldini, Pierre de Beaumarchais, Friedrich Schiller, Georg Büchner, Jacques Offenbach, Anton Chekhov, Luigi Pirandello, Roger Vitrac, Yukio Mishima, Samuel Beckett, Heiner Müller, Harold Pinter, Olov Enquist, David Mamet, Yasmina Reza, and Martin McDonagh. These are voices from across Europe and further afield that have been used by the Teatre Lliure to develop an appreciation for world drama among Catalan audiences and to help Catalans to see their local problems with fresh eyes – that is to say, through these plays Catalan theatregoers have seen how issues relevant to their lives have been handled in other national contexts.

The Gate Theatre

Contrary to what is often suggested in histories of Irish theatre, the early Gate Theatre was as concerned with Irish national identity as the Abbey, and explicitly asserted its wish to be accepted as a national theatre on a par with its counterpart. In many ways, the project that was underway at the Gate had as much to do with reflecting and culturally defining the nascent Free State of Ireland as it did with staging international theatre in an attempt to broaden a perceived parochial national perspective. Mary

---

[26] Serra, 'La Perla 29.'
[27] Serra, 'La Perla 29.'

Manning, a crucial figure in the early years, reflected on the project for an American newspaper in 1935:

> We are going through the difficult process of becoming a nation once again [...] We can never again be described as an Abbey kitchen interior, entirely surrounded by the bog! And with all this rebuilding and re-organisation a new generation has arisen [...] young writers, dramatists and actors who have found their inspiration and life in work in the Dublin Gate Theatre [...] We hope to portray in some small degree the mind and soul of Ireland.[28]

Manning also edited the Gate's house magazine *Motley*, which laid out the core beliefs of the theatre in its first issue. Lord Longford sketched his outline of the function of the Gate in a piece entitled 'A National Asset,' and Norman Reddin's contribution, 'A National Theatre,' defined his vision of this entity, and proposed that the Gate should assume the duty:

> A National Theatre should primarily be a source of intellectual education and refinement, and a patron would expect to be the recipient of these benefits when he pays for his seat ... It is certainly my ambition to see the 'Gate' not merely conforming with that definition of being a National Theatre, but one day of meriting it. Not merely Dublin only, but Ireland as well, will then have a possession of which they may be justly proud.[29]

It is clear from the content and tone of these contributions to *Motley* that the project being undertaken by those in charge at the theatre was not to provide a programme that would embrace both the modern and the international as a means of counteracting the Abbey Theatre or any perceived insularity in the political milieu of the time. What was intended rather was that their outward-looking and modern methods must be seen as part of a fundamentally intrinsic project forming part of the whole enterprise of nation-building post-independence.

Part of the Gate's concern over Irish nationalist matters was the interest shown by key figures from its early years in the Irish language. Lord Longford, the self-styled Éamonn de Longphort, did much to promote the language at a local political level. But, most notably, there are the Irish-language activities of the Gate's co-founders, Micheál mac Liammóir

---

[28] Manning, 'Dublin has also its Gate Theater.'
[29] Reddin, 'A National Theatre,' 8.

and (the non-Irish-speaking) Hilton Edwards. Prior to founding the Gate in Dublin, mac Liammóir and Edwards ('The Boys') helped to found Ireland's national Irish-language theatre, An Taibhdhearc, in Galway. This occurred in August 1928 – that is, two months before the Gate mounted its first productions in Dublin. Mac Liammóir gamely helped produce, direct, and design shows at An Taibhdhearc while also getting the Gate on its feet right up until 1931. In July of that year, he oversaw a production of *Gaisge agus Gaisgidheach*, his translation of Bernard Shaw's *Arms and the Man* (1894) at An Taibhdhearc, and – as he puts it in his 1946 memoir *All For Hecuba* – 'that was the end of my work in the West.'[30] However, it was not the end of mac Liammóir's work in the Irish language.

As he goes on to state in *All for Hecuba*: 'I have never found life complete if it is lived with one language only, and when in the autumn of [1931 …] I was offered the producership of An Comhar Drámaíochta, the Gaelic Drama League of Ireland, I accepted eagerly, though I knew the work would be overwhelming.'[31] Between 1931 and 1942, mac Liammóir not only allowed An Comhar to use the Gate auditorium on Sunday nights (when the theatre would otherwise be dark), he was also heavily involved in many of the company's productions.[32]

In addition to serving as a producer with An Comhar, he directed the company's productions of his own translations of works by Bernard Shaw, Eugene O'Neill, Anton Chekhov, and Sacha Guitry (the Russian-born French playwright), as well as Irish-language translations by others of works by William Shakespeare, Richard Brinsley Sheridan, Gregorio Martinez Sierra, Molière, T.C. Murray, Rutherford Mayne, Lennox Robinson, T.H. Stafford, Leo Tolstoy, Lady Gregory, Lord Dunsany, Eça de Queirós, Harley Granville-Barker, Laurence Housman, the Quintero brothers, and the French writing teams of Labiche-Martin and Erckmann-Chatrian. Like the Gate's programming, An Comhar offered an eclectic fare: English, continental European, and American playwrights, as well as Irish playwrights with an uneasy or non-existent relationship with the Abbey. An Comhar had been producing the same heady mix even prior to the founding of the Gate, and mac Liammóir had occasionally directed productions for

---

[30] Mac Liammóir, *All for Hecuba*, 210.

[31] Mac Liammóir, *All for Hecuba*, 210.

[32] It should be noted that An Comhar would also mount shows at the Peacock (the Abbey's experimental space) during these years. This occurred much more frequently starting in late 1934, when mac Liammóir stepped down from his An Comhar producer position. From 1936, the fact that Longford Productions were in residence at the Gate for six months of each year added further complications.

them between 1923 and 1930. It is therefore easy to see why 'The Boys' would be interested in effectively absorbing An Comhar into their Gate project. After all, both An Comhar and the Gate were seeking to fill gaps that the Abbey was ignoring – that is, work in the Irish language and also international work that was experimental and/or that would have much to say about a newly independent Ireland.

During An Comhar's years at the Gate, one prominent example of the company using an international play to speak to local socio-political concerns is its immensely popular production of *Scapin na gCleas*, Tomás Ó hÉighneacháin's translation of Molière's *Les Fourberies de Scapin* (1671). This play was directed by mac Liammóir and premiered at the Gate on 16 November 1931. Gearóid Ó Lochlainn, one of the Gate's original directors, starred as Scapin, and music for the production was provided by Bay Jellett, sister of the well-known visual artist Mainie Jellett. This production was a standout favourite for An Comhar's audience members,[33] and Ó hÉighneacháin's translation became something of a seminal text in Irish-language theatre circles: the play went on to be produced on four occasions at An Taibhdhearc between 1933 and 1950.

This popularity is perhaps unsurprising, given how much this Molière play had to say to the puritanically Catholic Irish Free State. After all, it is a work in which the hero Scapin comes up with schemes to literally undermine patriarchal authority: he outwits the fathers of two young suitors in order to obtain a degree of sexual freedom for the young couples that he seeks to assist. As Franco Tonelli notes, 'Molière was [often] under heavy attack from his contemporaries, who saw or wanted to see in the author the subversive spokesman of libertinage and of counter-cultural values.'[34] While commentators over recent decades have debated the exact nature and extent of Molière's political intentions, what cannot be denied is the significant and lasting socio-political impact of *Les Fourberies de Scapin* across the Western world. In addition to the play's implicit attack on constraining natural sexual attraction, it is also remembered as the work that features 'the first occurrence of [the verb] *se camper* in the modern sense,' thus marking 'the de facto birth of the camp aesthetic,' with its emphasis on subversive representations of gender, 'artifice and exaggeration.'[35] In newly independent Ireland, sexuality was heavily policed by the Catholic Church (with assistance from the state) – note for example the incarceration of

[33] O'Leary, *Gaelic Prose*, 395.

[34] Tonelli, 'Molière's "Don Juan,"' 463.

[35] Bolton et al., *Camp: Notes on Fashion*, 1/39; Michallon, '*Camp: Notes on Fashion* review'; Sontag, 'Notes on Camp,' 275.

young women in Magdalene Laundries, the use of the confessional and pulpit to control the sexual behaviour of young people, and even the 'supervision' provided by priests at dances. Marriage – especially in rural areas – was often contracted with financial considerations taking precedence over romance, and, as regards the queer sexuality conventionally associated with camp performance, homosexuality would not be decriminalised in the Irish state until 1993. As such, the topics handled in Molière's play were extremely pertinent to the Irish people attending An Comhar's production at the Gate in 1931.

A second prominent example of An Comhar using an international play to address Irish matters is its staging of *Gaisge agus Gaisgidheach*, mac Liammóir's translation of Shaw's *Arms and the Man* (mounted twice at the Gate during the latter half of 1931). As noted above, this translation had previously premiered in Galway at An Taibhdhearc, and – as on that occasion – the play was directed by mac Liammóir himself. Since Shaw was born and raised in Dublin and expressed pride in his Irish identity throughout his lifetime, it might seem odd to use a play of his as an example of 'international' drama. However, this is not one of Shaw's plays set in Ireland (such as *John Bull's Other Island*, *O'Flaherty, V.C.*, or *Tragedy of an Elderly Gentleman*), and it is not one of his English society plays that features an important Irish character (such as *Man and Superman*, *The Doctor's Dilemma*, or *Press Cuttings*). It is a play set in Bulgaria, in the wake of a war between the Bulgarians and the Serbs and in which a Swiss mercenary and a young Bulgarian woman fall in love.

While it seems that there is no clear link made to Ireland at all in the play, mac Liammóir and An Comhar knew that Shaw's script would have much to say to a newly independent Ireland. *Gaisge agus Gaisgidheach* (*Arms and the Man*) is set in 1885, only seven years after Bulgaria gained its freedom from the Ottoman Empire after five centuries of subjugation. Throughout the play, Shaw mocks the faux-sophistication of the Bulgarian family at the heart of the play: they do not realise how ridiculous they seem when they brag about having a library, a staircase, and an electric bell, or when they boast that they wash their hands nearly every day. Shaw suggests that their ineffectual aping of Viennese fashions only shows up their parochialism. By contrast, he compliments *true* Bulgarian culture when, for example, he praises the traditional Bulgarian outfits worn by the servants Louka and Nicola in the stage directions. Shaw is therefore implicitly calling for the Bulgarian characters to marry true Bulgarian culture to the political sophistication and genuine cosmopolitanism of the Swiss mercenary. This mirrors the Gate's own desire to show Irish people that Irish authenticity and European sophistication are not mutually exclusive. As Desmond Rushe has persuasively argued, mac Liammóir's 'vision was of an Ireland at once more Gaelic and more European, more connected with the Continent in spirit and, by being bilingual, having more sympathy with other languages and other cultures.'[36]

The Gate's Irish-language activities were not confined to the An Comhar productions on Sunday nights. The theatre also included Irish-language and bilingual plays in its revues (whether at Christmas, Easter, or over the summer). These occasional items, however, were written originally in Irish (or Irish and English) and dealt very directly with Irish issues. For example, two important examples of such work from the revues – *An All-Gaelic Talkie: 'An Gúm'* from 1931's *Dublin Revue* and *Caoine Nua Gaelach* from 1943–44's *Masquerade* – both deal with the Irish government's ineffectual attempts to revive the Irish language. Of course, the fact that these playlets were staged alongside English-language translations of plays originating everywhere from England and France to China, as part of these revues, once again emphasised the Gate's commitment to stressing that Gaelic pride did not preclude world citizenship.

Conclusion

The Teatre Lliure's success in the years after its founding meant that, in 1988, following a series of discussions and symposia involving local municipal and regional Catalan authorities, it was decided to abandon the cooperative format and create a private foundation. The intention was to expand dramatically the activities of the theatre to include building new premises; developing its participation in theatre for young audiences, music, and dance; engaging in more teaching and training; building and organising an archive; and fostering more research and publication. All of this was achieved by the foundation being taken under the wing of the official governmental authorities. Like the Gate, with its courting of politicians from the major political parties (through social events and opening night invitations) during its early decades and its decision to start taking an Irish government subsidy from 1972, the Teatre Lliure was accused of having its creative control diluted by the interests of the state, and of being part of a wider problem of funding going to a couple of approved institutions thereby causing hardship to competing independent theatre groups.

The main such 'approved' group was, of course, the National Theatre of Catalonia, which opened in 1996 under the direction of actor Josep Maria

---

[36] Rushe, Untitled, in *Enter Certain Players*, 67.

Flotats. The founding of this new organisation consolidated Teatre Lliure's position as an alternative national theatre – despite its government subsidy. The relationship between the National Theatre of Catalonia and the Teatre Lliure can be compared to that which persists between Ireland's national theatre, the Abbey, and the Gate. Just as the Abbey is more associated with plays by Irish playwrights and the Gate with international fare, the National Theatre of Catalonia's programme is more heavily composed of Catalan writers than its counterpart, the Teatre Lliure.

This crude contrasting of these Irish and Catalan theatres is reductive and ultimately misleading. After all, the Gate has introduced important Irish playwrights such as Denis Johnston, Mary Manning, Christine Longford, Maura Laverty, Brian Friel, and (of course) mac Liammóir to the world. Furthermore, the seven plays written originally in Irish that were staged by An Comhar Drámaíochta during its years based at the Gate are important, unjustly neglected, and influential Irish works.[37] Likewise, the Abbey has produced numerous international classics since its founding: consider Lady Gregory's translations of Molière or even Catalan director Calixto Bieito's famous, or infamous, challenging production of Ramón María del Vallé-Inclán's *The Barbaric Comedies* at the Abbey in 2000. Along similar lines, the Teatre Lliure has regularly produced Catalan writers (going right back to its premiere production, *Camí de nit*, written

---

[37] Although they vary in genre from short comedies to longer tragedies, those plays written in Irish are remarkable for the fact that they are almost all set in the present and to a greater or lesser extent provide a commentary on contemporary life. *Aintí Bríd* (1932) by Annraoi Saidléar is a comic play in the Abbey's naturalistic style about an avaricious family, yet it differs from the traditional Abbey mode by being set in the parlour of a Dublin house. Séamas de Bhuilmot's *An Ráidhteas Oifigeamhail* (1942) is an anti-war drama set in a lighthouse during the Second World War, which accepts Irish neutrality while dealing with the actuality of the national experience. Possibly the most complicated engagement with the aftermath of independence is found in Mícheál Ó Siochfhradha's *Dia 'Á Réidhteach* (1931), in which a drama set during the War of Independence provides an unsettling backdrop for a meditation on the dangers of certainties in war. Mirroring Frank O'Connor's celebrated short story 'Guests of the Nation,' published in the same year, the narrative depicts two Black and Tan officers being taken hostage by an IRA unit. The men become friendly with their captors as all discover a shared humanity. When an order is received to execute the men, the captors decide to refuse and stage an escape that ultimately fails, leading to the death of the Englishmen. Starker than O'Connor's story, given that the IRA men wholly sympathise with their captives, and given the fact that there was a mere ten years between the events depicted and the play's debut, it must have made startling viewing for any audience.

by co-founder Lluís Pasqual), and the National Theatre of Catalonia opened with a production of Tony Kushner's *Angels in America* and has produced versions of international classics by the likes of Shakespeare, Chekhov, and Shaw throughout its existence. However, the accusation still lingers that these alternative national theatres are somehow 'less' nationalist than the official national theatres to which they are frequently compared, due to their interest in international classics. As this chapter has shown, translated works produced at the Teatre Lliure and the Gate Theatre were speaking directly to contemporary political realities in Catalonia and Ireland, respectively. They were in no way distracting local people from nationalist concerns. What's more, these organisations were demonstrating through their theatre-making in a minority language that true cosmopolitanism – as scholars such as Janssens and Steyart have argued – consists of deep engagement with one's very specific local culture *and* with ideas, trends, and languages from beyond one's borders. Intercultural exchange of this kind somehow manages to simultaneously strengthen a local culture's sense of its own uniqueness while also helping to illuminate the important connections that all human beings have in common.

Bibliography

Appadurai, Arjun. *Modernity at Large: Cultural Dimensions of Globalization.* Minneapolis: University of Minnesota, 1996.

Balfour, Sebastian and Alejandro Quiroga. *The Reinvention of Spain: Nation and Identity.* Oxford: Oxford University Press, 2007.

Beck, Ulrich and Natan Sznaider. 'Unpacking Cosmopolitanism for the Social Sciences: A Research Agenda.' *The British Journal of Sociology* 57, no. 1 (2006): 1–23.

Benjamin, Walter. *Understanding Brecht.* Trans. Anna Bostock. London: Verso Books, 1983.

Bolton, Andrew, Karen Van Godtsenhoven, Amanda Garfinkel, and Fabio Cleto. *Camp: Notes on Fashion.* New York: Metropolitan Museum of Art, 2019.

Carr, Raymond and Juan Pablo Aizpura. *Spain: Dictatorship to Democracy.* London: George, Allen & Unwin, 1981.

Cronin, Mike. 'Projecting the Nation through Sport and Culture: Ireland, Aonach Tailteann and the Irish Free State, 1924–32.' *Journal of Contemporary History* 38, no. 3 (2003): 395–411.

Dean, Joan FitzPatrick. *All Dressed Up: Modern Irish Historical Pageants.* Syracuse, NY: Syracuse University Press, 2014.

Deane, Seamus. *Heroic Styles: The Tradition of an Idea.* Derry: Field Day, 1984.

Gallén, Enric. 'Catalan Theatrical Life: 1939–1993.' In *Contemporary Catalan Theatre*, edited by David George and John London, 19–42. Sheffield: Cromwell Press, 1996.

Hogan, Robert. Untitled. In *Enter Certain Players*, edited by Peter Luke, 13–18. Dublin: Dolmen Press, 1978.

Janssens, Maddy and Chris Steyaert. 'Re-considering Language Within a Cosmopolitan Understanding: Toward a Multilingualfranca Approach in International Business Studies.' *Journal of International Business Studies* 45, no. 5 (June/July 2014): 623–39.

Kennedy, S.B. *Paul Henry*. New Haven: Yale University Press, 2007.

Mac Liammóir, Micheál. *All for Hecuba*. Dublin: Lilliput, 2008.

Manning, Mary. 'Dublin has also its Gate Theater.' *Boston Evening Transcript*, 17 January 1935.

Michallon, Clémence. '*Camp: Notes on Fashion* review – A much-needed celebration of a profoundly queer, profoundly political aesthetic.' *The Independent*, 8 May 2019.

O'Leary, Philip. *Gaelic Prose in the Irish Free State: 1922–1939*. University Park, PA: Pennsylvania State University Press, 2010.

Pasqual, Lluís. 'Backpages 17.3.' *Contemporary Theatre Review* 17, no. 3 (2007): 471–73.

Pine, Richard, 'Micheál macLíammóir: The Erotic-Exotic and the Dublin Gate Theatre.' In *The Gate Theatre, Dublin: Inspiration and Craft*, edited by David Clare, Des Lally, and Patrick Lonergan, 147–59. Dublin: Carysfort Press/ Oxford: Peter Lang, 2018.

Reddin, Norman. 'A National Theatre.' *Motley* 1, no. 1 (March 1932): 6–8.

Rigola, Àlex. 'Backpages 17.3.' *Contemporary Theatre Review* 17, no. 3 (2007): 474–75.

Rushe, Desmond. Untitled. In *Enter Certain Players*, edited by Peter Luke, 66–68. Dublin: Dolmen Press, 1978.

Serra, Laura. 'La Perla 29 recupera la màgica "Dansa d'agost."' *ARA*, 4 March 2016. https://www.ara.cat/cultura/Perla-recupera-magica-Dansa-dagost_0_1534046616.html.

Sirera, Rodolf. 'Drama and Society.' In *Contemporary Catalan Theatre*, edited by David George and John London, 43–72. Sheffield: Cromwell Press, 1996.

Smyth, Denis. *Diplomacy and Strategy of Survival: British Policy and Franco's Spain, 1940–41*. Cambridge: Cambridge University Press, 1986.

Sontag, Susan. 'Notes on Camp.' In *Against Interpretation and Other Essays*, ed. Susan Sontag, 275–92. New York: Picador, 2001.

Tecglen, Eduardo Haro. 'La llamada de Eduardo II.' *El País*, 18 October 1988. https://elpais.com/diario/1988/10/18/cultura/593132403_850215.html.

'Timeline.' History of Teatre Lliure. https://www.teatrelliure.com/en/general/
    history.
Tonelli, Franco. 'Molière's "Don Juan" and the Space of the Commedia dell'Arte.'
    Theatre Journal 37, no. 4 (December 1985): 440–64.
Torreiro, Casimiro. 'Lluís Pasqual estrena la obra "Eduardo II," montaje para el
    Centro Dramático Nacional.' *El País,* 29 November 1983. https://elpais.com/
    diario/1983/11/29/cultura/438908412_850215.html.

PART IV
Deconstructing Aesthetics

✦ 9 ✦

Mogu and the Unicorn

Frederick May's Music
for the Gate Theatre

Mark Fitzgerald

On 26 December 1931, a new production of Padraic Colum's play *Mogu of the Desert* opened at the Gate Theatre. Recalling the production fifteen years later, Micheál mac Liammóir ruefully noted:

> On [Colum's] lips spoken with that slow Midwestern voice of his in the quiet grey summer afternoon among stone walls and fields that were yellow with buttercups and fairy horses, the story had pulsed with glowing alien enchantments; a magical Arabian carpet seemed to unroll itself before us, gay with flowers and jewels, alive with impossible adventure. On the stage it lost much: the story was involved, the characters shadowy, the imagery forced and derivative as in so many pseudo-Oriental plays. I think he felt this too, and shared with us a certain disappointment, though he never blamed us for our part in a production that showed no one at his best, and was only memorable for Hilton's grand bulging, lecherous, oily performance as Ali the Beggar, the incidental music by a new Irish composer called Frederick May, and Orson Welles's astonishing makeup as the Grand-Vizier, which involved several pounds of nose putty, a white turban at least two and half feet in diameter, and three inch fingernails of peacock-blue and silver.[1]

Frederick May (1911–85) was indeed a 'new' composer for Irish audiences, as this was the first important commission the twenty-year-old

---

[1] Mac Liammóir, *All for Hecuba*, 145. In reality, Edwards had played the part of Mogu and Welles was the King of Persia.

had received. In a country with no musical infrastructure, the Gate acted as an important launch-pad for the young composer, offering opportunities and experience that someone at his stage could not otherwise have obtained in Ireland. It was also to play an important role in shaping May's later career. Examining the music for the two productions to which May was asked to contribute in the early 1930s gives us interesting insights not just into his development as a composer, but also into working conditions at the Gate at this period. The theatre's promotion of a young and inexperienced gay artist via such substantial and high-profile theatrical commissions is demonstrative of the emancipatory role the Gate played in the wider artistic scene of Dublin in this period.

It is currently impossible to determine exactly how May came to the attention of the Gate Theatre's directors. The connection could have come via musical, literary or, as May was gay, homosexual circles in Dublin. On the literary side, May had been commissioned to write a song for a broadcast in memory of Katherine Tynan given by Lennox Robinson earlier in 1931.[2] May's recollection in a late interview that, around 1929, Irene Haugh asked Æ (George Russell) to arrange a meeting with James Stephens on his behalf, when he wished to get permission to set Stephens's poem 'Hesperus' to music, might also suggest connections with the Dublin literary scene, though it may simply be a reflection of his friendship with Haugh's brother Kevin.[3] May's younger sister Sheila was later to become an actor working at the Gate and other Dublin theatres, which could suggest a familial interest in theatre. On the musical front, May could have been recommended by his teacher John Larchet (1884–1967), who was director of music at the Abbey Theatre and had also provided music for some early Gate productions.[4] Furthermore, Pigott and Co. had published a song by May setting a text by Douglas Hyde in a translation by Lady Gregory in 1930, which might have caught someone's attention.[5] Unfortunately, no details of May's private life from this period survive, owing partly to the

---

[2] The song was entitled 'Drought.' For further information see Lennox Robinson papers, 1/4/MSS 091 Series: Non-fiction writings, 1919–24: Box 12, Folder 2, III – Katherine Tynan, 9.

[3] Ó Dúlaing, 'Interview with Frederick May.' Kevin O'Hanraghan Haugh was later to become Attorney General and judge in the High and Supreme Courts. The poet Irene Haugh studied at the Royal Irish Academy of Music and worked for AE at the *Irish Statesman*, for which she also provided music criticism. See White, 'Irene Haugh.'

[4] See for example Lally, Clare and Van den Beuken, 'Gate Theatre Chronology,' 343.

[5] May, *An Irish Love Song.*

illegality of homosexuality in the period, but also to the decision of fellow composer Brian Boydell (1917–2000) to consign May's personal papers to the bin rather than to the Manuscripts Library of Trinity College in the 1970s.[6]

The circumstances for a young composer trying to start a career in Ireland in the first half of the twentieth century were entirely unpropitious. Radio Éireann had formed an ensemble that would eventually become the first permanent full-time symphony orchestra in Ireland, but in 1931 consisted of five string players and a pianist.[7] A Dublin Philharmonic Society functioned between 1927 and 1936, but it would seem its infrequent concerts were marred by poor execution as large sections of the orchestra were filled by amateur musicians, while new music by young composers was not a feature of their performances.[8] Even composing for smaller formations was problematic due to a dearth of professionally trained musicians, as May was himself to discover: his String Quartet of 1936 had to wait until 1949 for its first Irish performance, when it was given by a visiting English quartet.[9] Opportunities to obtain the type of thorough technical musical education necessary to be a composer or professional performer were limited, not just (as they are today) to those with the economic capacity to invest in local specialised education, but only to those who were in a position to travel abroad to complete their study. May was lucky to win a new scholarship at the Feis Ceoil in 1930 worth £100 to be spent on further study abroad and registered as a composition student in the Royal College of Music London, where Ralph Vaughan Williams was his principal composition teacher.[10] In this context, the larger Dublin theatres provided rare opportunities for a young composer to have their work performed in front of a potentially large audience over a number of nights. Admittedly the evidence suggests that the performance standard of the musicians involved in some of these ventures was also variable, though at least the repetition of work over a number of performances presumably led to increased confidence of delivery.

[6] See the correspondence between Brian Boydell and Ralph G. Walker of Hayes and Sons Solicitors, TCD MS 11128/1/23/66–70.

[7] Kehoe, 'Evolution of the Radio Éireann Symphony Orchestra,' 31.

[8] See Dibble, *Michele Esposito*, 171–72, and Fitzgerald, 'A Belated Arrival,' 349.

[9] Fitzgerald, 'Retrieving the Real Frederick May,' 48.

[10] Dorothy Stokes, honorary secretary of the Student's Musical Union at the Royal Irish Academy of Music congratulated May on receiving the scholarship to study in London in their annual report, noting that 'Dublin cannot offer the same advantages.' For more on this period of May's education see Fitzgerald, 'Retrieving the Real Frederick May,' 33–36.

For the production of *Mogu of the Desert*, May was asked to provide music for a group consisting of flute, violin, cello, double bass and piano, while the various songs were to be performed by the actors.[11] For a twenty-year-old with no experience of working in the theatre, the commission to compose music for *Mogu* was a very large and potentially daunting task. It may be seen to indicate a measure of confidence in this young composer on the part of the directors, or it may simply be the case that by choosing someone young and inexperienced, the company was able to get a substantial amount of music for little or no money. By the winter of 1931, May had embarked on his second year of studies in London, but he had returned to Dublin in December to take his final exam for the Bachelor in Music (Mus. B.) at Trinity College Dublin, which at the time was an external degree.[12] The degree was conferred on 10 December, and on the same day May began work on the music for *Mogu*.[13]

The surviving sketches, score, and parts for the music give some interesting insights into the manner in which the production was put together. While today the play is problematic, containing as it does all the worst orientalist tropes of violent sadistic male rulers, barbarous practices, and sexually objectified women lumbered with names such as 'Moon-of-Love' or 'Food-of-Hearts,' this would not have been problematic at the time. Indeed, Colum was convinced that Edward Knoblock's hit play *Kismet* (1911), which went on to became a successful musical in the 1950s, was based on ideas taken from the first version of his *Mogu*.[14] The problems for the Gate audience were rather more fundamental. It is evident that once work began on the production, it dawned on producer Hilton Edwards that the play, which traces the rise of the vagabond Mogu to the position of Vizier after his daughter attracts the love of the King of Persia and the subsequent reversal of his fortunes, was lacking in the individual characterisation or strength of plot that might have made it stage-worthy. A decision had therefore been taken to enliven the work with a series of songs for the principal characters, drawing the play closer to the world of the musical and potentially making it more inviting for a post-Christmas

---

[11] The full score and sketches for the *Mogu* music are held by the Manuscripts and Archives Department of Trinity College Dublin Library, TCD MS 11495/5/1/1–7.

[12] Fitzgerald, 'Retrieving the Real Frederick May,' 37.

[13] May, 'Music for *Mogu*,' TCD MS 11495/5/1/1.

[14] See 'Colum's Secret Lay in Bare and Stony Tracks of Connaught Bogs,' *Irish Times*, 19 January 1972, which records mac Liammóir's comments at Colum's funeral regarding *Kismet*. See also '*Kismet* and Mr Padraic Colum,' *Irish Times*, 2 April 1912, and a further letter from Colum printed alongside one from Thomas Kettle, '*Kismet* and Mr Padraic Colum,' *Irish Times*, 6 April 1912.

theatre audience. One of these songs, sung by Mogu's daughter Narji, took its text from a passage in the first act of Colum's play where she recalls what she describes as 'the words in the song.'[15] This was then moved to the opening of the work to provide a vocal curtain raiser, its text focusing on a dream of escape from ordinary life ('I perceive it was only a dream, the thought that came to me / The thought that the desert was passed, that we were on the couches / I thought we had dainty food, that singing and wine were around us'), and perhaps also acting as a subliminal 'author's apology' for the orientalist fantasy that followed. An 'Ethiopian Chant' for two Ethiopian captives also took its text from Colum, transplanting lines of a conversation from the end of his third act to the second act. For the rest of the songs, new words not relating to anything in the Colum play were written by an unknown hand, providing May with a range of texts of dubious quality to set. Mogu therefore introduces himself with a 'Desert Song,' beginning:

> I come from lands are [sic] hard and bare, the desert lands
> Where scanty fruits are thorn encased, in desert lands,
> where they are lone the beasts that prowl
> From shade to shade across the waste
> of desert lands
>
> Where the mad ostrich wheels in haste through desert lands
> Where men are like the desert rocks
> that yield no herbage to the flocks
> Men that for hopes have stripes and mocks
> in desert lands.[16]

An even greater challenge for the composer was provided by the texts to a 'Mouse Song' ('O little runner on four feet, / spirit of unobtrusiveness / Thou who are always at a task / Who hast wise eyes and modest dress') and a 'Nose Song' ('O nose that is the king of kings / O nose of Mogu firm and high / O'er all the noses of mankind / This song gives thee supremacy / No force can ever cut thee off / Nor root thee up O deep based nose'), also sung by Mogu.[17]

---

15 Colum, *Mogu the Wanderer or The Desert*, 17.

16 May, 'Music for *Mogu*,' TCD MS 11495/5/1/1.

17 May, 'Music for *Mogu*,' TCD MS 11495/5/1/1. At some point in the rehearsals the first four lines seem to have been cut, judging by the vocal parts. The bizarre words relate to a twist in the plot whereby Mogu finds, after he has agreed to

May's sketches show that he initially composed ten pieces for the play. These can be divided into songs for the principal actors, scene-setting pieces, and short instrumental pieces required directly by the text. In the first category come four songs for Mogu (the 'Desert Song' and 'Song of deliverance from the desert' in the first act and the 'Mouse' and 'Nose' songs in the third), Narji's Song 'I perceive it was only a dream,' court poet Nuseyr's song 'O forest bird,' and the duet for two of the Ethiopian Captives (Ethiopian Chant: 'Our boat floats on the water'). In terms of more general scene setting, a short 'Fruit Seller's Cry,' which is used to enliven the lengthy first scene, takes its cue from a stage direction that refers to a passing fruit seller. A chorus titled 'The Mighty Indian' is used at the end of Act I to indicate Mogu's transformation from vagabond to Vizier while also providing a suitably loud ending to the act and is used again as an effective curtain number to close the first scene of the last act and a second time as Mogu's status is reversed. A flute solo is required directly by the text as Mogu in Act III asks the Vizier's Historiographer Kassim-Farraj to play something on the flute to soothe him.[18]

By the time the play had gone into production, a number of other pieces had been added to the score. A 'Persian Dance' is used to signal the presence of Chosroes, the King of Persia. It is heard at his first appearance and is used again at the opening of the second act, which begins with a scene between Chosroes and Nuseyr. It also appears after Narji has been chosen by Chosroes to be his wife, as she exits stating 'the King awaits me at the Pavilion.' A short passage titled 'Melodrama' seems to have been used to accompany a portion of the scene for the Ethiopian slaves, but a substantial amount of this scene may have been cut, as other musical cues relating to it are crossed out on the running order. A second flute solo was also provided. A 'Butterfly Dance,' which in Colum's text is performed by Narji in the first act, seems to have been used instead for the dance at the Act III banquet performed by the slave Moon-of-Love. While this piece is included in May's full score, the handwriting is John Larchet's, suggesting that he was the author. The *Irish Times* review mentions that John Larchet composed one song for the production and some of the parts for this piece entitled 'Kisses of Women' are to be found inserted loosely

---

marry Gazeleh, a woman of the King's harem, that men who marry ladies from the harem must have their nose cut off. While the number of songs for Mogu reflects the centrality of the role, it also takes advantage of the fact that Edwards had been trained vocally, unlike some of the other actors. See Fitz-Simon, *The Boys*, 47–49.

[18] May, 'Music for *Mogu*,' TCD MS 11495/5/1/1–3.

in the instrumental part-books.[19] It was placed after a scene between Mogu and Gazelah, a woman from the King's harem with whom Mogu has fallen in love.

In total, the surviving full score of the music indicates that there were thirty separate musical cues, and a further three that were deleted at some point in the rehearsals.[20] Many of these consisted of repetitions of earlier cues or sections of the songs, sometimes played as purely instrumental pieces. Both this, and the fact that several of the shorter pieces such as the 'Fruit Seller's Cry' or 'The Mighty Indian' have notes on the score to say they have to be played through twice, suggests that, as rehearsals progressed, more music was incrementally added to enliven the production. The cuts to the second act and the decision to alter it from a three-act to a four-act production all took place at a relatively late point. The fact that Larchet had to assist with the provision of music also suggests that the various additional pieces were requested at the last minute, leaving May without enough time to complete the work himself. Perhaps more interestingly, in May's sketch for the 'Ethiopian Chant,' the vocal line alternates between a group of men, a group of women and passages for both, indicating that May was unaware that this was a text for two male slaves and not a large group of actors. This suggests that, while composing the main cues, May was not actually certain how these specially written texts were to fit into the dramatic action of the play.

While the use of the Phrygian scale for the 'Persian March' and its alternation between harmonised and unharmonised phrases could be seen to have given the music a mildly 'orientalist' sound, most of the songs are composed in May's customary musical language, which is indebted to contemporary English music, somewhat lushly harmonised and chromatic. That May briefly considered making his music sound in some way exotic is suggested by a note at the top of the sketch for Nuseyr's song, which states: 'In a Persian mode.' However, this was crossed out and no attempt was made to make the song sound in any way Persian. True grand opera orientalism was reserved for the intervals; after Act II, violinist Bay Jellet performed solos from the Camille Saint-Saëns opera *Samson and Delilah*,

---

[19] The *Irish Times* review states: 'The music of *Mogu of the Desert* is the work of Dr J.F. Larchet and Mr Fred M. May, Dr Larchet's contribution being the setting of one song and Mr May's the settings of several beautiful lyrics.' See '*Mogu of the Desert*: New Play at Gate Theatre.'

[20] This includes an overture, listed in the index, which does not appear in the score. Presumably this role was played by one of the other pieces from the score, possibly an instrumental version of Narji's song.

while in between the scenes of the final act an arrangement by Larchet for the ensemble of the 'Song of the Indian Guest' from Nikolai Rimsky-Korsakov's *Sadko* was performed.[21]

May made a number of concessions to the fact that he was not writing for professional musicians. The violin is used to double the solo voices in all the songs to aid the actors with pitching the melody and in general the string and flute parts are quite straightforward. Despite this, one or two slightly more challenging moments in the cello line had to be rewritten and simplified, presumably to suit the capability of the player. Also, it seems that the careful doubling did not save all of the actors, as the *Irish Times* noted that John Stephenson, who played Nuseyr, 'did get somewhat out of tune in his singing.'[22]

While reviews seem to have mentioned the music favourably, not everyone was impressed by this refashioning of the play. In George Yeats's scathing report to her husband, she notes:

> It was a bad performance, the music was quite intolerable, it turned the play into something approaching light opera although there was not a great deal of it. The music should have been flute only, the songs almost spoken. No difference was made between the dressing of the Romans and that of the Persians, nor was their acting different so one lost a most necessary sense of balance in the first act and in the 3rd. Hilton Edwards played Mogu as he played the jew in *Jew Suss*, the women were atrocious, the scenery and lighting excellent, the dresses and colours ditto; Colum said to me as we were going out 'I don't recognise my play'. (They had cut an essential part of the second act, he told me.)[23]

While Colum's bewilderment at the cutting, reordering and wholesale alteration of the play is understandable, George Yeats's comments can be seen as a reflection of some of W.B. Yeats's earlier pronouncements on music and certainly, in this case, the quality of the words would suggest that a clear declamation would not have been any help to the success of the production. May himself was happy with at least some of the music, as Nuseyr's song 'O forest bird' from Act II was a feature in recitals May gave four years later in 1935. Mac Liammóir and Edwards must also have

---

21   The flute part for the Rimsky-Korsakov arrangement is to be found in the instrumental part-books entitled 'Hindoo Song.'

22   '*Mogu of the Desert*: New play at Gate Theatre.'

23   See Saddlemeyer, "'Yours affly, Dobbs,'" 294.

been happy with May's music, as in 1933 he was asked to provide music for the first production of a new play by Denis Johnston, *A Bride for the Unicorn*.

From a surviving letter that May sent to Johnston after the initial run, we can gather some facts about the preparation for the production. May notes that while he was at one, or possibly more, of the early rehearsals, he could not stay in Dublin to see the performances, as he had to return to college in London. In addition, he notes, 'I read the play over in such a hurry that I only received a confused impression from it, and I very much hope it will be produced in London.'[24] It would seem that, once more, there was not a lot of time for May to compose the music. Unlike *Mogu*, where the music was draped hastily over Colum's text to hide some of its inadequacies, in *A Bride for the Unicorn*, the music was intended as an integral structural element from the outset. Johnston's subtitle for the 1933 version of the play was 'fantasia and fugue in two parts' – two musical terms referring to both a free form (fantasia) and a strict contrapuntal form: in other words, music with two or more independent voices combined. In an essay on production, Hilton Edwards drew explicit links to this idea of musical form, describing the play as a development of 'the symphonic form' of *The Old Lady Says 'No!'*, and observed that the themes of the play unfolded 'simultaneously in the manner of counterpoint.'[25] He added that 'this contrapuntal construction depended upon the audience receiving a general impression such as one receives at the first hearing of a musical work rather than a concise unfolding of a story.'[26]

The self-conscious linking of the play to musical forms by author and producer was also a reflection of the importance actual music played in the unfolding of the performance. It is clear that Johnston did not write the play with the Gate Theatre in mind, as his stage directions indicate a larger theatre with much greater musical and technical resources. The play begins with an overture that Johnston requests should consist of 'slow music in chords of modern timbre that are intimately connected with the plot – cold wintry music.' He adds that 'as the orchestra draws to its climax, the theme is taken up by an unseen Player at a piano. To a series of arpeggios, a spotlight rises upon a baby grand piano downstage, at which a girl is seated.' Having described the set, the player, and an elderly gentleman who sits by her, additional descriptions of the music state that it rises 'to a series of chords faintly suggestive of the chiming

---

[24] May, 'Letter to Denis Johnston, 7 June 1933,' TCD MS 10066/287/2083.
[25] Edwards, 'Production,' 36.
[26] Edwards, 'Production,' 36.

of the hours.' At this point, the Player stumbles over a phrase, retries it and writes on the manuscript from which she is playing, like a woman practising diligently at home. Further attempts follow, before 'the phrase she is attempting is taken up and played through successfully upon an unseen piano in the Orchestra.'[27] After a passage in which the two pianos play in duet, the Player on stage finds that there is 'a well-dressed man in party clothes, seated at another piano' in the orchestra.[28] Even if we interpret the word orchestra liberally to mean a small group such as that used for *Mogu*, the use of two pianos in addition to the orchestra would present issues of space and expense for a small theatre like the Gate. The orchestra and pianos have to provide music in a wide range of musical styles, some of it drawn from pre-existing sources such as Wagner's 'Wedding March' and any 'well-known hotel air,' while at another point Johnston requests 'the dreary strains of a provincial orchestra.' In addition to this, the eleventh scene requires a group playing dance music behind a curtain on the upper level of the stage. Various passages were designated to be sung by the actors and one of the characters, Egbert the Eccentric, has to play the violin at two points in the play.

Faced with such demands, a series of practical and innovative solutions had to be found. May was commissioned to write music for two pianos and timpani as well as a solo violin piece for Egbert. With no orchestra available for the opening, Johnston's production notes state that 'the orchestral introduction for the first Dublin production had to be played upon an electric gramophone wired for three loudspeakers.'[29] The music was the first side of a recording on 78s of 'Uranus' from Gustav Holst's suite *The Planets*.[30] The opening brass and timpani figure would certainly convey a sense of cinematic drama as the house lights were dimmed, but it is harder to reconcile the genial music that follows with Johnston's request for cold wintry music and slow chords. At the climactic moment of the eleventh scene, when midnight strikes and the Masked Woman reappears, Johnston notes 'orchestral music is preferable to the piano' and adds that, in the first production, the last side of 'Neptune' from Holst's

---

[27] All indications are taken from the unpublished 1933 version of Johnston, *A Bride for the Unicorn*, TCD MS 10066/3/1.

[28] Johnston, *A Bride for the Unicorn*, TCD MS 10066/3/1.

[29] Johnston, 'Notes for music of *A Bride*,' TCD MS 10066/3/55.

[30] This was presumably Holst's 1926 recording with the London Symphony Orchestra and Chorus, though it may have been a copy of his earlier acoustic recording with the same forces. Johnston's consistent misspelling of the composer's name in his notes suggests the 78s may have been provided by Edwards and mac Liammóir.

The Planets was used. In this case, the unusual harmonic and orchestral textures (including a distant female choir) would have been extremely novel, modern, and unusual for a Dublin audience in 1933.[31] When one considers the surface noise of the 78s and the further distortion created by the amplification process one can imagine how this contributed to what one critic described as the violently experimental form of the play.[32]

May provided five pieces of original music for the play. The first piece, entitled 'Clock theme,' was to be played as the side of 'Uranus' came to an end. It is not clear if May was aware that his music would be prefaced by an extract from 'Uranus,' but it is possible that he was, as the low B to which Holst's music descends at the natural point where one could cut it off (bars 108–16) forms the bass of the first of the series of harmonically ambiguous chords with which May's music begins. It would also explain why, after only four bars, he moves to a series of chords directed to be played 'with a chime-like sonority,' corresponding with the second paragraph of Johnston's directions. After seventeen bars of this music, we hear a simple phrase in octaves that seems to be the phrase that the on-stage Player has to stumble over and try repeatedly. Scrawled out in the manuscript are a series of variations on this phrase, presumably to guide the Player in playing it *in*correctly. The second part of the cue then consists of a piano duet that is based on this little phrase, again corresponding to Johnston's directions.

The other cues composed by May offer fewer complications. There is a monumental setting for the chorus of the seven companions of the hero John Phosphorus at the close of the first scene, titled 'Sing, oh children of triumphant Zeus.' Johnston's stage directions indicate that they should be accompanied by both pianos, the on-stage piano to be played by Egbert the Eccentric. May provides a setting for the two pianos and timpani in which the on-stage piano closely follows the sung parts, while the orchestra piano has a more independent harmonic function, thus following the stage direction while also helping to ensure the chorus of actors stays together and in tune. In the third scene, the Drunken Swell has a song called 'The shoes stand sentry at the door,' which is scored for voice and piano. For the

---

[31] There was a performance of five of the movements in Belfast in 1931 by a specially augmented BBC orchestra. See 'In the Northern Capital: A Holst Masterpiece.' While three movements (Venus, Mercury, and Jupiter) were performed by the Radio Éireann Symphony orchestra in 1949 and Mars was performed (with Jupiter) in 1954, it would seem the first complete Dublin performance of *The Planets* took place only in 1963. See Kehoe, 'The Evolution of the Radio Éireann Symphony Orchestra,' 303 and 356, and Acton, 'R.E. concert at Gaiety Theatre.'
[32] D.M. 'New Play's Success.'

tenth scene, May provided a short violin solo which is played by Egbert.
The remainder of May's cues belong to the final scene, a largely musical
coda in which a chorus titled 'Woe, woe, Adonis is dead!' is followed by a
short song for the Drunken Swell, 'The sun has set,' before the play ends
with a repeat of the first scene chorus ('Sing, oh children of triumphant
Zeus'). Apart from the use of pre-existing music, as with the *Mogu* music,
extracts of May's cues were used at other points in the play. For example,
in the eleventh scene, which begins with 'a blare of any new popular
dance tune,' Johnston asks for 'a syncopated version of Triumphant Zeus
played softly by the dance orchestra.'[33] In May's scrawled list of cues, there
is a note that this is 'to be played in the same key as the [gramophone]
dance,' so it seems that the pianist had to fill the role of Johnston's dance
orchestra, taking over from a recording of a dance tune.[34]

By the time May composed the music for *A Bride for the Unicorn*,
he had developed substantially as a composer. He had almost completed
his training at the Royal College of Music and his first orchestral work,
the *Scherzo for Orchestra*, had been rehearsed in public in London.[35] The
music reflects this growing confidence and is more individual in character
than much of the music for *Mogu*. Unfortunately for May, the ambitious
nature of his settings caused problems for the cast. As he had returned to
London, he was not able to provide solutions to the difficulties caused in
particular by his flamboyant setting of 'The shoes stand sentry in the hall,'
in which the piano has a strongly independent role rather than acting as
sympathetic support for an amateur singer. Art Ó Murnaghan, who was
playing Egbert (a character that has to play the piano in the first scene
and mime playing the violin in the tenth scene) was drafted in to compose
an alternative easier setting of 'The shoes stand sentry.'[36] He preceded this
with a short, almost atonal instrumental passage to mark the point where
John enters the bedroom of the mysterious lady, which contrasts bizarrely
with his plain and undemanding setting of 'The shoes stand sentry in the
hall.' Ó Murnaghan also provided a simple chant setting of a text in the
fourth scene that was originally to be recited 'in unison with stiff stylised
gestures,'[37] presumably as the decision to chant the text was taken after
May's departure. Despite these problems, it is notable that the most positive

[33] Johnston, 'Notes for music of *A Bride*,' TCD MS 10066/3/55.
[34] May, 'Sing O Children' and sequence of cues, TCD MS 10066/3/16.
[35] Fitzgerald, 'Retrieving the Real Frederick May,' 39.
[36] Ó Murnaghan also worked at the Gate in a variety of other capacities including
   stage manager and designer.
[37] Johnston, 'Notes for music of *A Bride*,' TCD MS 10066/3/55.

of the reviews not only singled out 'the gravely poetic lament for Adonis,' but also highlighted the way in which 'music and rhythmic sounds played on our nerves,'[38] indicating the vital part the music played in conjunction with the challenging text, dazzling scenography, and flexible direction to 'cut clean away from the old 'realistic' stage tradition.'[39]

The play itself was not successful and Johnston decided to rewrite it, publishing the new version in 1935.[40] A production was mounted at the Gate in April of that year. Due to the substantive nature of the revisions, new music was required and a decision was taken to commission this from Arthur Duff (1899–1956) rather than from May. It is possible that May was not in Ireland at the time the work went into production, but it is also possible that the problems posed by some of his settings were responsible for the change of composer. On the other hand, it is possible that Duff was put forward by Johnston, who had heard and admired some of his earlier work.[41] That May never composed for any Gate production after this date may be due to the fact that in January 1936 he became director of music at the Abbey Theatre, having already deputised there for John Larchet at the end of 1935. It is not impossible that there was some personal falling out between May and the directors of the Gate; his next recorded appearance at the Theatre was in a song and piano recital presented by Lord Longford in 1937, at which he performed a number of piano works, while the singer Hamlyn Benson premiered a song by May titled 'By the bivouac's fitful flame.'[42]

Whatever the reason for May's lack of further engagement with the Gate Theatre, the two commissions he received in the early 1930s were extremely important in bringing the young composer's music to the attention of the wider Dublin audience.[43] Undoubtedly the experience he gained was crucial in helping him to secure the job at the Abbey Theatre ahead of other candidates such as Arthur Duff, who had worked with Yeats at the Abbey on the music for *The King of the Great Clock Tower* and *Resurrection* and who had also composed a ballet for the Abbey School of Ballet.[44] The appointment at the Abbey, while providing a secure income,

---

[38] D.M., 'New Play's Success.'

[39] 'Mr Johnston's New Play *A Bride for the Unicorn.*'

[40] Johnston, *Storm Song and A Bride for the Unicorn.*

[41] Duff, undated letter to Denis Johnston, TCD 10066/287/1126.

[42] 'Gate Theatre: Song and Piano Recital.'

[43] The *Irish Independent* review of *Mogu*, for example, after naming the composers, stated that 'the songs are among the best things in the play.' D.S., 'Gate Players Have Difficult Task.'

[44] O'Meara, 'A Gentle Musician: Arthur Duff,' 19.

proved to be artistically unfulfilling as well as personally very difficult for
May. His principal duty was not to provide incidental music but rather to
provide musical entertainment during the intervals of plays as director of
the grandly named Abbey 'orchestra' – at the time of May's appointment,
this group had been reduced from five players to three, namely May at the
piano, a violinist, and a cellist. The music performed during the intervals
usually consisted of popular classical pieces in reduced arrangements and
some Irish airs.[45] The surviving manuscripts in the TCD (Trinity College
Dublin) and Abbey archives suggest that, for most productions that May
was involved in, he was only required to provide short cues, a handful of
bars in length, to set a mood or cover a scene change. On no instance
did he have to provide a score as substantial as had been required at the
Gate, illustrating perhaps the difference between the role of music as part
of the overall experience in each theatre at this time. The Gate Theatre had
provided a young gay composer with his first professional engagements,
the freedom to compose a wide variety of music and, in the Johnston
production, the experience of engaging with innovative theatre practice all
of which was undoubtedly invaluable for his development as a composer.

Bibliography

Acton, Charles. 'R.E. concert at Gaiety Theatre.' *Irish Times*, 14 October 1963.
Boydell, Brian. 'Letters to Ralph G Walker of Hayes and Sons Solicitors.' Brian
    Boydell Papers, TCD MS 11128/1/23/66–70. Manuscripts and Archives
    Department of Trinity College Dublin Library.
Colum, Padraic. *Mogu the Wanderer or The Desert: A Fantastic Comedy in Three
    Acts*. Boston: Little, Brown and Company, 1917.
'Colum's Secret Lay in Bare and Stony Tracks of Connaught Bogs.' *Irish Times*,
    19 January 1972.
D.M. 'New Play's Success: Brilliant Experiment at the Gate.' *Irish Press*, 10 May
    1933.
D.S. 'Gate Players Have Difficult Task: *Mogu of the Desert*.' *Irish Independent*,
    28 December 1931.
Dibble, Jeremy. *Michele Esposito*. Dublin: Field Day Publications, 2010.
Duff, Arthur. Undated letter to Denis Johnston. Denis Johnston Papers, TCD
    10066/287/1126. Manuscripts and Archives Department of Trinity College
    Dublin Library.

---

[45] Full details of the music performed at the intervals in Abbey Theatre performances
can be found at the online database compiled by Dr Maria McHale: www.
abbeytheatremusic.ie.

Edwards, Hilton. 'Production.' In *The Gate Theatre*, edited by Bulmer Hobson, 21–45. Dublin: The Gate Theatre, 1934.

Fitzgerald, Mark. 'A Belated Arrival: The Delayed Acceptance of Musical Modernity in Irish Composition.' *Irish Studies Review* 26, no. 3 (2018): 347–60.

Fitzgerald, Mark. 'Retrieving the Real Frederick May.' *Journal of the Society for Musicology in Ireland* 14 (2019): 31–73.

Fitz-Simon, Christopher. *The Boys: A Biography of Micheál MacLíammóir and Hilton Edwards*. Dublin: New Island Books, 2002.

'Gate Theatre: Song and Piano Recital.' *Irish Times*, 5 April 1937.

'In the Northern Capital: A Holst Masterpiece.' *Irish Times*, 16 June 1931.

Johnston, Denis. *A Bride for the Unicorn*. Unpublished, 1933. Denis Johnston Papers, TCD MS 10066/3/12–24. Manuscripts and Archives Department of Trinity College Dublin Library.

Johnston, Denis. 'Notes for music of *A Bride*.' Denis Johnston Papers, TCD MS 10066/3/55. Manuscripts and Archives Department of Trinity College Dublin Library.

Johnston, Denis. *Storm Song and A Bride for the Unicorn*. London: Jonathan Cape, 1935.

Kehoe, Patrick Joseph. 'The Evolution of the Radio Éireann Symphony Orchestra, 1926–1954.' PhD dissertation, Dublin Institute of Technology, 2017.

'*Kismet* and Mr Padraic Colum.' *Irish Times*, 2 April 1912.

'*Kismet* and Mr Padraic Colum.' *Irish Times*, 6 April 1912.

Lally, Des, David Clare, and Ruud van den Beuken. 'Gate Theatre Chronology (1928–1982): The Edwards–macLíammóir and Longford Directorates.' In *The Gate Theatre, Dublin: Inspiration and Craft*, edited by David Clare, Des Lally, and Patrick Lonergan, 341–85. Oxford: Peter Lang, 2018.

Lennox Robinson papers, 1/4/MSS 091. Non-fiction writings, 1919–24: Box 12, Folder 2, III – Katherine Tynan, 9. Special Collections Research Center, Morris Library, Southern Illinois University, Carbondale.

Mac Liammóir, Micheál. *All for Hecuba*. Dublin: Progress House, 1961.

May, Frederick. 'Frederick May's Music for *A Bride for the Unicorn*.' Denis Johnston Papers, TCD MS 10066/3/12–24. Manuscripts and Archives Department of Trinity College Dublin Library.

May, Frederick. *An Irish Love Song*. Dublin: Pigott and Co., 1930.

May, Frederick. 'Letter to Denis Johnston, 7 June 1933.' Denis Johnston Papers, TCD MS 10066/287/2083. Manuscripts and Archives Department of Trinity College Dublin Library.

May, Frederick. 'Music for *A Bride for the Unicorn*.' Frederick May Papers, TCD MS 11495/5/2/1–2. Manuscripts and Archives Department of Trinity College Dublin Library.

May, Frederick. 'Music for *Mogu the Wanderer*.' Frederick May Papers, TCD MS 11495/5/1/1–7. Manuscripts and Archives Department of Trinity College Dublin Library.

'*Mogu of the Desert*: New Play at Gate Theatre.' *Irish Times*, 28 December 1931.

'Mr Johnston's New Play *A Bride for the Unicorn*: Expressionism at the Gate.' *Irish Times*, 10 May 1933.

Ó Dúlaing, Donncha. 'Interview with Frederick May, Three-O-One.' 18 February 1975. Contemporary Music Centre Library Ireland, uncatalogued.

O'Meara, Evin. 'A Gentle Musician: Arthur Duff.' B Mus Ed dissertation, Dublin Institute of Technology, 1999.

Saddlemeyer, Ann. '"Yours affly, Dobbs": George Yeats to her Husband, Winter 1931–32.' In *Essays for Richard Ellmann: Omnium Gatherum*, edited by Susan Dick, Declan Kiberd, Dougald McMillan, and Joseph Ronsley, 280–303. Buckinghamshire: Colin Smythe Limited, 1989.

White, W.J. 'Irene Haugh.' In *Catholic Authors: Contemporary Biographical Sketches*, Vol. 2, edited by Matthew Hoehn, 238. New Jersey: St Mary's Abbey, 1952.

✦ 10 ✦

Tartan Transpositions

Materialising Europe, Ireland, and Scotland in the Designs of Molly MacEwen

Siobhán O'Gorman

In 1960, Inverness-born artist Molly MacEwen designed the simple setting for a major Dublin Gate Theatre production: Micheál mac Liammóir's internationally successful tribute to Oscar Wilde, *The Importance of Being Oscar*. The show went to Broadway and was televised by RTÉ, airing first on Saint Patrick's Day 1964. MacEwen's design featured a few simple items of furniture, backed by a sumptuous gold and purple carpet that not only accompanied the production on its international tour, but was featured prominently in the Gate's Golden Jubilee exhibition at the Hugh Lane Gallery, Dublin, in October 1978. Mac Liammóir had passed away in March that year and, as *Irish Times* theatre critic David Nowlan put it, the 'Shade of MacLiammóir' presided over the exhibition.[1] MacEwen's simple setting for *The Importance of Being Oscar* was given a room to itself, with one green carnation on a table.

This room was a fitting tribute to mac Liammóir, not only because the set evoked his famous one-person show and affectively pointed to the absence of its star and author, but because MacEwen's tapestry showed an emphasis on sumptuous, textured details framed by a few basic set pieces – an approach that can also be traced back through mac Liammóir's own practice as a designer. Aoife Monks's reflections on costume and the memory of performance also seem applicable here: 'The work,' writes Monks, 'may appear to disappear, but the imprint of that work, as if in a faulty wax mould, continues in the textures, smells and shapes of the fabric left behind.'[2] In the case of the carpet and set discussed above, the

---

[1] Nowlan, 'Shade of MacLiammoir presides over Gate Theatre's Golden Jubilee.'
[2] Monks, *The Actor in Costume*, 140.

imprint left behind was not body-shaped, as in a costume, but still bodily in the sense of MacEwen and mac Liammóir's collaborative design labour at the Dublin Gate Theatre since the mid-1930s. MacEwen contributed significantly to designing for performance in Ireland and Scotland, and the shade of mac Liammóir – as well as other practitioners who advanced European scenography – can be seen to have haunted her work.

Nearly a decade before *The Importance of Being Oscar*, a weave that also materialised purple and gold tones had characterised a tartan that MacEwen designed for Clan Bracken in *The Highland Fair* – an adaptation of an eighteenth-century ballad opera presented at the Edinburgh International Festival in 1952 and 1953.[3] This 'Bracken Tartan' is now included in the official Scottish Registry of Tartans. Tartan is also a useful conceptual framework for understanding the crisscrossing transpositions of artistic practice that fed into, and emanated out of, MacEwen's highly significant (but under-acknowledged) designs for performance. Ian Brown, introducing his edited volume *From Tartan to Tartanry: Scottish Culture, History and Myth* (2010), traces possible etymologies of the word 'tartan' variously to Gaelic, Scots, and French languages, identifying themes of 'hybridity or crossing, even contrariness' in its linguistic genealogies; while some dictionaries propose that the Scots language may have derived the related word 'plaid' from Gaelic, Brown suggests that 'the journey may have been in the opposite direction.'[4]

Like the pattern of tartan, and like its etymology, practices coming from Europe to Ireland to Scotland, and going back in the opposite direction, can be traced between MacEwen's work at Dublin's Gate Theatre and a range of events in Scotland – several of which were large-scale European initiatives. Erika Fischer-Lichte also uses textile metaphors across several books and journal articles to illuminate historical genealogies of transnational performance traffic. The history of European theatre is, as Fischer-Lichte discusses, replete with examples of 'the interweaving of neighbouring cultures that share a number of features.'[5] Modern European theatre was also increasingly influenced by Asian performing arts practices from the mid-nineteenth century, and theatre artists such as Max Reinhardt, Edward Gordon Craig, Vsevolod Meyerhold, and Bertolt Brecht appropriated 'certain elements and practices' from Chinese and Japanese performing arts troupes who toured to Europe during the early twentieth

---

[3] MacEwen's designs for *The Highland Fair* (1952) can be found in the Scottish Theatre Archive, University of Glasgow: STA 2Fa 2/48–72.

[4] Brown, *From Tartan to Tartanry*, 2–3.

[5] Fischer-Lichte, 'Interweaving Cultures in Performance,' 392.

Figure 3. Purple and gold Bracken tartan designed by Molly MacEwen for
the Edinburgh Festival production of *The Highland Fair* (1951),
by permission of the Scottish Registry of Tartans.

century.[6] This particular interweaving of performance cultures, according
to Fischer-Lichte, 'created entirely new theatre forms' in Europe.[7]

This chapter advocates for MacEwen's importance as a designer and
situates her practice within a set of interwoven influences, including
mac Liammóir's mentorship at the Gate Theatre, twentieth-century
revivals of Early Modern stagecraft, design for large-scale outdoor and/or
site-responsive events, and the modern European theatrical innovations of
Craig, Adolphe Appia, and Leopold Jessner. I draw on a range of archival
research, mainly involving the Dublin Gate Theatre Papers at the Charles

[6] Fischer-Lichte, 'Interweaving Cultures in Performance,' 392–93.
[7] Fischer-Lichte, 'Interweaving Cultures in Performance,' 393.

Deering McCormick Library, Northwestern University, Illinois, and the
Molly MacEwen Collection at the University of Glasgow's Scottish Theatre
Archive.[8] Analysis of these materials reveals that MacEwen's work at
Dublin's Gate Theatre can be situated within wider international contexts
in terms of both its influences and its legacies, thus building on existing
feminist historical revisionism that illuminates the often overlooked (and
probably monumental) roles of women in the development of Irish and
Scottish theatre practice.[9]

MacEwen's Gate Productions

MacEwen made a substantial scenographic contribution to the Gate, but the
extent of that contribution is not entirely clear owing to the fragmentary
nature of evidence available, in addition to omissions within existing
published sources. Her design career appears to have taken off after serving
as mac Liammóir's apprentice at the Gate during the mid-1930s and
following her design work on the 1938 Empire Exhibition, an initiative held
at Bellahouston Park in Glasgow to celebrate trade in the British Empire
and to boost Scotland's economy. Although MacEwen's name appears in
relation to only three productions in the catalogue of the Dublin Gate
Theatre Papers, Richard Pine's research within that collection links her to
forty-eight productions up to 1978, beginning with the Gate's premiere
of Hazel Ellis's *Women without Men* in November 1938.[10] Yet MacEwen's
name first appears in the *Irish Times* in August that year for designing
costumes and settings for *Hollywood Pirate* (1938): mac Liammóir and Isa
Hughes's translation of Marcel Achard's *Le Corsaire* (1938), a metatheatrical
comedy in the style of Luigi Pirandello focusing on the absurdities of a
Hollywood film shoot.[11]

The same article reports that MacEwen had already been carrying out
mac Liammóir's designs at the Gate for three seasons, which suggests that
Hollywood Pirate may actually have been MacEwen's first independent design
at the Gate. Pine's list indicates that MacEwen also continued to collaborate

---

8   Research trips to Illinois and Glasgow were funded by the Irish Research Council
    and the Scottish Society for Art History, respectively. I am grateful for the support
    of these organisations.
9   My recovery of women's under-acknowledged roles in theatre history in this
    chapter and other publications builds on such volumes as Sihra, ed. *Women in
    Irish Drama*; and Angeletti, ed., *Nation, Community, Self.*
10 Pine and Cave, *The Dublin Gate Theatre 1928–1978.*
11 'Gate Theatre: A French Play.'

with others – particularly mac Liammóir – on the Gate's scenography. Collaboration itself has likely contributed to historical omissions regarding the extent of her work. As I have suggested elsewhere in relation to Pike Theatre co-founder Carolyn Swift and other women theatre practitioners who worked in Ireland throughout the twentieth century, intersecting issues of gender, authority, and attribution, have helped to form a situation in which women's significant practice has been overlooked in established theatre histories, especially in the context of collectively created work.[12] This chapter seeks to go some way towards addressing historical omissions in relation to MacEwen's theatre design in particular.

A 1978 *Irish Times* report, also responding to the Gate's Golden Jubilee, sheds further light on MacEwen's relationship with, and the extent of her work at, Dublin's Gate Theatre. This article credits MacEwen with 153 productions by the Gate Theatre Company (more than triple the amount to which Pine linked her in 1984), citing Pat Turner's list for the Gate's fiftieth anniversary of every production, playwright, and set designer associated with the Gate across the fifty years of its existence by 1978.[13] The article also reveals that MacEwen, having 'studied art in Edinburgh and London, and worked as a designer in Windsor,' heard about the Gate while in London; she 'wrote, came over for an interview, got the job, and worked out her apprenticeship for some months before she was allowed the run of the stage.'[14] MacEwen did 'a great deal of designing for the Empire Exhibition,' subsequently returning to work at Dublin's Gate.[15] Her sets were simple and, as such, ideal for touring; the *Irish Times* reports that she even accompanied Edwards and mac Liammóir to Egypt in the late 1930s (1936–38), 'on the excuse that they needed somebody to touch up the sets after they'd been hacked to pieces on the journey.'[16]

By 1942, what a journalist described as MacEwen's 'modern sets' were shown in an exhibition of Dublin Stage Designs called *In Theatre Street*; the event featured 'pictures of theatrical subjects, designs for stage sets, and masks.'[17] Although MacEwen left Dublin in 1947 'to work in the Citizens Theatre in Glasgow, the Gateway in Edinburgh, and on the Edinburgh Festival for Tyrone Guthrie,'[18] it seems that she returned to

---

12 O'Gorman, "'Hers and His,'" 121–38.
13 'An Irishman's Diary.'
14 'An Irishman's Diary.'
15 'Gate Theatre: A French Play.'
16 'An Irishman's Diary.'
17 'Dublin Stage Designs Theatre Exhibition.'
18 'An Irishman's Diary.'

design for the Gate annually from 1953 to 1955, and then on sporadic occasions such as the premiere of *The Importance of Being Oscar* as well as a commemorative production of mac Liammóir's *Where Stars Walk* (first produced in 1940), again following his death in 1978. The latter was costumed by Sarah Looney.

Following Edwards–mac Liammóir's Egyptian tours of the late 1930s, their Gate Theatre Company often presented work at a much larger, commercial venue: Dublin's Gaiety Theatre, which had a capacity of approximately two thousand. It appears that MacEwen played a significant role in the Gate's Gaiety Theatre offerings. She designed the set and costumes for Scottish writer J.M. Barrie's 1901 Broadway comedy *Quality Street* when it appeared on the Gaiety stage in 1941. In the Dublin Gate Theatre Papers, these set and costume designs appear in a folder with her designs for mac Liammóir's comedy *Home for Christmas* (1950), which concerns a Dublin aristocrat who decides to take his daughters on a grand tour of Europe. While the *Irish Playography* credits mac Liammóir with the production's design, archival research reveals that MacEwen must have played a significant role in visualising this work for the stage. The only set designs for *Home for Christmas* in the Dublin Gate Theatre Papers are attributed to MacEwen (although they are undated). Moreover, a design for a stage backdrop featuring birds holding a flower garland linked to *Home for Christmas* in the Gate Theatre Papers reappears as an unidentified design in the Scottish Theatre Archive's Molly MacEwen collection.[19] That collection also contains an undated sketch of a set for mac Liammóir's *Ill Met By Moonlight* (1946), set in an eighteenth-century big house built over a fairy fort in Connemara. Indeed, MacEwen designed the premiere of this play for the Gate on the Gaiety stage. Pine does acknowledge that MacEwen contributed to *Home for Christmas*, indicating that she co-designed the 1976 revival with mac Liammóir.[20]

However, the range of evidence above suggests that MacEwen may have played a more comprehensive role in designing Gate productions at the Gaiety from the 1940s up to at least 1950 than has previously been recognised. Her designs for such productions as *Home for Christmas* bear a close resemblance to her contemporaneous work in Scotland – for example her set design for the Citizen's Theatre Company's 1950 production of *The Merchant of Venice*.[21] It is possible that MacEwan designed the premiere of *Home for Christmas* or that she worked collaboratively on the production

---

[19] Scottish Theatre Archive, University of Glasgow: STA 2Fa 1/52.
[20] Pine and Cave, *The Dublin Gate Theatre*, 118.
[21] Scottish Theatre Archive, University of Glasgow: STA 2Fa 1/46.

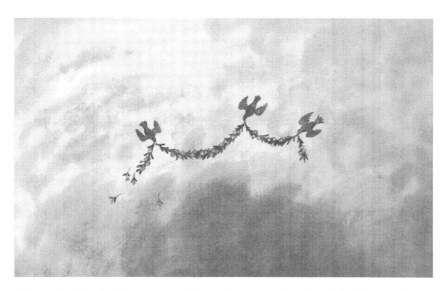

Figure 4. Sketch of a stage backdrop featuring three birds holding a flower garland, by Molly MacEwen (undated), by permission of the University of Glasgow Library, Archives and Special Collections. The same design appears in the Dublin Gate Theatre Archive and the Charles Deering McCormick Library, Northwestern University, where it is linked to Micheal mac Liammóir's *Home for Christmas* (1950).

with mac Liammóir. Either way, it appears that the styles of these two artists became remarkably similar and began in some ways to coalesce as they progressed on from their early collaborations in the 1930s. This situation may have facilitated a skating over of each designer's specific contribution – especially MacEwen's, as a younger woman and mac Liammóir's mentee.

Neo-Elizabethan Stagecraft and European Influences

Another key work presented on the Gaiety stage that Pine lists as co-designed by MacEwen and mac Liammóir is the Gate's 1945 revival of *Othello*, which embodied the Gate's contemporaneous development of a 'neo-Elizabethan' aesthetic – a term that Edwards used to describe his aspirations for the Gate. Pine locates Edward's stagecraft within a wider neo-Elizabethan movement, pioneered in the early twentieth century by William Pole, B. Iden Payne and others, who sought to rescue Shakespeare's plays from Victorian melodramatic distortion.[22] Robert Atkins, who had directed

---

[22] Pine and Cave, *The Dublin Gate Theatre*, 70.

Edwards in Shakespeare's work at the Old Vic, had also sought to revive Elizabethan stagecraft. These influences are evident in the whittling down to the barest essentials in structure and physical statement, which Pine sees as progressively characterising the Gate's Shakespeare productions. In these aspects of scenography, in addition to certain directorial approaches, the Gate of the early 1930s was looking, as Edwards wrote, 'not for something new, but for something once possessed and now mislaid'; this was partly a rejection of the kind of realism that was by then widely available through the proliferation of cinema, in favour of embracing 'the conscious realisation of the presence of the audience.'[23] The Gate honed these aspects of its style in subsequent productions, also in response to ongoing developments in cinema. In relation to the Gate's first production of *Othello* in 1935, for example, Edwards declared that the Gate had decided to 'dispense with everything remotely photographic' and with methods leading to confusion 'between the work of the stage and the work of the screen.'[24]

MacEwen joined the Gate at a key moment in the development of its neo-Elizabethan stagecraft in the mid-1930s, and she also furthered the Gate's increasingly stripped back approach for reasons that were practical as well as aesthetic. The Second World War, which the neutral Irish Free State referred to as the 'Emergency,' was underway for much of MacEwen's tenure at the Gate. This made increased simplification and the recycling of existing settings a necessity: MacEwen recalled in 1978 that, working as a designer during the Emergency, 'almost anything you could think of that you might need became unavailable.'[25] Yet she designed what she claimed were some of her favourite productions during or soon after that period, including Richard Brinsley Sheridan's *The School for Scandal* (1777) in 1943, and *The Merchant of Venice* in 1946.[26]

Although MacEwen designed other productions of Shakespeare's plays for the Gate (returning for a 1955 production of *Henry IV* for example), the simplified, neo-Elizabethan stagecraft that she helped to develop there is also evident in other wartime productions that she designed. Her 1943 design for George Bernard Shaw's *Arms and the Man* (1894), for example, achieved three different stage images through 'the simple adaptation of two basic set pieces,' building on mac Liammóir's use in the period of 'simple but emblematic objects ranged against black curtains.'[27] MacEwen's

---

[23] Hilton Edwards, 'Production,' 45.
[24] Hilton Edwards, quoted in Pine and Cave, *The Dublin Gate Theatre*, 73.
[25] MacEwen, quoted in 'An Irishman's Diary.'
[26] MacEwen, quoted in 'An Irishman's Diary.'
[27] Pine and Cave, *The Dublin Gate Theatre*, 60.

application of neo-Elizabethan stagecraft to Shaw's *Arms and the Man* is one of several examples of how the Gate gradually developed this approach across a range of productions – and particularly in relation to Shaw's work. Indeed, Patricia Goldstone, in her 1977 thesis on the Gate theatre held at Trinity College Library, notes that 'the Elizabethan stage typified those precepts towards which Edwards was constantly working in his method of selection and elimination; the use of scenery was scaled down to the barest essentials and locality most often indicted by a line in the script.'[28] It appears that MacEwen was also heavily involved in this process of selection and elimination, not just to hone the Gate's scenographic vision but as a way of accommodating to limited resources.

MacEwan's contribution to *Othello* (1945) indicates that her approach to Shakespeare was clearly situated within the Gate's then established style of staging his work; yet, it also advanced the Gate's modern sensibilities in ways that evidence MacEwen's growing knowledge of European stagecraft. Critic Gabriel Fallon's enthusiastic review of the Gate's 1939 Christmas production of *The Merry Wives of Windsor* hints that MacEwen was already developing beyond Edwards–mac Liammóir's modes of staging Shakespeare at that early stage in her career:

> A special tribute is due to Molly MacEwen for her settings and costumes. They are of the very best in Gate tradition. No doubt it is true that Miss MacEwen owes much to the influence of Michael MacLiammóir and Hilton Edwards (as what producer or designer does not?), but these settings and costumes are of a very high order.[29]

Images of MacEwen's model for *Othello* show that a central rostrum of concentric steps flanked by four square pillars served as the permanent setting, with single items of furniture – including a throne, a bed, and a tapestry – placed variously atop the rostrum to signal location.[30] Pine sees the influence of Craig on her designs here, as well as on the masks she designed for the Gate's 1942 production of Yeats's 1934 play, *The King of the Great Clock Tower*.[31]

---

[28] Goldstone, 'The Gate Theatre Dublin: 1928–1976,' 65–66.

[29] Fallon, 'Two Shakespeare Productions,' 100.

[30] Four images of MacEwen's model for *Othello* appear on slide 44 accompanying Richard Pine and Richard Allen Cave's *The Dublin Gate Theatre 1928–1978*, held at Special Collections, James Hardiman Library, NUI Galway.

[31] Pine and Cave, *The Dublin Gate Theatre*, 82.

What is most clearly echoed in MacEwen's composition for the Gate's *Othello*, however, is the well-known 1921 Schauspielhaus Berlin production of the play directed by Leopold Jessner, who was in turn influenced by both Appia and Craig. The Schauspielhaus production also centralised a stepped, circular rostrum, in this case flanked by two curved salmon-coloured screens.[32] Details and images of this production (as well as other staging practices that had become prominent in Europe) had spread across the anglophone world with the publication of Kenneth MacGowan and Robert Edmund Jones's 1922 volume based on their European theatre tour: *Continental Stagecraft*. Edwards had also been developing on such European trends as part of his scenographic vision for Gate since the company's inaugural production of *Peer Gynt* at the studio space of Dublin's Abbey Theatre, the Peacock, in 1928. In particular, Edwards had adapted Appian ideas with regard to formative lighting, evocative crowd patterning, and designing rhythmic spaces (often involving stepped or angled solid forms that created rhythm in interaction with moving human bodies).[33] Whether it was Edwards's suggestions or her own research that led MacEwen to also adapt such Appian conceptions of space, her simple, unified, architectonic vision for *Othello* on the large Gaiety stage, as well as her earlier design for *The Merry Wives of Windsor* at the Gate, were also likely informed by her experience of designing for large-scale outdoor events during Scotland's Empire Exhibition, in which architecture had occupied a central position.[34]

MacEwen's Legacy

MacEwen's set designs for the Gate's 1945 *Othello* might additionally be seen as influential on subsequent Irish design for performance. The stage image of a central rostrum flanked by four pillars was echoed ten years later, but for theatre in the round, in Michael O'Herlihy's design for the *Pageant of St. Patrick*, which opened An Tóstal Festival at Croke Park, Dublin, in 1955, with a cast of seven hundred.[35] An Tóstal, parent of the Dublin Theatre Festival (established in 1957), brought the Irish state's internationalising agenda into contact with culture, design and the arts

[32] MacGowan and Jones, *Continental Stagecraft*, 132–38.
[33] For detailed discussion of the Gate's adaptation of Appian techniques, see O'Gorman, *Theatre, Performance and Design*, Chapter 2.
[34] The importance of architecture is evident in *Empire Exhibition, Scotland – 1938, Bellahouston Park, Glasgow: Official Catalogue*, held at Special Collections, University of Glasgow.
[35] 'St. Patrick's Pageant Will Have Cast of 700.'

across the country, aiming to attract visitors – especially from an Irish diaspora of approximately twenty million – and to educate Irish people about 'the importance of industry, the country's proud cultural heritage, and the way in which Irish Landscapes should look.'[36] For the 1955 *Pageant of St. Patrick*, O'Herlihy is credited on the script as 'assistant producer,' as well as with décor and designing the 'King's, Queen's and St. Patrick's last costumes.'[37] Scale drawings for the pageant's settings (signed by O'Herlihy) reveal that the vast rectangular area of Croke Park, with seating on all four sides, was carefully considered in mapping the performance space.[38] It is possible that MacEwen had advised O'Herlihy on approaches to set and costume design. The pair had collaborated on the design for a new Gate production of Eugene O'Neill's *Anna Christie* in 1953. Moreover, MacEwen had by then been designing large-scale, national, site-responsive productions comparable to Edwards–mac Liammóir's *Pageant of St. Patrick* almost annually at the Assembly Hall of the Church of Scotland for the Edinburgh International Festival, beginning with Robert Kemp's abridged version of Sir David Lyndsay's morality play *Ane Satyre of the Thrie Estaites* (1540) in 1948.

The *Thrie Estaites* was the first Scottish drama to be staged at the Edinburgh Festival; it aspired, in a similar way to An Tóstal's Patrician pageants, to performing national identity on an international stage. Like the Dublin Theatre Festival ten years later, the Edinburgh Festival (established in 1947) was part of a series of European initiatives that sought to mobilise visual and performance arts in the service of promoting tolerance and understanding between cultures in the aftermath of the Second World War. The Edinburgh Festival – as one of the earliest of such enterprises – aimed initially to 'bolster a badly damaged sense of European identity by supporting the post-war revival of European arts and culture.'[39] Yet 'a number of prominent Scots' had heavily criticised the inaugural festival, claiming that 'there should have been far greater emphasis on Scottish music and drama.'[40] Programming *The Thrie Estaites* in the second year of the festival was a direct response to such criticisms. Kemp established the

---

[36] Zuelow, *Making Ireland Irish*, 68.

[37] The typescript for *The Pageant of St. Patrick* (1955) is in Box 86 in 'P: Productions' (P 190), Dublin Gate Theatre Collection, Charles Deering McCormick Library of Special Collections, Northwestern University Library.

[38] Stage plans for *The Pageant of St. Patrick* (1955) are in Box 86 in 'P: Productions' (P 190), Dublin Gate Theatre Collection. Subsequent references to designs and stage plans for *The Pageant of St. Patrick* (1955) draw on materials in this box.

[39] Harvie, 'Cultural Effects of the Edinburgh International Festival,' 14.

[40] Miller, *The Edinburgh International Festival, 1947–1996*, 13.

Scottish Theatre Company to resurrect *The Thrie Estaites*, which had not been performed since 1554. Its author, Lyndsay, was considered Scotland's first dramatist, and the play had its first outing as a private performance for King James V and Queen Mary of Guise. *The Thrie Estaites* engaged with social tensions in its original production context – a pivotal moment in Scottish history. The title refers to 'the three bodies represented in the old Scottish Parliament: the Lords Spiritual, the Lords Temporal and the Merchants'; Lydsay's satire protests the 'unprincipled authority of all three' and particularly the Church.[41] Following a couple of public performances in the 1550s, the Scottish clergy banned *The Thrie Estaites* in 1558.

MacEwen's scenographic work was central to the heraldic revival of Scottish cultural heritage that *The Thrie Estaites* embodied in 1948. Guthrie was invited to direct and, since the best theatres in Edinburgh were scheduled to accommodate other Festival productions, he decided to find 'somewhere completely out of the ordinary,' finally securing the Assembly Hall. To adapt this rather bleak setting towards accommodating his festive vision, he asked: 'Can we build an apron stage over the moderator's throne?'[42] The resultant stage resembled those of the sixteenth century and, as such, was ideal for the pageantry of *The Thrie Estaites*: 'Built on three levels with surrounding flights of steps it projected into the centre of the auditorium. The audience sat round the stage on three sides, the actors making their entrances and exits down the aisles between the sections of the audience.'[43]

Guthrie is largely credited with creating this mode of staging, which became a mainstay of future Edinburgh Festival performances and 'was to revolutionize theatre building in Britain and America.'[44] Yet it is possible that he collaborated with MacEwen in a similar way to his work with Tanya Moiseiwitsch, with whom he worked between 1946 and the late 1960s.[45] Like the Edwards–mac Liammóir director–designer duo, Guthrie's professional relationship with Moiseiwitsch (whose career had taken off at the Abbey from 1935) was often characterised by artistic negotiation, even though he pulled directorial (and masculine) rank at times. If his relationship with MacEwen was comparable, then MacEwen probably had a hand in designing the stepped apron stage that went on to convert the Assembly Hall regularly into an Edinburgh Festival theatre. She was billed

41 Miller, *The Edinburgh International Festival*, 14.
42 Guthrie, quoted in Miller, *The Edinburgh International Festival*, 14.
43 Miller, *The Edinburgh International Festival*, 14.
44 Miller, *The Edinburgh International Festival*, 14.
45 The collaborations of Moiseiwitsch and Guthrie are discussed in Edelstein, ed. *The Stage is All the World*, 47–116.

Figure 5. Production image of *The Thrie Estaites*,
Assembly Hall, Church of Scotland, Edinburgh (1948), by permission of
the University of Glasgow Library, Archives and Special Collections.

as designer on the programme, and there is a photograph of a model for
the stage in the Scottish Theatre Archive's Molly MacEwen collection.[46]
Moreover, MacEwen had by then garnered at least a decade of relevant
experience in neo-Elizabethan stagecraft incorporating modern Appian
approaches while working for the Gate in Dublin.

Her costume designs for *The Thrie Estates* also reveal attention to
movement and crowd patterning – suggesting close collaboration with
the director.[47] Production shots show that costumes, in conjunction with
red and brown scenery, imbued *The Thrie Estates* with a sense of reddish
monochrome – although MacEwen also used other colours to attractive
effect.[48] These costumes and furnishings worked well with the spatial
design, as well as Cedric Thorpe Davie's music, to create a theatrical
extravaganza that became 'the smash hit of the Festival.'[49] Whether or not

[46] Scottish Theatre Archive, University of Glasgow: STA 2Fa 1/57.
[47] See, for example, Scottish Theatre Archive, University of Glasgow: STA 2Fa 1/21.
[48] Scottish Theatre Archive, University of Glasgow: STA 2Fa 1/57.
[49] Miller, *The Edinburgh International Festival*, 15.

Figure 6. Sketches of period costumes by Molly MacEwen for three
merchants played by James Gilbert, Randolph Kennedy, and
Sam D. Stevenson in the Citizens' Theatre Company's production
of *The Thrie Estaites*, Assembly Hall, Church of Scotland,
Edinburgh (1951 revival), by permission of the University of Glasgow
Library, Archives and Special Collections.

some of MacEwen's labour was subsumed under Guthrie's (and, if so, this
likely resulted from a combination of contemporary directorial authority
and gender politics), the scenography of this production of *The Thrie
Estaites* was a complex collaborative achievement. Moreover, this particular
scenography was central to the cultural revivalism of the production –
for which Kemp maintained the Lowland Middle Scots dialogue of the
original. Much like Modern Irish pageants employing Gaeilge (including
several devised by Edwards–mac Liammóir), scenographic spectacle enabled
Edinburgh Festival productions of *The Thrie Estaites* to convey meaning
to large audiences who spoke a different mother tongue.

MacEwen designed revivals of *The Thrie Estaites*, in addition a to a
range of other productions of indigenous Scottish work, for the Edinburgh
Festival from the late 1940s to the late 1950s. As such, she made a
significant contribution to the performance of Scottish identities on an
international platform throughout that period. Her contemporaneous work

Figure 7. Molly MacEwen's design for the Citizens' Theatre Company production of *Douglas* (1950), by permission of the University of Glasgow Library, Archives and Special Collections.

at Glasgow's Citizen's Theatre regularly involved designing collectively created pantomimes and other devised popular performances, and – to a lesser extent – canonical classics. The Molly MacEwen collection at the Scottish Theatre Archive contains hundreds of period costume designs, often undated and not labelled in relation to any specific production. Several of these designs are richly detailed, carefully annotated, and shown from more than one angle. Who these characters were, and what theatrical worlds they inhabited, remain to be further evidenced.

However, these designs, many of which include facial expressions and attention to movement as well as other details, already reveal the effort that MacEwen directed towards imagining – towards visually conjuring – the characters in question. MacEwen's costume sketches often incorporate tartan, and fabric swatches suggesting a blend of different materials and textures, are attached to several of her designs. It appears that mac Liammóir also adopted the practice of including fabric swatches during the 1950s. This is exemplified in a costume design, attributed to mac Liammóir, for the London Westminster Theatre's premiere of *The Heart's A Wonder* (1958), Máirín and Nuala O'Farrell's musical adaptation of *The Playboy of the Western World*.[50] The swatch for Una Collins's character in *The Heart's A Wonder* interestingly features both tartan and plaid. Mac Liammóir's use of a swatch here, and the specific fabric samples included, might suggest that the sharing of approaches from mentor (mac Liammóir) to mentee (MacEwen) went back in the opposite direction. Indeed, the Gate offered an emancipatory space for collaboration and international exchange that endured beyond an artist's tenure there: MacEwen maintained close ties with mac Liammóir, as shown in the correspondence between the pair in collections relating to mac Liammóir held at the National Library of Ireland.[51] The familiar, reassuring surfaces of tartan belie detailed intersections of diverse contributing threads. Similarly, the familiar, reassuring surfaces of theatre history obscure the intricacies of collaborative relationships – particularly the offerings of important women artists such as MacEwen – that await further disentangling.

---

[50] Dublin Gate Theatre Collection, Charles Deering McCormick Library of Special Collections, Northwestern University Library: L Folder 3a, no. 9. Catalogue description: 'Design for Una Collins in color, swatches. For *The Heart's A Wonder?* 33 X 42 CM. Tempera?'

[51] See, for example: National Library of Ireland, Papers of Micheál MacLiammóir: MS 41,288/5; and National Library of Ireland, Additional Micheál MacLiammóir and Hilton Edwards Papers: MS 45,860/7.

Figure 8. Sketch of a female period costume, by Molly MacEwen (undated), by permission of the University of Glasgow Library, Archives and Special Collections.

Bibliography

Additional Micheál MacLiammóir and Hilton Edwards Papers. National Library of Ireland, MS 45,860/7.

'An Irishman's Diary.' *Irish Times*, 28 December 1978. 7.

Angeletti, Gioia, ed. *Nation, Community, Self: Female Voices in Scottish Theatre from the Seventies to the Present*. Milan: Mimesis International, 2018.

Brown, Ian. *From Tartan to Tartanry: Scottish Culture, History and Myth*. Edinburgh: Edinburgh University Press, 2010.

Coffey, Fiona Coleman. *Political Acts: Women in Northern Irish Theatre, 1921–2012*. Syracuse, NY: Syracuse University Press, 2016.

Dublin Gate Theatre Collection, Charles Deering McCormick Library of Special Collections, Northwestern University Library.

'Dublin Stage Designs Theatre Exhibition.' *Irish Times*, 3 December 1942. 3.

Edelstein, T.J., ed. *The Stage is All the World: The Theatrical Designs of Tanya Moiseiwitsch*. Chicago: David and Alfred Smart Museum of Art, 1994.

Edwards, Hilton. 'Production.' In *The Gate Theatre*, edited by Bulmer Hobson, 21–45. Dublin: The Gate Theatre, 1934.

Empire Exhibition, Scotland – 1938, Bellahouston Park, Glasgow: Official Catalogue. Special Collections, University of Glasgow.

Fallon, Gabriel. 'Two Shakespeare Productions.' *The Irish Monthly* 68, no. 800 (1940): 95–101.

Fischer-Lichte, Erika. 'The Body as Site of Interweaving Performance Cultures: Between Being a Body and Having a Body.' *Indian Theatre Journal* 1, no. 2 (2017): 107–21.

Fischer-Lichte, Erika. 'Interweaving Cultures in Performance: Different States of Being In-Between.' *New Theatre Quarterly* 25, no. 100 (2009): 391–402.

Fischer-Lichte, Erika, Torsten Jost, and Saskya Iris Jain, eds. *The Politics of Interweaving Performance Cultures: Beyond Postcolonialism*. New York: Routledge, 2014.

'Gate Theatre: A French Play.' *Irish Times*, 13 August 1983. 5.

Goldstone, Patricia. 'The Gate Theatre Dublin: 1928–1976.' MLitt dissertation, Trinity College Dublin, 1977.

Harvie, Jen. 'Cultural Effects of the Edinburgh International Festival: Elitism, Identities, Industries.' *Contemporary Theatre Review* 13, no. 4 (2003): 12–25.

MacGowan, Kenneth and Robert Edmund Jones. *Continental Stagecraft*. London: Benn Brothers, 1923.

Miller, Eileen. *The Edinburgh International Festival 1947–1996*. Aldershot: Scolar Press, 1996.

Monks, Aoife. *The Actor in Costume*. Basingstoke: Palgrave Macmillan, 2010.

Nowlan, David. 'Shade of MacLiammoir presides over Gate Theatre's Golden Jubilee.' *Irish Times*, 5 October 1978. 5.

O'Gorman, Siobhán. "'Hers and His': Carolyn Swift, Alan Simpson and Collective Creation at Dublin's Pike Theatre.' In *Women, Collective Creation, and Devised Performance: The Rise of Women Theatre Artists in the Twentieth and Twenty-First Centuries*, edited by Kathryn Syssoyeva and Scott Proudfit, 121–38. New York: Palgrave Macmillan, 2016.

O'Gorman, Siobhán. *Theatre, Performance and Design: Scenographies in a Modernizing Ireland*. Basingstoke: Palgrave Macmillan, forthcoming.

Papers of Micheál MacLiammóir. National Library of Ireland, MS 41,288/5.

Pine, Richard, and Richard Allen Cave. *The Dublin Gate Theatre 1928–1978*. Teaneck, NJ: Chadwyck-Healey, 1984.

Scottish Theatre Archive, University of Glasgow. STA 2Fa 1.

Sihra, Melissa, ed. *Women in Irish Drama: A Century of Authorship and Representation*. Basingstoke: Palgrave Macmillan, 2007.

'St. Patrick's Pageant Will Have Cast of 700.' *Irish Times*, 26 April 1955. 10.

Zuelow, Eric G.E. *Making Ireland Irish: Tourism and National Identity since the Irish Civil War*. Syracuse, NY: Syracuse University Press, 2009.

PART V
Contesting Traditions in Contemporary Theatre

From White Othello to Black Hamlet

A History of Race and Representation
at the Gate Theatre

Justine Nakase

In 2018, Selina Cartmell marked her inauguration as the artistic director of the Gate Theatre by announcing that the recently Oscar-nominated Ethiopian-Irish actress Ruth Negga would be playing the title role in the Gate's upcoming production of *Hamlet*. Billed as 'a Hamlet for our time,' the production's marketing implied that Negga – a Black Irish woman – was the most fitting representative for the current Irish nation.[1] While Negga's star power was certainly a significant factor behind this casting choice, it was nevertheless a bold move to so clearly highlight an Irish actress of colour in a theatrical ecology and national brand that continues to be overwhelmingly white, despite the country's increasing diversity.[2] However, rather than being a radical departure for the Gate, Negga's casting can be seen as a return to the original ethos of the company, which has from the very first demonstrated an interest in querying the borders of Irish theatre.

Discussions of the Gate's internationalism have tended to focus on its relationship with America and continental Europe, often 'as a means of counteracting the Abbey Theatre or any perceived insularity in the political milieu of the time.'[3] What is overlooked in this framing – and in explorations of Ireland's theatrical history in general – is how this

---

[1] Blake Knox, '"Hamlet of Our Times" – Ruth Negga Confirmed to Play Hamlet in Gate Theatre Production.'

[2] The most recent Census in 2016 records that nearly 20 per cent of the usually resident population identify as non-White Irish, with 57,850 respondents identifying as Black Irish or Black African, 19,447 as Chinese, and 79,273 as Other Asian. Central Statistics Office, 'Census 2016 Summary Results – Part 1,' 60.

[3] Whelan, 'Lord Longford's Yahoo,' 148.

internationalism extended beyond a white European exchange to include engagements with racial and cultural Others. This chapter thus seeks to act as an initial survey of the history of race and theatrical representation at the Gate, with a focus on the material practices of casting. Drawing on archival holdings, this chapter traces the various attitudes and approaches towards racial diversity on the Gate's stage under multiple directorships and in conversation with contemporaneous understandings of race, culture, and performance in Ireland.

It is important to acknowledge that for this survey I focus on a mere handful of productions within the Gate's eighty-five years of programming. As such, my intention is not to claim that the Gate consistently – or even consciously – championed racial diversity. Indeed, the plays under discussion are few and far between, often separated by long stretches of time and with issues of appropriation, orientalism, and racial stereotype woven into their production and reception. However, much as layers of sedimentation can reveal the actions of currents, climate, or past civilisations, in its shifting but sustained engagement with other cultures the Gate acts as a theatrical record of larger attitudes towards race and representation, both in Ireland and abroad. It also makes clear the key role that cultural gatekeepers play in creating opportunities for diversity in the arts. Ultimately, by bringing to light these pivotal moments of the theatre's history, this chapter hopes to encourage further exploration of these emancipatory themes and issues, both at the Gate and beyond.

Cross-Racial Performance in the Early Gate Years: 1930–54

Ever since the foundation of the Gate Theatre, its programming demonstrated its artistic directors' interest in cultures beyond the pale. In its first year, 1930, the theatre staged a Christmas variety show that included two Chinese plays: *Princely Fortune* and *Little Sister*, written by Su Ting Po and translated into English by Kwei Chen. *Princely Fortune* would prove to be particularly popular and was revived in 1933 as an opening piece for Richard Brinsley Sheridan's *St Patrick's Day* and Mary Manning's *Storm Over Wicklow*. In 1931, Orson Welles appeared as the King of Persia in Padraic Colum's *Mogu the Wanderer*, and 1932 saw a staging of R.E. Goddard's melodrama *Obsession in India*, with artistic director Micheál mac Liammóir performing the role of the manipulative Indian servant, Bharat Singh. In 1934 another Chinese drama, *Lady Precious Stream* by London-based playwright Hsiung Shih-I, would round out the theatre's first five seasons, and Lord Longford's own Chinese drama, *Armlet of Jade* (1936), was among the first of the Longford Productions' plays when the theatre split into two directorships. The Orient, then, was a significant and sustained feature of the Gate's formative years.

In all of these productions, white actors portrayed non-white characters through the use of costume and makeup. Press photographs show mac Liammóir playing Bharat Singh with a turban and darkened skin, and with exaggerated eyebrows and eyeliner to give an 'Asian' look in his performance for *Princely Fortune*.[4] Generally, these racial impersonations were cosmetic rather than mimetic – the intention was not to 'pass' as Asian, but rather to augment one's appearance in order to better fit the scenery and setting. Mac Liammóir playfully acknowledged the artifice of his appearance, inscribing a photograph of himself from *Princely Fortune* with Chinese-esque characters, followed by the note 'Not really Chinese' – a tongue-in-cheek reference to both his invented script and his pictorial representation.[5]

This cross-racial casting was, of course, common practice at the time. Yellowface – white performances of Asian characters that were 'comprised of dialect, makeup, posture, and costuming' – had been a staple of American vaudeville since the mid-1800s.[6] These early Gate performances did not carry the same derogatory implications of their American counterparts, however, which pointedly used cross-racial performance as an opportunity to 'mark the Chinese body as inferior and foreign.'[7] Rather, the theatre's orientalism was more aligned with British *chinoiserie*, that 'idealization of Chinese culture, which was Anglicised in the English romantic and sentimental traditions.'[8] Lord Longford in particular was fascinated by China, having redecorated his home of Pakenham Hall in a Chinese style, and is acknowledged in the programme for *Lady Precious Stream* as he 'kindly lent many genuine garments for this production' from his personal collection.[9] Reviews of *Princely Fortune* praised the short play as 'beautifully produced' and commended the actors for a piece 'presented with a brilliant simplicity' where '[w]ith demure, formal gesture and grave voice they conjured a bird-haunted garden before our eyes.'[10] If the Gate's

---

[4] 'Press photographs of *Obsession in India*,' ITA/206/01/20/A; 'Photograph of *Princely Fortune*,' 1661-PH-0001.

[5] 'Photograph of Micheál mac Liammoir dressed up as a Chinese,' ITA/268/03/25.

[6] Moon, 'Lee Tung Foo and the Making of a Chinese American Vaudevillian, 1900s–1920s,' 25.

[7] Moon, 'Lee Tung Foo and the Making of a Chinese American Vaudevillian, 1900s–1920s,' 25.

[8] Min, 'Lady Precious Stream,' 161.

[9] 'Programme for *Lady Precious Stream*,' 1655_MPG_0001, 2.

[10] 'Programme and press cuttings for *Princely Fortune*; *Storm over Wicklow*; *St Patrick's Day*,' ITA/206/01/28, Turner Collection/Mac Liammoir Papers, ITA/206/01/28.

engagement with Chinese theatre was in some ways superficial, then, it still strove for a certain authenticity that sought to honour rather than debase the original theatres that inspired it.

More importantly, this orientalism was also closely tied with the theatre's modernism and echoed its formal experiments with symbolist and expressionist performance styles. In her analysis of Ria Mooney's acting at the Gate, Ciara O'Dowd notes how the performance of *Lady Precious Stream* adapted Chinese theatrical devices such as visible stage hands, the separation of performer and character, and non-realistic staging techniques, while also attempting to recreate Chinese music and costume.[11] Much like theatrical modernism in general, Asian theatrical forms acted as an early interculturalism for the Gate, an opportunity to explore non-realist staging techniques for a company interested in expanding its creative boundaries. Unlike at the Abbey, where these Asian influences were subsumed within an Irish context due to that theatre's particularly nationalist project, the Gate embraced the very Otherness that Chinese theatre represented.[12] Indeed, its recurring engagement with Chinese formal aesthetics in the first five years acted as a shorthand for the very internationalism of the theatre's mission.

After the split between the Longfords and Edwards–mac Liammóir, the programming of the Gate would never again feature such a diversity of plays. But through one play in particular we can trace the theatre's transition from cross-racial performance to an emphasis on self-representation: the Gate's multiple productions of Shakespeare's *Othello*. The Gate first produced *Othello* in 1935, placing it *in situ* with the orientalist dramas discussed above. Like many of the Gate's other Shakespearean productions, *Othello* was a chance to showcase mac Liammóir's acting prowess, with the added benefit of allowing him to play across his partner Edwards, who often took on the foil of Iago to mac Liammóir's leading man. Mac Liammóir was also widely known for taking on the role of Iago in Orson Welles's 1951 film adaptation.

In Ireland, Othello was a role that was highly associated with another key Gate figure, the actor Anew McMaster. McMaster's productions of *Othello* were often hosted at the Gate, and in 1941 he played the role for the Gate's own revival, with Ronald Ibbs as Iago. As a reviewer for the *Evening Herald* noted in 1952, '[t]he greatest Irish portrayer of Othello is

---

[11] O'Dowd, 'Magic Windows,' 143–44.

[12] For example, W.B. Yeats was heavily influenced by Japanese *noh* theatre; however, rather than staging extant *noh* plays in a Japanese style the Abbey produced Yeats's dance plays, which combined elements of *noh* performance within a narrative framework of Ireland. See Murray and Sekine, *Yeats and the Noh*.

Anew McMaster: following in his prodigious footsteps is an unenviable task.'[13] The programme note for the Gate's final production of *Othello* in 1962 observes that 'Othello has always been a favourite in the Dublin Gate Theatre repertory, both Hilton Edwards and Michael MacLiammoir having each alternately played both Othello and Iago,' and that '[h]is performance of Othello was the brightest jewel in the crown of the late Anew McMaster.'[14]

In all of these productions, the actors playing Othello used stage make-up to darken their faces and bodies for the role. In a press photograph from the 1935 production, mac Liammóir appears in dark face make-up with a black beard and exaggerated eyebrows and eyeliner.[15] In an even more striking image, a photograph of Anew McMaster's *Othello* depicts the actor shirtless and in profile with arms crossed, wearing metal arm cuffs and earrings, bronzed completely from face to waist.[16] This cosmetic augmentation was in keeping with the general representation of Othello at the time, which had moved from performances in full blackface to interpretations of Othello as a lighter Arabic- or Indian-inspired presentation – a 'bronze age of *Othello*' that began in the early 1800s as a response to contemporary hostility towards miscegenation on stage.[17] In Ireland this convention was observed at other theatres as well: a review of the Globe Theatre's 1952 production of *Othello* starring Godfrey Quigley critiqued the actor's 'tight-lipped performance, too closely confined,' which was not helped by the fact that '[t]here was a grievous handicap on the first night as regards make-up (which became streaky) robbing the actor of dignity.'[18] Here it is not the use of make-up to impersonate blackness that troubles the performance, but rather its inexpert application that robs the actor (and the character) of dignity on stage.

However, by the time that mac Liammóir and McMaster stepped into the role, high-profile Black actors had also begun to tackle *Othello*. A century earlier, Ira Aldrige 'achieved his first great success in Dublin at the Theatre Royal in 1831–32,' where he found a more ready acceptance of his *Othello* than in his later appearances in England.[19] Furthermore, the breakthrough performance of Paul Robeson as Othello in 1930 – 'whose

---

[13] 'Othello Review.'
[14] 'Programme for *Othello*,' 1974_MPG_0002, 8.
[15] 'Press photographs for *Othello*,' ITA/206/01/39.
[16] 'Programme for *Othello*,' 1974_MPG_0002, 8.
[17] Kaul, 'Background: Black or Tawny?' 8.
[18] 'Othello Review.'
[19] Kaul, 'Black or Tawny?' 12–13.

mere presence transformed and re-politicized the play' – marked a sea change moment that would ultimately result in a general consensus today that the role should only be played by a Black actor.[20] However, during the Gate's run of *Othellos*, it was still common practice for white actors to step into the lead role. Indeed, Lawrence Olivier himself appeared as Othello in full blackface in the 1965 film version of the play[21] – by which time Edwards and mac Liammóir had turned to the African American actor William Marshall to fill the role for their 1962 production.

Imported Authenticity:
Othello (1962) and *Black Man's Country* (1974)

The shift from racial impersonation to importing actors of colour happened under the Edwards–mac Liammóir tenure by unhappy accident. When the pair initially planned to stage *Othello* again in 1962, Anew McMaster was set to renew the role for which he was so well known. However, McMaster unexpectedly passed away the week before rehearsals began, leaving the artistic directors in need of a new star. The theatre reached out to African American actor William Marshall, who stepped into the production at the last minute. Despite rumoured interpersonal tensions between Marshall and mac Liammóir, the show was a great success – during its tour to England, Marshall was hailed by the London press as the 'best Othello of our time.'[22]

Though the casting of the theatre's first Black Othello was prompted by pressing and unforeseen circumstances, the seed of this choice might be traced back to two significant experiences mac Liammóir had in the years just preceding. First, mac Liammóir was present for the appearance of Paul Robeson as the first Black actor to play Othello at Stratford-Upon-Avon in 1959, a performance that he reviewed for the Irish papers. According to mac Liammóir:

> Paul Robeson has a majesty of voice and presence that illumines everything he does with magical fires, and if he and the director could agree that he should remain for the greater part of the

---

20 Potter, *Shakespeare in Performance*, 106. Indeed, Robeson's impact on the performance history of the play is so significant that Potter divides her book on the play into two parts: '*Othello* before Robeson' and 'Robeson and after.'

21 '[A]n unashamed tour de force of impersonation; widely praised, it would soon become (on film and video) a source of embarrassment itself.' See Potter, 135.

22 Kaul, 'Black or Tawny?' 18.

play immobile and magnificent as the Sphinx, cutting away those small abrupt movements of the hands which reduce his leonine grandeur, and allowing him to rely for interpretation mainly on the profound reality of his voice, the black lightening of his eyes, the sorcery of his tortured and smiling face, he would be the finest Othello of his day.[23]

Mac Liammóir must have been aware of the historic significance of the event, and personally witnessing a Black actor in the role could certainly have impacted his casting considerations. Coincidentally, Robeson was almost unable to play the role in Stratford due to illness; poised to step in and take on the role if Robeson was unable was none other than the Othello that would grace the Gate stage three years later – William Marshall.

The second experience that may have influenced mac Liammóir's approach to casting and representation was his theatrical tour of his one-man show *The Importance of Being Oscar* in South Africa in 1962. In an interview with the Irish press, mac Liammóir spoke out about the racial injustice he had witnessed during his travels, and he was particularly critical about the lack of access South Africa's Black population had to the theatre, both as audience and artists. He noted that when playing to Black audiences, he 'wanted to make a speech saying how happy I had been to play – if only for three times in a long tour of more than three weeks and eight shows a week – to an audience truly representative of *all* the peoples of South Africa.'[24] When questioned about the existing system of Apartheid, mac Liammóir observed that 'though not as ubiquitous as I feared, [it] was horrible,' and felt that the 'real tragedy of South Africa [is that they] cannot express themselves in life or in the theatre. They are not allowed, except on special ocasions [*sic*], even to attend it, far less take their share in its development from within.'[25] He then concludes the interview with the observation, 'I hope for a brief rest before I start rehearsing for "Othello" for the Dublin Theatre Festival.'[26] It is worth considering, then, whether his experiences in South Africa, paired with his exposure to Robeson's performance three years earlier, contributed to his decision to reach out to William Marshall.

[23] Micheál mac Liammóir, 'Review of *Othello*,' ITA/268/05/03.
[24] However, '[t]his was not encouraged and I didn't do it.' See 'Home after Tour,' ITA/268/05/46.
[25] 'Home after Tour,' ITA/268/05/46.
[26] 'Home after Tour,' ITA/268/05/46.

Marshall's Othello marked a new moment at the Gate Theatre, in which actors of colour were brought in from America and England to represent racialised characters on stage.[27] However, it would be over a decade before the Gate would repeat this approach. In 1974, Edwards and mac Liammóir produced *Black Man's Country* by Desmond Forristal, a play about the role of Irish missionaries in the Nigeria–Biafra war. Forristal, himself a Catholic priest, was inspired by his visit to Biafra in 1968 when making a documentary for the *Rasharc* series on RTÉ. Centred on the interpersonal conflicts between the older Irish priest Father Mitchell and the idealistic new arrival, Father O'Brien, as well as the local Igbo priest, Father Zachary Azuka, the play 'expose[d] the intergenerational differences that existed between Irish missionaries as well as the difficulties inherent in handing over the Church to the African clergy.'[28]

Correspondence between the Gate board members and Forristal reveals that casting was one of the primary concerns about the play's producibility. While Terence de Vere White seems to have felt that the play 'would be easy to cast,' Christine Longford countered that 'I've no idea how you get black actors, but I'm sure you [Edwards] know and so would he [Forristal].'[29] Edwards confirmed that 'I like the play in spite of the difficulty [of getting] three coloured actors for it,' and mac Liammóir concurred: 'The only difficulties I see in putting on to our stage this most interesting play are as follows: The three negro actors,' as well as doubts that 'our sweet Irish public care more about any problem outside this island of Saints and Scholars.'[30]

While the board accepted the value of producing the play based on its lively dialogue and timely subject matter, Edwards wrote to Forristal, 'One thing is certain: I have no black people on my list of casts and I would be very much in your hands about getting hold of them.'[31] He conceded that 'if necessary, we would have to import from England (where I understand the population is now predominantly black) but this is unsatisfactory because it often means buying a pig in a poke ... Most of them

[27] A notable exception was the 1965 production of *Rashomon*, a stage adaptation by Fay and Michael Kanin of the film by Akira Kurosawa. Though set in Japan, all of the roles were played by white actors, which was in keeping with the casting of the original 1959 New York run as well as the Gate's earlier tradition of orientalist cross-racial performance.

[28] Bateman, 'Biafra in the Irish Imagination,' 310.

[29] 'Correspondence and press information for the Gate Theatre's production of *Black Man's Country*,' 1973–74, GADM_00002172, 4.

[30] 'Correspondence and press information,' 4–5.

[31] 'Correspondence and press information,' 7.

tend to have a talent, but we naturally want everybody good.'[32] Forristal responded to this concern with the suggestion that 'it might be possible to get some black students ... if Equity would permit this'[33] – a reference to the significant population of Black medical and law students in Dublin, many of whom would have been Nigerian.[34] However, while this solution might be an option for the smaller roles, Forristal expressed reservations about casting a non-professional for the main role and older character of Zachary. He notes that '[o]ne possibility would be Louis Mahony, who is at present appearing in Jesus Christ Superstar as Caiaphas, and will be in the Gaiety from next week so you could see him in action if you wished.'[35] In Mahony's favour, Forristal notes, is his 'good presence and appearance, good voice and plenty of experience of Irish conditions – he did the part of Lumumba in the Conor Cruise O'Brien play "Murderous Angels" a couple of years ago, if I am not mistaken.'[36] Forristal was mistaken; Mahony *was* in O'Brien's play, which dramatised the 1961 assassination of Congolese prime minister Patrice Lumumba, but played Diallo Diop, the aide to UN Secretary General Dag Hammarskjöld, rather than Lumumba himself.

In the end, the Gate did have to 'buy a pig in a poke,' as all of the Black actors that they employed were sourced through the London-based CC Oriental Casting Agency, 'Specialists in Afro Asian Artists.' When staged in 1974, the play featured 'special guest artists' Olu Jacobs as Father Zachary Azuka, Kwesi Kay as Cyprian Akuta, and Fred Brobby as Gregory Olume.[37] Jacobs, a Nigerian British-based actor, had appeared in Dublin before as Kasavubu in O'Brien's aforementioned *Murderous Angels*, and in the Abbey's 1972 tour of Brendan Behan's *Richard's Cork Leg*. Kay and Brobby were both British-based Ghanaian actors; this seems to have been their first (and only) Irish engagement.

What is telling about the pre-production exchange around *Black Man's Country* is the unspoken agreement that the Nigerian roles needed to be played by Black actors. Forristal had earlier suggested potentially double-casting the two smaller roles, a suggestion that was quickly dismissed

---

[32] 'Correspondence and press information,' 7. Edwards's comments, though likely written in the jesting vein that characterises his general correspondence with Forristal, also reveal a certain casual racism that is worth noting considering the themes of this chapter.

[33] 'Correspondence and press information,' 9.

[34] See Brannigan, *Race in Modern Irish Literature and Culture*; Fanning, *Migration and the Making of Ireland*.

[35] 'Correspondence and press information,' 9.

[36] 'Correspondence and press information,' 9.

[37] 'Correspondence and press information,' 1.

by Edwards and mac Liammóir. Yet no one ever considered the idea of a white actor taking on any of the Black characters through the use of blackface. This is not because blackface performance was a completely outdated practice. One need only note the mainstream popularity of the BBC's *The Black and White Minstrel Show*, which ran until 1978, or the Irish show band The Zulus, who in 1972 changed their name (and image) from The Royal Earls to tour the country 'dressed in animal skins,' and who 'bore spears and shields on stage, wore afro-wigs, and were blacked up.'[38] Even the Abbey Theatre, when first staging Behan's *Richard's Cork Leg* in 1972, used the white actor Barney McKenna to play the role of 'A Coloured Gentleman.' Rather, the genre of the play itself foreclosed the possibility of cross-racial performance. Blackface is necessarily a racist parody, and the examples cited above spoke to popular forms of entertainment such as the music hall.[39] In contrast, the straightforward realism of Forristal's play required a degree of authenticity, particularly considering the weighty subject matter of civil conflict, ethnic identity, and the suffering of famine.

The fact that the Gate chose to proceed with staging *Black Man's Country* despite the perceived difficulty in casting Black actors speaks to the important role that cultural gate keepers can play in encouraging diversity in the arts. In contrast, Conor Cruise O'Brien's *Murderous Angels* had allegedly been rejected by the Abbey in 1969 on the grounds that 'there are no Negro actors in the Abbey company,' forcing O'Brien to take the play abroad for production.[40] The Abbey's rejection of O'Brien's play spoke more to the theatre's unwillingness to outreach to new communities than to an actual lack of talent, as subsequent stagings of the play in Ireland would attest. In contrast, the Gate's collaboration with William Marshall on *Othello* and its commitment to producing Forristal's play created opportunities that, though certainly limited, still opened the door for an exploration of race on the Irish stage.

---

[38] Brannigan, "'Ireland, and Black!'", 240–41.

[39] As Michael Pickering writes in his book on blackface in Britain, '[m]instrelsy specialized in mock blacks and racial mockery.' Pickering, *Blackface Minstrelsy in Britain*, 3. For an excellent overview of the larger racist histories and ongoing legacies of blackface in a global context, as well as key scholarship in the field, see Catherine Cole and Tracy Davis's introduction to their special issue of *TDR*. Cole and Davis, 'Routes of Blackface,' 7–12.

[40] Simpson, 'Murderous Angels.' *Murderous Angels* was originally staged at the Mark Taper Forum in 1970, and was brought to the Dublin Theatre Festival in 1971.

Hidden Histories: *Jane Eyre* (2003, 2010), Bertha Mason, and Race in Celtic Tiger Ireland

After mac Liammóir's death in 1978 and Edwards's passing in 1982, the artistic directorship at the Gate was taken on by Michael Colgan, who stepped into that role in January 1983. Unlike the previous tenures, Colgan's artistic direction was less interested in exploring global influences and experiences, and more focused on developing the canons of white male playwrights from Ireland, the United States, and Britain, such as Samuel Beckett, Arthur Miller, and Harold Pinter. Ironically, the moment in which the Gate was the least diverse in its programming was the very moment when the rest of Irish theatre was engaging with this 'new' issue. In the 1990s and 2000s, plays such as Donal O'Kelly's *Asylum! Asylum!* (1994), Roddy Doyle's *Guess Who's Coming for the Dinner* (2001), Ken Harmon's *Done up Like a Kipper* (2002), Charlie O'Neill's *Hurl* (2003), and Gary Duggan's *Shibari* (2012) explored how a nation of historical emigration was reacting to inward migration for the first time.[41] If the Gate's status as an alternative to the national theatre had previously given it the freedom to push the racial boundaries of the Irish stage, it also released it from the responsibility of addressing immigration as a contemporary social issue.

However, although the Gate did not directly address the shifting demographics of the country, there was one particular casting choice during the Colgan years that revealed the longer history of Irish diversity. In 2003 Alan Stanford adapted and directed *Jane Eyre*, which would be restaged in 2010. One significant change that Stanford made to previous productions of *Jane Eyre* at the Gate was writing in the stage appearance of the character Bertha Mason, and casting Bertha as a Black woman.[42] Unlike the productions of *Othello* and *Black Man's Country* discussed above, Stanford did not need to look abroad for racially 'authentic' actors to play the role. Instead, he cast Mary Healy in 2003 and Donna Anita Nikolaisen in 2010, both of whom are Black Irish women. As such, the existence of Bertha on the Gate's stage is a glimpse into the often hidden community of Irish citizens of mixed-race heritage.

---

[41] This was of course itself a canon of white male playwrights reflecting on their experiences of encountering the Other rather than perspectives authored from within minority ethnic or migrant communities in Ireland. See McIvor, 'White Irish-Born Male Playwrights and the Immigrant Experience,' 37–49.

[42] Previous productions of *Jane Eyre* were staged in 1944, with mac Liammóir playing Rochester, and 1990, with Stanford playing Rochester under the direction of Helena Kaut-Howson.

While today Irishness tends to be equated with whiteness, there is a significant mixed-race Irish population that challenges the myth of a racially homogeneous nation. Though only recently emerging, initial documentation of this population can be seen in the collection of interviews entitled *My Eyes Only Look Out: Experiences of Irish People of Mixed Race Parentage* and the ongoing *#IamIrish* project.[43] Furthermore, the establishment of the Mixed Race Irish campaign in 2013 to 'raise awareness of the experiences of mixed race children … in the Irish institutional care system during the 1940s, 50s, 60s, and 70s' indicates that generations of Irish diversity were lost through practices of state containment.[44] In other words, one of the reasons the mixed-race Irish community has seemed to be invisible for so long is that they *were* invisible, being historically hidden away in Irish industrial schools and orphanages. Bertha Mason and her enforced confinement, then, could be seen as an apt embodiment of the experiences of many people of mixed race in Ireland.

However, rather than attempting a commentary on this hidden history or the country's growing diversity, the Gate's choice to cast Bertha as a Black woman was more likely influenced by Jean Rhys's novel *Wide Sargasso Sea* (1966), which describes the background of Rochester's marriage to the Creole heiress Antoinette Cosway. Tracing the emergence of Bertha as a character in literary and dramatic adaptations of *Jane Eyre*, Patsy Stoneman argues that 'the impact of *Wide Sargasso Sea* on readings and reproduction of *Jane Eyre* is enormous' and includes a shift towards depictions of Bertha that were not only more sympathetic, but also particularly raced.[45] Though the inspiration behind Bertha's casting might have originated in a feminist and postcolonial critique, in practice Stanford's *Jane Eyre* worked to reinscribe the Black female body with historic and pejorative stereotypes of racial difference.

Throughout Stanford's script, the language surrounding Bertha paints her as monstrous and animalistic. Jane wonders aloud, 'What creature is it … that utters the laughter of a demon, the cry of a caged beast?'[46] When Rochester finally reveals Bertha on stage, he laments how she 'dragged me through hell. I was bound to a wife, intemperate and … unchaste.'[47] The production's staging further emphasised Bertha's animalistic nature – in the 2003 production, she emerges from her attic room restrained by a rope

[43] McCarthy, *My Eyes Only Look Out*; '#IamIrish,' https://iamirish.org/.
[44] Mixed Race Irish, 'Experience of Persons of Mixed Race in State Institutions.'
[45] Stoneman, 'Jane Eyre's Other,' 205.
[46] 'Script for *Jane Eyre*,' 43.
[47] 'Script for *Jane Eyre*,' 60.

leashed around her wrist and moves about the ground on all fours.[48] The implicit connection between these descriptions and the visual presentation of a (bound and imprisoned) Black female body on stage is problematic enough, yet even worse is the way that blackness itself is mobilised. After being confronted by Bertha in the night, Jane weeps to Rochester, 'I never saw a face like it! Discoloured ... savage ... The red eyes ... the fearful blackened skin.'[49] Later, Rochester defends his actions by imploring his audience to hold Jane beside Bertha: 'Compare these clear eyes, this face with that mask ... this perfect being with that monster of insanity.'[50] While intended to draw attention to the difference in character and temperament, the production's racial casting ultimately invoked historical and hierarchical binaries of race, with Jane's whiteness acting as a shorthand for her chastity, purity, and rationality in contrast to Bertha's Black sexuality, corruption, and madness.

It is worth noting that this depiction of Bertha appeared on the Gate's stage just one year before the 2004 Citizenship Referendum, a constitutional amendment that changed the right to Irish citizenship from *jus soli* to *jus sanguinis*. The debates on the right to Irish citizenship, which were in full swing by 2003, centred on racist and xenophobic fears about the female Black body as hypersexual and threateningly fecund.[51] Phrases such as 'pregnancy tourism' and 'maternity hospital crisis' were triggered by 'highly publicized cases of African women arriving in the latter stages of pregnancy allegedly to avail of the provision within Irish law that children born on Irish soil had a right to Irish citizenship.'[52] As Ronit Lentin argues, these racialised anxieties around legitimacy and maternity 'signifie[d] not only the moral panic about "floods of refugees," but also the insidious positioning of sexually active "Irish" and "non-national" women alike as a danger to themselves, to men, and "the nation."'[53] Bertha Mason, with her 'intemperate' and 'unchaste' ways – as well as her 'fearful blackened skin' – seems to be a prescient anticipation of the larger social and political discourses around race in the Celtic Tiger. Ultimately, the 2003 and 2010 productions of *Jane Eyre* revealed both

---

[48] 'Production video of *Jane Eyre*.'

[49] 'Script for *Jane Eyre*,' 53.

[50] 'Script for *Jane Eyre*,' 58.

[51] For analyses of the gendered and racialised discourses that shaped the Citizenship Referendum, see Tormey, '"Everyone with Eyes Can See the Problem,"' 69–100; Brandi, 'Unveiling the Ideological Construction of the 2004 Irish Citizenship Referendum,' 26–47.

[52] Dianna Shandy, 'Irish Babies, African Mothers,' 808.

[53] Lentin, 'Black Bodies and '"Headless Hookers,"' 8.

the existence of a longer history of diversity in Ireland in the form of its mixed-race Irish actresses, as well as an underlying conservativism that tended to characterise the Colgan-era Gate.

A Return to Interculturalism?: Ruth Negga's *Hamlet* (2018)

Selina Cartmell named her inaugural season at the Gate 'The Outsider,' a theme that 'aim[ed] to see doors, windows and hearts flung open in a spirit of inclusiveness and diversity.'[54] This emphasis on diversity became fully apparent when a production of *Hamlet* was added to the season, with Ruth Negga stepping into the role of the Danish prince. The production would mark Negga's first appearance on the Irish stage since she last played at the Abbey in 2008, and her first stage performance since being nominated for Best Actress at the 2016 Academy Awards. It would also be her very first performance at the Gate Theatre, despite a prolific early acting career in Ireland that included leading roles at the Abbey and Druid.

Commentators noted how *Hamlet*, one of the Gate's most revived Shakespearean productions, 'draws a line back to the theatre's legacy of Michael MacLiammoir and Hilton Edwards ... but also marks a break from tradition' – ostensibly through the non-traditional casting of Negga as a woman of colour.[55] Yet in many ways, Negga's casting was actually a drawing together of and breaking away from multiple threads that have woven through the history of the Gate. As a 'colourblind' performance,[56] Negga's Hamlet echoes both mac Liammóir's and Marshall's Othellos: at once a cross-racial characterisation of the Danish prince and an actor of colour stepping into a Shakespearean lead. As a mixed-race Irish woman, Negga represents that hidden history of Irish diversity, but centre stage as Hamlet rather than doubly hidden on the periphery, as with Bertha in *Jane Eyre*. But perhaps most importantly, Negga's Hamlet harkens back to the

---

[54] O'Rourke, 'The Outsider: The Gate Theatre Programme 2017/18.'

[55] Knox, "Hamlet of Our Times."

[56] Though the production cast Black Dublin-based actor Steve Hartland as Hamlet's father, the rest of the characters (including Hamlet's paternal uncle, Claudius) were portrayed by white Irish actors and Negga's racial identity was not commented upon or incorporated into the stage action itself. I thus argue that Negga's casting in *Hamlet* is a continuation of Irish theatre's tendency to colourblind cast Negga in ways that both mobilise and deny her racial identity. See Nakase, 'Performing Scalar Interculturalism'; McIvor, *Migration and Performance in Contemporary Ireland*.

Gate's original emancipatory project (flawed and sporadic as it sometimes has been) of pushing at the boundaries of who could or should be represented on the Irish stage. As Negga notes, director Yaël Farber's description of the production as a 'Hamlet for our times' was 'about me being brown and a woman, quite explicitly and obviously.'[57] This emphasis on diversity and inclusion indicates a return to the theatre's initial openness, while simultaneously speaking to the changing demographics of the contemporary Irish nation.

It remains to be seen whether this engagement with diversity will be sustained over the course of Cartmell's tenure, or if it will be another ten years until we see another production featuring actors of colour. However, if the Gate Theatre 'can be seen as a microcosm for the development of independent Ireland, operating as a laboratory in which could be explored such issues as gender, Europeanisation, and the rise of the Irish middle class,' this chapter suggests that this view can also be extended to that theatre's investigation of issues such as race and diversity, inclusion and exclusion, and the right to representation on the Irish stage and beyond.[58]

Bibliography

'#IamIrish.' https://iamirish.org.

Bateman, Fiona. 'Biafra in the Irish Imagination: War and Famine in Banville's *An End to Flight* and Forristal's *Black Man's Country*.' In *Writing the Nigeria-Biafra War*, edited by Toyin Falola and Ogechukwu Ezekwem, 284–313. Suffolk: James Currey, 2016.

Brandi, Sylvia. 'Unveiling the Ideological Construction of the 2004 Irish Citizenship Referendum: A Critical Discourse Analysis.' *Translocations* 2, no. 1 (2007): 26–47.

Brannigan, John. '"Ireland, and Black!": Minstrelsy, Racism, and Black Cultural Production in 1970s Ireland.' *Textual Practice* 22, no. 2 (2008): 229–48.

Brannigan, John. *Race in Modern Irish Literature and Culture*. Edinburgh: Edinburgh University Press, 2009.

Central Statistics Office. 'Census 2016 Summary Results – Part 1.' Central Statistics Office. www.cso.ie/en/csolatestnews/presspages/2017/census2016 summaryresults-part1/.

Clare, David, Des Lally, and Patrick Longergan. 'Introduction.' In *The Gate Theatre, Dublin: Inspiration and Craft*, edited by David Clare, Des Lally, and Patrick Lonergan, 1–9. Oxford: Peter Lang, 2018.

---

[57] Negga, 'Ruth Negga Talks Diversity, Hamlet and her Split from Dominic Cooper.'
[58] Clare, Lally, and Lonergan, 'Introduction,' 9.

Cole, Catherine M. and Tracy C. Davis. 'Routes of Blackface.' *TDR/The Drama Review* 57, no. 2 (June 2013): 7–12.

'Correspondence and press information for the Gate Theatre's production of *Black Man's Country*,' 1973–74, GADM_00002172, Gate Theatre Digital Archive. National University of Ireland, Galway.

Fanning, Brian. *Migration and the Making of Ireland*. Dublin: University College Dublin Press, 2018.

Kaul, Mythili. 'Background: Black or Tawny? Stage Representations of Othello from 1604 to the Present.' In *Othello: New Essays by Black Writers*, edited by Mythili Kaul, 1–22. Washington, D.C.: Howard University Press, 1997.

Knox, Kirsty Blake. '"Hamlet of Our Times" – Ruth Negga Confirmed to Play Hamlet in Gate Theatre Production.' *Independent.ie*. https://www.independent.ie/entertainment/theatre-arts/hamlet-of-our-times-ruth-negga-confirmed-to-play-hamlet-in-gate-theatre-production-36905125.html.

Lentin, Ronit. 'Black Bodies and "Headless Hookers": Alternative Global Narratives for 21st Century Ireland.' *The Irish Review*, no. 33 (2005): 1–12.

Mac Liammóir, Micheál. 'Home after Tour McLiammoir on African odyssey.' *The Herald*, July 1962. ITA/268/05/46, Sheila and Carmel Leahy: Edwards–macLiammoir Papers, Irish Theatre Archive, Dublin City Library, Ireland.

Mac Liammóir, Micheál. 'Review of *Othello*.' 1959. ITA/268/05/03, Sheila and Carmel Leahy: Edwards–macLiammoir Papers. Irish Theatre Archive, Dublin City Library, Ireland.

McCarthy, Margaret. *My Eyes Only Look Out*. Dingle: Brandon Books, 2001.

McIvor, Charlotte. *Migration and Performance in Contemporary Ireland: Towards a New Interculturalism*. Basingstoke: Palgrave Macmillan, 2016.

McIvor, Charlotte. 'White Irish-Born Male Playwrights and the Immigrant Experience.' In *Literary Visions of Multicultural Ireland: The Immigrant in Contemporary Irish Literature*, edited by Pilar Villar-Argaiz, 37–49. Manchester: Manchester University Press, 2013.

Min, Tian. 'Lady Precious Stream: A Chinese Chinoiserie Anglicized on the Modern British Stage.' *Comparative Drama* 51, no. 2 (2017): 158–86.

Mixed Race Irish. 'Experience of Persons of Mixed Race in State Institutions: Mixed Race Irish.' 22 October 2014. http://oireachtasdebates.oireachtas.ie/debates%20authoring/DebatesWebPack.nsf/committeetakes/JUJ2014102200002.

Moon, Krystyn R. 'Lee Tung Foo and the Making of a Chinese American Vaudevillian, 1900s–1920s.' *Journal of Asian American Studies* 8, no. 1 (2005): 23–48.

Murray, Christopher and Masaru Sekine. *Yeats and the Noh: A Comparative Study*. Gerrards Cross: Smythe, 1990.

Nakase, Justine. 'Performing Scalar Interculturalism: Race and Identity in Contemporary Irish Performance.' PhD Thesis. National University of Ireland, Galway, 2018.

Negga, Ruth. 'Ruth Negga Talks Diversity, Hamlet and her Split from Dominic Cooper.' https://www.marieclaire.co.uk/entertainment/people/ruth-negga-diversity-dominic-cooper-610595.

O'Dowd, Ciara. 'Magic Windows: Ria Mooney at the Gate Theatre.' In *The Gate Theatre, Dublin: Inspiration and Craft*, edited by David Clare, Des Lally, and Patrick Lonergan, 131–45. London: Peter Lang, 2018.

O'Rourke, Chris. 'The Outsider: The Gate Theatre Programme 2017/18.' *The Arts Review*. 18 May 2017. https://www.theartsreview.com/single-post/2017/05/18/The-Outsider-The-Gate-Theatre-Programme-201718.

'Othello Review.' *Evening Herald*, 11 July 1952.

'Photograph of Micheál Mac Liammoir dressed up as a Chinese, n.d.' ITA/268/03/25, Sheila and Carmel Leahy: Edwards–macLiammoir Papers. Irish Theatre Archive, Dublin City Library, Ireland.

'Photograph of *Princely Fortune*, 14 March 1933.' 1661_PH_0001, Gate Theatre Digital Archive. National University of Ireland, Galway.

Pickering, Michael. *Blackface Minstrelsy in Britain*. London: Routledge, 2017.

Potter, Lois. *Shakespeare in Performance: Othello*. Manchester: Manchester University Press, 2002.

'Press photographs for *Othello*, 26 March 1935.' ITA/206/01/39, Turner Collection/Mac Liammoir Papers. Irish Theatre Archive, Dublin City Library, Ireland.

'Press photographs of *Obsession in India*, 4 March 1932.' ITA/206/01/20/A, Turner Collection/Mac Liammoir Papers. Irish Theatre Archive, Dublin City Library, Ireland.

'Production video of *Jane Eyre*, 2003.' Gate Theatre Digital Archive. National University of Ireland, Galway.

'Programme and press cuttings for *Princely Fortune*; *Storm over Wicklow*; *St Patrick's Day*, 14 March 1933.' ITA/206/01/28, Turner Collection/Mac Liammoir Papers. Irish Theatre Archive, Dublin City Library, Ireland.

'Programme for *Lady Precious Stream*, 1934.' 1655_MPG_0001, 2. Gate Theatre Digital Archive. National University of Ireland, Galway.

'Programme for *Othello*, 10 October 1962.' 1974_MPG_0002, 8. Gate Theatre Digital Archive, National University of Ireland, Galway.

'Script for *Jane Eyre*, 2 December 2003.'1239_S_0001. Gate Theatre Digital Archive, National University of Ireland, Galway.

Shandy, Dianna. 'Irish Babies, African Mothers: Rites of Passage and Rights in Citizenship in Post-Millennial Ireland.' *Anthropological Quarterly* 81, no. 4 (2008): 803–31.

Simpson, Gerry. 'Murderous Angels.' *Irish Times*, 3 February 1969.

Stoneman, Patsy. 'Jane Eyre's Other: The Emergence of Bertha.' In *The Brontës in the World of the Arts*, edited by Sandra Hagan and Juliette Wells, 197–212. Burlington: Ashgate, 2008.

Tormey, Anwen. '"Everyone with Eyes Can See the Problem": Moral Citizens and the Space of Irish Nationhood.' *International Migration* 45, no. 3 (2007): 69–100.

Whelan, Feargal. 'Lord Longford's Yahoo: An Alternative National Myth from an Alternative National Theatre.' In *The Gate Theatre, Dublin: Inspiration and Craft*, edited by David Clare, Des Lally and Patrick Lonergan, 147–59. Oxford: Peter Lang, 2018.

Bending the Plots

Selina Cartmell's Gate
and Politics of Gender Inclusion

Marguérite Corporaal

'It's really exciting to be there under Yaël and Selina … It's great
to see [Selina] at the helm of the Gate, "womaning" it.' Thus stated
Irish-Ethiopian Ruth Negga, who starred in the title role of Yaël Farber's
production of *Hamlet* in the autumn of 2018, in an interview with
University Times.[1] The transference of the artistic directorship from
Michael Colgan to Selina Cartmell in April 2017 indeed led to what
Nicola Anderson in the *Irish Independent* called a 'theatre sea-change' at
the Dublin Gate Theatre:[2] 'women-led projects have taken centre stage
at the Gate,' as Victoire Lemaire likewise noted in *The Irish Tatler*.[3]
Such progress is also marked by the fact that the Gate explicitly engages
with the Gender Equality in Practice in Irish Theatre campaign, which
was launched on 9 July 2018 in the trail of the #WakingTheFeminists
movement, and seeks 'to enhance the possibilities for women in the Irish
theatre sector.'[4] This has, among others, led to an increasing involvement
of women actors, directors, and playwrights at the Gate over the past
few years: examples include collaborations with actors in lead roles
Marie Mullen (Lucy Kirkwood's *The Children*) and Eileen Walsh (*The
Beginning*), stage designer Susan Hilferty (*Hamlet*), emerging director
Oonagh Murphy (*The Children*, *Tribes*), and playwrights Nancy Harris
(*The Red Shoes*) and Nina Raine (*Tribes*).

---

[1] Farrell, 'Ruth Negga on Plunging Shakespeare into the 21st Century.'
[2] Anderson, 'How Gate's Director Selina Cartmell Set the Stage for a Theatre
Sea-Change.'
[3] Lemaire, 'Ruth Negga as Hamlet Riffs on the Feminising of Hollywood.'
[4] Gate Theatre, 'Launch of Gender Equality in Practice in Irish Theatre.'

Under Cartmell's leadership, the Gate has thus become a more inclusive theatre than in previous decades, especially in terms of the scope it has given to female theatre-makers and their artistic visions. However, as this chapter will argue, the Gate Theatre has also invested in 'womaning' through recent stage productions that intervene in repertoires of cultural representations by including perspectives that bend existing plotlines, discourses, and roles from the perspective of gender, and its intersections with class and ethnicity. This chapter will analyse two of these, Yaël Farber's *Hamlet* (2018) and Nancy Harris's *The Red Shoes* (2017), exploring how both productions raise issues of marginality, empowerment, and processes of in- or exclusion. In doing so, these analyses illustrate what theatre scholars Mireia Aragay and Nicholas Ridout have described as the increasing 'ethical turn' in contemporary theatre:[5] forms of theatre that stage 'an ethical encounter ... with the other.'[6] This reveals the ways in which these two plays call for an ethical engagement on the part of the spectator.

'The oppressor's wrong ... the law's delay': Yaël Farber's *Hamlet*

Let us start with the production of an existing play: Yaël Farber's *Hamlet*. There is a long tradition of women who have performed the role of Shakespeare's Danish tragic hero, also on the Irish stage: Fanny Furnival (1774), Siobhán McKenna (1957), and Olwen Fouéré (1993) preceded Irish-Nigerian actor Ruth Negga in playing the role of Hamlet.[7] There is, likewise, a long-standing tradition of female playwrights and directors who have rewritten Shakespeare's drama from feminist perspectives: Ann-Marie MacDonald, Paula Vogel, and Djanet Sears and their reworkings of *Othello* come to mind.[8] Farber's *Hamlet* goes one step further by casting a black female actor as Shakespeare's tragic protagonist, but this does not imply gender swapping, as Victoire Lemaire noted in *The Irish Tatler*:[9] the play stays close to Shakespeare's original play in spirit, while cutting some of the original text. It can be argued, however, that by casting Ruth Negga as Hamlet, Farber accentuates the issue of powerlessness against outrage and the illegitimate usurpation of authority as a way to reflect upon present-day political climates, and the Trump administration in particular.

---

[5] Aragay, 'To Begin to Speculate: Theatre Studies, Ethics and Spectatorship,' 3–5.
[6] Ridout, *Theatre & Ethics*, 54.
[7] Howard, *Women as Hamlet*, 127, 222–24.
[8] See Friedman, *Feminist Theatrical Revisions of Classical Works*.
[9] Lemaire, 'Ruth Negga as Hamlet.'

This becomes clear in multiple ways. The costume and boots that Owen Roe, performing the role of Claudius, is wearing are strongly reminiscent of uniforms worn by those connected to dictatorial regimes, such as Hitler's Third Reich, Stalin's communist state, and Franco's Spain. This outfit not only endorses his illegal usurpation of state power; the contrast between the brutal white, masculine power that he embodies and a Hamlet who can be identified with cultural marginality in terms of ethnicity and gender stresses the central theme of the play: the vulnerability of the human subject in the face of personal loss and political injustice. That this was the interpretation of Shakespeare's drama that Farber sought to convey is evident from the fact that, in an interview with Peter Crawley of the *Irish Times*, she described Elsinore – the play's setting – as 'any place where there has been an illegitimate takeover of the rightful transmission of power,'[10] with Hamlet as the individual confronted with the ethical dilemma of political agency and duty in times of political transgression. As Farber said in this interview, 'I wanted to hear from a Hamlet who has the true, deep experiential understanding of saying, "The time is out of joint. O cursèd spite, That ever I was born to set it right!"'[11]

Those lines from the play were also used in marketing the production, creating the impression that, for Farber, the marginalised individual's struggle against power is what she perceives to be the play's major concern, and its primary connection to our own time. Several aspects of the production emphasise Farber's interpretation. The set, designed by Susan Hilferty – an enclosed space with twelve doors – suggests that Hamlet's Denmark is a prison. This 'mix of Kafka's the Trial and Bartók's Bluebeard's Castle,' as Michael Billington wrote in *The Guardian* of 7 October 2018,[12] is a place where characters are under constant surveillance by state authorities, and where those who are not holding power are figuratively confined by the marginal roles that society allocates to them. The fact that Farber's Ophelia – played by Aoife Duffin – stares into an open grave from the onset of the play, not only implies the 'deadness' of a society under a patriarchal regime, but also the few options left for women in such a society: they are preferably reduced to non-existence, to silence.

The depiction of Gertrude resonates with Melania Trump's fashion style, thereby evoking analogies with misogyny and gender oppression in our own times, as conveyed by today's political leaders. Like America's First Lady at the time, Melania Trump, Gertrude appears to occupy a position

---

[10] Crawley, 'Directing Ruth Negga as Hamlet.'
[11] Crawley, 'Directing Ruth Negga as Hamlet.'
[12] Billington, '*Hamlet/Richard III* Review.'

of influence that actually disguises powerlessness in a male-dominated world. According to Crawley, Farber is obsessed with 'post-truth' politics and Trumpian misrule, and thus the feminine figure of a Hamlet who is trying to bring uncomfortable truths into the open enables reverberations of the #MeToo movement. This holds wider implications for the Gate Theatre as well, with accusations launched at its former creative director Michael Colgan, as Crawley also implies: 'an emboldened movement bringing hidden stories to public attention; something the Gate knows only too well.'[13] Farber's female Hamlet can thus be analysed in light of the ongoing marginalisation of women, and their quest to bring such injustice into the public sphere.

The fact that Farber grew up under Apartheid in South Africa – a divided society that contributed to her 'political awakening,' as she said in the interview with Crawley[14] – adds a further interpretative layer to the production. Choosing a black female actor to play Hamlet, it appears that Farber also frames Hamlet's quest for agency in the light of marginalised ethnic groups and their battle to bring out stories of past and present injustice. The fact that Roe's Claudius resonates with contemporary populist leaders such as Donald Trump points to ways in which ethnic minorities today – including migrants – are deprived of societal authority and equality, struggling against the 'oppressor's wrong.' In view of today's Black Lives Matter movement, these resonances of Farber's staging are even stronger; and the tensions between ethnic diversity and Trump's politics may have been brought out more profoundly when the Gate stage production briefly toured St Ann's Warehouse in Brooklyn in February 2020.

It is particularly significant that Farber has omitted asides by all the other characters in *Hamlet* from this production, instead solely rendering those by Ruth Negga's Hamlet: Farber argued that she was 'concerned that only Hamlet alone should have direct access to the audience.'[15] As such, the production manipulates and activates ethical 'commitment to response and responsibility' on the part of the theatre audience with the 'Other' and his or her social inequality in ways outlined by Helena Grehan.[16]

[13] Crawley, 'Directing Ruth Negga as Hamlet.'
[14] Crawley, 'Directing Ruth Negga as Hamlet.'
[15] Crawley, 'Directing Ruth Negga as Hamlet.'
[16] Grehan, *Performance, Ethics and Spectatorship in a Global Age*, 175.

'Just put her in a corner, you won't know she's there': Nancy Harris's *The Red Shoes*

As Nancy Harris stated in an interview with RTÉ on 12 April 2017, her aim in reworking Hans Christian Andersen's fairy tale 'The Red Shoes' for a stage production under the same name was to reveal the brutal class and gender politics of the original narrative. At the same time, Harris wanted to offer an approach 'for a contemporary audience' and a 'new generation' without 'white washing' the problematic ideologies of Andersen's story, which was first published in *New Fairy Tales* by C.A. Reitzel in Copenhagen, on 7 April 1845.[17] In Andersen's tale, the orphan Karen's main weakness, from the perspective of the narrative, is her self-centred vanity. Karen is obsessed by looking in the mirror, and when she gets the red shoes and anticipates her confirmation in church it is clear that admiration of her beauty is all she craves:

> And everyone inside looked at Karen's red shoes, and all the pictures looked down on them and when Karen knelt at the altar and placed the golden chalice to her lips, all she could think of was the red shoes and it was as if they floated around in the chalice; and she forgot to sing her hymn, she forgot to say the Lord's Prayer.[18]

Karen meets a soldier while dancing out of the church, and the shoes start to lead a life of their own. Subsequently, Karen becomes oblivious to her adoptive mother's illness, even failing to attend her funeral. An angel appears to her, bearing a sword, and condemns her to dance even after she dies, as a warning to vain children everywhere. Karen has her feet chopped off by an executioner, but can only find grace after she passes away.

As Harris indicates in the interview,

> Hans Christian Anderson's original story is set against a background of oppressive Christianity, in which an orphan's passion for a pair of sinful red shoes and the wild dancing which follows, seems like an unconscious rebellion against the stifling environment she finds herself in. In the fairy tale, Karen is brutally punished for her transgression, but did she transgress at all?[19]

---

[17] RTÉ, 'The Red Shoes.'
[18] Andersen, 'The Red Shoes.'
[19] RTÉ, 'The Red Shoes.'

Figure 9. Stephanie Dufresne in Nancy Harris's *The Red Shoes*.
Photograph by Ste Murray. Image reproduced by permission of
the Gate Theatre, Dublin.

This is a question she explores in her 2017 play, which, in contrast to
Andersen's tale, is set in present-day Ireland. As the following discussion
will demonstrate, Harris's *The Red Shoes* not only challenges the strong
gender and class bias in the original narrative, but also criticises the
marginalisation of identities in our own time, exposing the hypocrisy of
charity, tolerance, and Christian morality.

     As in Andersen's narrative, Harris's main protagonist Karen is an
orphan who, in this case, is taken in by the very affluent couple Bob and
Mariella Nugent. From the start of the play, it becomes obvious that society
ostracises Karen because of her ethnic and class background, but also
because of the gender role model that her mother represented. The group
of mourners – that seems to function as a dramatic chorus representing
society and its rigid values[20] – strongly critiques Karen's recently deceased
mother for what they see as her sexually transgressive behaviour: they
warn Karen not to repeat her mother's sin of vanity, which led her to
becoming a single mother. They also attribute Karen's indecency of dress
at her mother's funeral to the latter setting a bad example: 'Sure think of

---

[20] See Travis, *Allegory and the Tragic Chorus in Sophocles' Oedipus at Colonus*, 2–3;
    Dewar-Watson, *Tragedy*, 26–28.

what she used to wear herself.'[21] As the mourners imply, Karen's mother was lascivious, having many lovers, or perhaps even clients who came to her house, since 'half the men in town [were] knocking on her door.'[22] The mourners attribute the mother's deviancy in gender and sexuality primarily to the fact that she is an ethnic 'Other,' coming from an exotic, though unidentified, Continent: 'Of course they dressed differently where her mother was from ... It was very hot there.'[23]

The priest who oversees Karen's adoption echoes similar ethnic bias towards the girl's mother when he remarks to Bob and Mariella that the woman was 'off her trolley' and 'strayed from the flock,' alluding to the mother's status as a foreigner to explain her 'unwomanly' behaviour: 'Of course she wasn't from here. No family or support. And some of the things they say she got up to to make ends meet ...'[24] In fact, the society depicted in the play frowns upon the 'otherworldliness' of Karen in a similar vein, connecting her ethnic exoticness to inappropriate gender and sexual identities. For example, when Karen expresses herself through dance – a form that is reminiscent of Argentinian tango and suggests Latin American roots – Mariella voices her determination to have her 'fixed up and looking normal,'[25] and she perceives the sensual way in which Karen dances with her husband Bob as both a threat to her marriage and a sin against decency. Harris's play thus reveals the complex ways in which gender, ethnicity, class, and issues of sexuality intersect in processes of societal marginalisation: the ethnic 'Other' is often viewed as aberrant in terms of femininity, in mutually reinforcing ways. In demonstrating this, *The Red Shoes* at the same time painfully draws attention to current racial prejudice and the stigmatisation of immigrants in Ireland, even though the country itself has a history as a colonised nation subjected to poverty-induced emigration– a theme that is increasingly explored not only by cultural historians such as Steve Garner and Sinead Moynihan,[26] but also by scholars and dramatists in relation to present-day theatre and issues of 'historical duty': a current sense of social responsibility that is rooted in historical experiences.[27]

As *The Red Shoes* makes clear, Irish society tends to objectify the marginalised: the ethnic 'Other,' women, and people of lower classes.

[21] Harris, *The Red Shoes*, 8.
[22] Harris, *The Red Shoes*, 8.
[23] Harris, *The Red Shoes*, 9.
[24] Harris, *The Red Shoes*, 62.
[25] Harris, *The Red Shoes*, 25.
[26] See Garner, *Racism in the Irish Experience*; Moynihan, *Other People's Diasporas*.
[27] See McIvor, *Migration and Performance in Contemporary Ireland*, 123.

While the mourners literally lean forward to Karen as if she might not understand English, the priest presents her to Bob and Mariella as if she has no voice: 'Just put her in a corner, you won't know she's there.'[28] Mariella is more annoyed than pleasantly surprised when she finds out that Karen will not just nod and gesture, but 'speaks. And perfect English too.'[29] Finding Karen's grief about her bereavement a burden she is not willing to face, Mariella is only too happy to exploit Karen's vocal abilities as a way to serve her personal interests. Karen is to express her gratitude towards Mariella during a dinner with the Orphan Foundation, acting as the mouthpiece to proclaim her adoptive mother's greatness and enhance her social status: 'Make sure to mention that at the dinner.'[30] The scene literally draws attention to the performativity of marginalised identity, in line with Judith Butler's concepts:[31] those who are considered to be the disenfranchised 'Other' have to enact the scripts by those empowered by their money, status, sex, or race. For Mariella, Karen is just 'our orphan': she should remain without a name, will, or individual identity.[32]

Karen's marginalised 'double,' the domestic servant Mags, is likewise denied any claim to personal desires by her employers, the Nugent couple. When she has a heart attack, the Nugents ardently wish for her recovery not because they care for her as a person, but because they miss her cheap labour: 'We need you back to full health ASAP, Mags, cos honestly the state of this house since you got sick …'[33] Mags herself is remarkably expressive about her marginalisation in the play. She voices awareness of the fact that Bob and many of his class have no idea about the person she really is and what secret ambitions she cherishes: 'Being left with no state pension / Scrubbed a million floors / Washed dishes till I'm raw / I made my choice, stifled my voice / Became invisible.' As Mags bitterly confesses to both Karen and the theatre audience, the fact that she herself is a 'human being' like them, who once 'had hopes and dreams' has always been ignored by those who were wealthy or were her employers.[34] Lacking the means to support a family, society has even denied Mags motherhood, taking away her child born out of wedlock when she was a young woman. Mags thus functions as the symbol of the exploitation of the lower classes in the play.

---

[28] Harris, *The Red Shoes*, 17.
[29] Harris, *The Red Shoes*, 35.
[30] Harris, *The Red Shoes*, 35.
[31] Butler, 'Performative Acts and Gender Constitution,' 519–31.
[32] Harris, *The Red Shoes*, 14.
[33] Harris, *The Red Shoes*, 98.
[34] Harris, *The Red Shoes*, 89–90.

By focusing on the rights of the individual to ambitions and dreams, *The Red Shoes* takes an overtly critical stance towards the marginalisation of certain societal groups and their desires. Harris's play reinforces this critique by addressing the hypocrisy of those who assume moral superiority, especially with regard to Karen. The group of mourners may warn Karen against the pitfalls of vanity, but, at the same time, they grab the precious possessions of her dead mother, preying upon her jewellery like a group of vultures. Furthermore, while the priest condemns Karen's mother for reputedly selling her body to make a living, he does not refrain from accepting money from the Nugents for his services in getting them an orphan who will enhance their public influence and status.

The Nugents are the epitome of capitalism – especially Clive, who looks upon his job in 'property development' as a magical trick to increase his fortune.[35] Their charity is, in fact, a thin veneer overlaying their ambitious self-promotion: as Mariella says to Bob, it is 'just blind luck' they can have 'an orphan of our own' now, for the Save the Orphans Foundation 'cannot ignore that … They'll have to take us seriously now!'[36] The Nugents chastise Karen for desiring a beautiful dress and shoes, arguing that 'we don't want to give her notions about herself,'[37] that she should know her place, and that 'vanity is a dangerous thing.'[38] While they feel that Karen is entitled just to shoes that are 'plain, simple, modest, sensible even to the point of dull,'[39] they themselves are presented in grotesquely rich attire, are often in the vicinity of a big magical speaking mirror that recalls the fairy tale of Snow White, and they even throw a sumptuous party with marshmallow table cloths to impress their guests with 'the orphan we rescued from devastating impoverishment.'[40]

However, when Karen seeks to release herself from the curse of the continuously dancing red shoes by having her legs chopped off by their son Clive, the Nugents refuse to invest money in prosthetics, instead supplying Karen with a cheap pair of wooden pegs. To them, Karen has just turned into damaged goods which they would love to return if they could: 'Are there no places that would take her?'[41] The rich, then, treat the poor as sheer commodities, and the fact that they will not provide Karen with a

---

[35] Harris, *The Red Shoes*, 60.
[36] Harris, *The Red Shoes*, 21.
[37] Harris, *The Red Shoes*, 46.
[38] Harris, *The Red Shoes*, 136.
[39] Harris, *The Red Shoes*, 46.
[40] Harris, *The Red Shoes*, 61.
[41] Harris, *The Red Shoes*, 123.

good replacement of her legs, but would rather confine her to her bed, symbolise the fact that they will not grant any social mobility to the lower classes, even if they themselves – as the *nouveaux riches* – have apparently benefitted from the capitalist economy during the Celtic Tiger era. The red miniature Santa hats that the couple wear are not only reminiscent of the consumerist excesses that mark Christmas ads, but ironically suggest a benevolence that the couple fail to demonstrate.

The play also highlights the sexual hypocrisy of Irish society: while society disapproves of the sexual life of Karen's deceased mother as well as Karen's sensuality in dancing, Bob is evidently aroused by her shortened dress, sudden confidence, and enchanting movements. The red shoes that Karen wears on stage and that contrast with the dull, darker tones of the rest of the setting and costumes suggest a vitality and vibrancy that Bob cannot help surrendering to. Furthermore, as pictures of the stage production illustrate, the setting of the ball that Karen eventually decides to go to, behind Mariella's back, is erotically charged. The voluptuous king is reminiscent of a Bacchian worshipper, and the dance in which the prince leads Karen is suggestive of copulation. Karen herself looks like an Oriental belly dancer in her bright blue outfit, and the stage setting and costume, designed by Monica Frawley, convey how she is eroticised and exoticised by the men around her, made into an object of gratification and availability. If Karen seeks to explore pleasure, feeling that people like her and Mags have as much right to 'parties' and 'balls' as the rich and powerful, the stage setting creates the impression that society inevitably sexualises women who pursue their desires.

The hypocrisy of male-dominated society, the play suggests, is that on the one hand it seeks to derive pleasure from women's sexuality, while on the other condemning women's sexual desire and autonomy. This becomes clear from the prince's brutal rejection of Karen once he offers her one of the red shoes – in line with the plotline of the fairy tale Cinderella – in order to see whether it fits and she is his destined wife. When he is confronted with Karen's amputated legs, he calls her 'a freak,'[42] and the unconditional love he once confessed to her proves to be a sham. What the scene illustrates is not just that the fairy tale 'drill' of 'happily ever after' is a pack of lies when it comes to love. This point is also made by Sylvestor's rhetorical question to the audience at the onset of the play ('And everything turns out alright at the end. ... Doesn't it?'[43]), and by Mariella herself in a song that gives expression to her profound disillusionment at

---

[42] Harris, *The Red Shoes*, 137.
[43] Harris, *The Red Shoes*, 7.

being neglected by the 'prince' she once 'married' and gave up her career for: 'He's been distracted and he's disappeared.'[44] He no longer dances with Mariella, as her song implies ('Why don't we dance anymore?'); a statement that seems to point out a sexless existence.[45] Instead, Bob looks for alternative – especially *younger* – partners.

Yet while men have the freedom to chase their desires, this does not seem to be the case for women. The enactment of the scene in which Karen's feet are chopped off illustrates as much: the way she is lying down, with Clive holding the axe high in the direction of the split between her legs, suggests a phallic assault. Some of the witnesses of this implied rape are, among others, the prince and king, and their presence creates the impression of patriarchal retribution: if a woman expresses her sexuality, she will be punished. Thus the play engages with the discussions that have been taking place in the wake of the #MeToo campaign, and that also resonate in the theatre world. Furthermore, the prince's outrageous response to Karen's mutilation once again underlines the hypocrisy of today's society: once a woman is 'damaged goods,' in terms of lost beauty or lost reputation, she is brutally cast off.

So what does Harris's *The Red Shoes* eventually do with the idea of transgression in Andersen's original tale? The ending of the play initially seems rather bleak. Karen looks beaten down, subdued, and her numbness appears to be intensified by the medication that Mariella forces her to take. The priest presents her with a Bible as a Christmas gift, claiming that Karen should learn to be morally disciplined and resigned: 'have you been saying your prayers?'[46] The scene may seem to suggest that those from marginal social groups who trespass social codes and seek to defy the inequality they face will be punished: the red shoes, which made Karen kick off the cutlery from the dinner table, confront Mariella with her vanity and walk away from the cares that the upper-class Mariella and Bob force upon her, symbolise how rebellion against social disempowerment results in defeat. This is in line with what Rebecca-Anne Do Rozario argues about the symbolism of red shoes in fairy tale traditions: 'The tension between red fabric shoes and those of wood is played out in a variety of fairy tales, where wooden shoes indicate a hero's poverty or disenfranchisement.'[47] As Sylvestor tells Karen when she picks the red shoes in his shop, she cannot continue to be submissive and 'good' in the eyes of society if she wants to

---

[44] Harris, *The Red Shoes*, 58.
[45] Harris, *The Red Shoes*, 58.
[46] Harris, *The Red Shoes*, 124.
[47] Do Rozario, *Fashion in the Fairy Tale Tradition*, 189.

claim her own pleasure and right to live: 'You just want to be the nice girl. Speak when you're spoken to, do as you're told. You don't want to cause trouble ... or let anyone see the fire that rages beneath.'[48] If that fire of revolt leads to harm, the ending of the play does offer a more optimistic note, suggesting Karen's resilience. Karen may now have to rely on a pair of wooden pegs, but this does not prevent her from dancing. As Sylvestor says, 'She transcends / her limitations / Though it is bittersweet.'[49] While social conditions may not change overnight, those at the margins of power and wealth may have the strength to fight back, even if some, like Mags, were too 'exhausted from a lifetime of toil – and tragedy' to step out of the role of Cinderella.[50]

Conclusion

According to Helen Meany, who wrote about the #WakingTheFeminists movement in *The Guardian* on 5 January 2018, Cartmell's inaugural 2017–18 season explored the many guises of 'the outsider.'[51] The two productions by Harris and Farber that marked the early stages of Cartmell's career at the Gate certainly confirm this view, as both plays explore the role of the marginalised, displaying the intricate ways in which issues of ethnicity, class, gender, and sexuality are intertwined. Both plays also draw analogies with our present-day society, suggesting that despite several emancipatory movements, the position of the lower classes, women, and ethnic minorities is still very vulnerable, and that age-old prejudices have remained persistent. Interestingly, both productions also allude to current debates about sexual harassment, thereby indirectly reflecting upon a recent, dark episode from the Gate's ninety-year history.

'While the Gate's commitment is to the international classical canon, I want to reimagine that – to reframe the classics by bringing in great female directors, playwrights and actors.'[52] Cartmell's observation to Meany indeed illustrates her mission to work with female theatre-makers from Ireland and abroad, as she did for *Hamlet* and *The Red Shoes*. Giving opportunities to female designers, choreographers, actors, and playwrights, just like the theatre's original founders Edwards and mac Liammóir did, Cartmell's leadership also heralds a new era of what Adrienne Rich would

---

48 Harris, *The Red Shoes*, 49.
49 Harris, *The Red Shoes*, 140.
50 Harris, *The Red Shoes*, 47.
51 Meany, 'Waking the Feminists.'
52 Meany, 'Waking the Feminists.'

have called 'revisionist mythmaking.'[53] Canonical texts are reimagined and remembered in startlingly fresh ways on the Gate stage, enabling a dissection of processes of marginalisation and exclusion. Cultural repertoires become reperformed memories, as Diana Taylor would argue,[54] and, as such, both productions stage what Ridout calls 'an ethical encounter, in which we come face to face with the other,'[55] while looking into the mirror of self-reflection upon our responsibility within society and the processes of inclusion and exclusion that we are implicated in as well. The magical mirror in *The Red Shoes* is also a metaphorical mirror that is held up to the audience: whichever way we look, we cannot escape seeing our own, sometimes distorted, perceptions. As such, the play offers a mode of emancipation that complements the Gate's long-standing tradition in casting actors and enlisting playwrights from marginalised backgrounds.

Bibliography

Andersen, Hans Christian. 'The Red Shoes.' http://hca.gilead.org.il/red_shoe.html.

Anderson, Nicola. 'How Gate's Director Selina Cartmell Set the Stage for a Theatre Sea-Change.' *Irish Independent*, 14 November 2018. https://www.independent.ie/entertainment/theatre-arts/how-gates-director-selina-cartmell-set-the-stage-for-a-theatre-seachange-37526638.html.

Aragay, Mireia. 'To Begin to Speculate: Theatre Studies, Ethics and Spectatorship.' In *Ethical Speculations in Contemporary British Theatre*, edited by Mireia Aragay and Enric Monforte, 1–22. Houndmills: Palgrave Macmillan, 2014.

Billington, Michael. '*Hamlet/Richard III* Review.' *Guardian*, 7 October 2018. https://www.theguardian.com/stage/2018/oct/07/hamlet-richard-iii-review-gate-abbey-theatre-dublin-ruth-negga.

Butler, Judith. 'Performative Acts and Gender Constitution.' *Theatre Journal* 40, no. 4 (1988): 519–31.

Crawley, Peter. 'Directing Ruth Negga as Hamlet.' *Irish Times*, 26 September 2018. https://www.irishtimes.com/culture/stage/directing-ruth-negga-as-hamlet-theatre-either-puts-you-to-sleep-or-wakes-you-up-1.3636867.

Dewar-Watson, Sarah. *Tragedy*. Basingstoke: Palgrave, 2014.

Do Rozario, Rebecca-Anne. *Fashion in the Fairy Tale Tradition: What Cinderella Wore*. Basingstoke: Palgrave, 2018.

Farrell, Jack. 'Ruth Negga on Plunging Shakespeare into the 21st Century.' *University Times*, 11 September 2018. www.universitytimes.ie/2018/09/ruth-negga-on-plunging-shakespeare-into-the-21st-century/.

---

53 Lattimore, '*New Ways to See Ancestral Lands*,' 9.
54 Taylor, *The Archive and The Repertoire*, 13.
55 Ridout, *Theatre & Ethics*, 54.

Friedman, Sharon. *Feminist Theatrical Revisions of Classical Works: Critical Essays.* Jefferson, NC and London: McFarlane, 2009.

Garner, Steve. *Racism in the Irish Experience.* London: Pluto, 2004.

Gate Theatre. 'Launch of Gender Equality in Practice in Irish Theatre.' https://www.gatetheatre.ie/gender-equality-in-practice/.

Grehan, Helena. *Performance, Ethics and Spectatorship in a Global Age.* Basingstoke: Palgrave, 2009.

Harris, Nancy. *The Red Shoes, Stage Version.* London: NHB Modern Plays, 2017.

Howard, Tony. *Women as Hamlet.* Cambridge: Cambridge University Press, 2007.

Lattimore, Carol Ann. *'New Ways to See Ancestral Lands': Revisionist Myth-making in the Poetry of Sylvia Plath, Muriel Rukeyser, and Adrienne Rich.* Austin: Texas Christian University, 1991.

Lemaire, Victoire. 'Ruth Negga as Hamlet Riffs on the Feminising of Hollywood.' *Irish Tatler,* 6 October 2018. https://irishtatler.com/news/ruth-negga-hamlet-female-reboot.

McIvor, Charlotte. *Migration and Performance in Contemporary Ireland: Towards a New Interculturalism.* London: Palgrave Macmillan, 2016.

Meany, Helen. 'Waking the Feminists: The Campaign that Revolutionised Irish Theatre.' *The Guardian,* 5 January 2018. https://www.theguardian.com/stage/2018/jan/05/feminist-irish-theatre-selina-cartmell-gate-theatre.

Moynihan, Sinéad. *Other People's Diasporas: Negotiating Race in Contemporary Irish and Irish-American Culture.* Syracuse: Syracuse University Press, 2013.

Ridout, Nicholas. *Theatre & Ethics.* Basingstoke: Palgrave, 2009.

RTÉ. 'The Red Shoes – Nancy Harris on The Gate's Modern Fairy Tale.' https://www.rte.ie/culture/2017/1204/924910-the-red-shoes-nancy-harris-on-the-gates-modern-fairytale/.

Taylor, Diana. *The Archive and The Repertoire: Performing Cultural Memory in the Americas.* Durham and London: Duke University Press, 2003.

Travis, Roger. *Allegory and the Tragic Chorus in Sophocles' Oedipus at Colonus.* New York: Rowman & Littlefield, 1999.

Index

Abbey Theatre 29n11, 81, 83, 100, 107, 108n48, 134–35, 141, 152, 163–64, 178, 202
  and ballet 163
  and the Dublin Gate Theatre 9, 11, 12, 27–28, 41, 57, 81, 93, 139–40, 142, 145, 189, 192, 198
  and socio-cultural climate 83, 123, 140, 198
  as venue 9, 10, 13, 107, 145, 176, 192n12, 197
  and women in theatre 1, 8–9, 39, 57
Academy Awards 202
Achard, Marcel
  Le Corsaire (*Hollywood Pirate*) 16, 170
Alcañiz, Muntsa 139
Aldrige, Ira 193
Allen, Nicholas 3
Amalgamated Artists 103, 107
Andersen, Hans Christian
  'The Red Shoes' 16, 211–12, 217
  see also Harris, Nancy, *The Red Shoes*
Anderson, Nicola 207
Anouilh, Jean
  Cher Antoine 96n16
  Ornifle 96n16
Antient Concert Rooms 14
apartheid 195, 210
Appia, Adolphe 169, 176, 178

Aragay, Mireia 208
Archer, Kane 104
Aron, Geraldine
  The Stanley Parkers 12
Artaud, Antonin 95
Arts Centre project 107
Atkins, Robert 173
Atkinson, Brooks 26n3

Baker, Stanley 102
Bannard Cogley, Desirée 'Toto' 1, 25, 28, 135n13
Barba, Eugenio 95
Barnett, David 86
Barrie, J.M.
  Quality Street 172
Bartók, Béla
  Bluebeard's Castle 209
Baudelaire, Charles 117
Bayon, Job Le 15
Beaumarchais, Pierre de 139
Beck, Ulrich 132
Beckett, Samuel 95, 100, 139, 199
Bedford, Patrick 98
Behan, Brendan 115
  Richard's Cork Leg 197–98
Benet i Jornet, Josep María 133
Benjamin, Walter 137
Benson, Hamlyn 163
Bhuilmot, Séamas de
  An Ráidhteas Oifigeamhail 145n37

Bieito, Calixto 145
Billington, Michael 209
birth control 9–11, 39–52
The Black and White Minstrel Show
  (TV programme) 198
Black Lives Matter 210
blackface 193–94, 198
Bolger, Dermot 91
Bond, Edward 95
Boothby, Frances
  *Marcelia; or the Treacherous
  Friend* 6
Boydell, Brian 153
Boyle, Roger (Earl of Orrery) 6
Brandi, Sylvia 201n51
Breathnach, Micheál
  Seilg I Measc na nAlp 125
Brecht, Bertolt 91–92, 94, 131,
  136–37, 139, 168
Bresler, Liora 59–60, 64, 68, 73
Brobby, Fred 197
Brontë, Charlotte
  Jane Eyre 17, 199–202
Brontë, Emily
  Wuthering Heights 25
Brown, Christy 78
Brown, Ian 168
Browne, Noel 51
An Buachaillín Buidhe (pseud.) 118
Büchner, Georg 139
Burgan, Mary 69
Burke Brogan, Patricia
  Eclipsed 10
Butler, Judith 214
Byrne, David 98

Cadic, Louis 15
Canavan, Joseph 80
Carlson, Marvin 13
Carmichael, Coralie 2, 29, 35
Carr, Marina
  The Mai 10
Carroll, Niall 49

Cartmell, Selina 5, 16–17, 189,
  202–3, 207–8, 218
Catholic Truth Society of Ireland
  46–48, 51
Catholicism 40–41, 45–48, 50–51,
  116, 118, 138, 142–43, 196
CC Oriental Casting Agency 197
Celtic Tiger 201, 216
censorship 11, 30n13, 39–41, 45,
  47–48, 50–51, 61, 71, 118
  see also Irish Censorship
  Publications Board
Cervantes, Miguel de
  Don Quixote 125
Chancellor, Betty 2, 11, 29, 34, 37
Chaucer, Geoffrey 123
Chekhov, Anton 15, 125, 139, 141,
  146
  A Marriage Proposal 126
'Cinderella' (fairytale) 216, 218
Citizen's Theatre 171–72, 180–82
Citizenship Referendum (2004) 201
Clann na Poblachta 39, 51
Clare, David 3, 15, 40
class 3–5, 11–13, 16, 40–42, 50,
  52, 58, 77–88, 91–108, 203, 208,
  211–19
Clear, Caitriona 42, 47–48
Coffee, Lenore
  Family Portrait 103
Coffey, Fiona Coleman 4
Cole, Catherine 198n39
Colgan, Michael 5, 17, 199, 202, 207,
  210
Colleary, Suzanne 96
Collins, Una 182
Collinson, Peter 102
Collis, Robert 50
  The Barrel Organ 80
  Marrowbone Lane 13, 77–88,
  107
  The Silver Fleece 80
  To be a Pilgrim 80

Colum, Padraic
  Mogu of the Desert 15, 151–64,
    190
An Comhar Drámaíochta 14–15,
  113, 126, 132, 135n13,
  141–45
Compton, Fay 103
Constitution of Ireland (1937) 2,
  85
contraception *see* birth control
Coogan, Amanda
  The Fountain 10
Corneille, Pierre
  Pompei, a Tragedy 6
Corporaal, Marguérite 16
Covent Garden Theatre 6
Craig, Edward Gordon 168–69,
  175, 176
Crawley, Peter 10, 209–10
Cronin, Anthony 50
Cruise O'Brien, Conor
  King Herod Explains 103
  Murderous Angels 197–98
Cummins, Geraldine
  Fidelity 8

Daly, Mary E. 45, 50–51
An Damer 14
Davie, Cedric Thorpe 179
Davis, Tracy 198n39
Day, Susanne R.
  Fidelity 8
De Valera, Éamon 85, 119
De Vere White, Terence 196
Dean, Joan FitzPatrick 27
Deeney, John F. 30n13
Diamond, Elin 86
Dinner, William
  The Late Edwina Black 93n9
Do Rozario, Rebecca-Anne 217
Dolan, Jill 27
Donnelly, Donal 102, 105
Doolan, Lelia 93

Dowling, Ann 29
Dowling, Vincent 99n26
Doyle, Roddy
  *Guess Who's Coming for the
    Dinner* 199
  The Snapper 10
Druid Theatre 12, 202
Drury Lane (Theatre Royal) 6
Dublin Arts Company 103
Dublin Drama League 27, 135n13
Dublin Gate Theatre
  and class 13, 77–88, 91–108
  as emancipatory institution 1–5,
    11–17
  and ethnicity 16–17, 189–203
  and gay, lesbian, and queer
    identities 12, 25–37, 57–75,
    151–53, 163–64
  and gender 1–5, 11, 39–52,
    207–19
  and minority languages 13–15,
    113–29, 131–32, 139–46
  and scenography 167–82
  see also expressionism
Dublin Repertory Theatre 135n13
Dublin Theatre Festival 9, 96n16,
  99n26, 176–77, 195
Duff, Arthur 163
Duffin, Aoife 209
Dufresne, Stephanie 212
Duggan, Dave
  Makaronik 115
Duggan, Gary
  Shibari 199
Dunne, Lee 107
Durkan, Neil 7

Eagleton, Terry 98
Eblana Theatre 99, 103, 107
Eça de Queirós, Jose Maria 126,
  141
Edinburgh International Festival
  168–69, 171, 177–80

Edwards, Hilton 12, 17, 28, 33n21,
    39–40, 49–50, 52, 92, 96, 105,
    108, 158–59, 160n30, 171–73,
    175, 178, 180, 192, 194, 199, 202
  as actor 103–5, 151, 158, 174,
    192–93
  and establishment of the Gate
    Theatre 1, 113, 218
  as head of drama at RTÉ 92–93,
    97, 102–3
  and management of the Gate
    Theatre 11, 14, 83, 88, 96n16,
    102, 107, 159, 173–74, 176
  as producer 13, 41, 77
  as stage director 34, 35, 99, 154,
    177, 196, 198
  and An Taibhdhearc 141
Ellis, Hazel 29
  Women without Men 170
Empire Exhibition (1938) 170–71, 176
Enable Ireland see National
  Association of Cerebral Palsy
Enquist, Olov 139
Erckmann-Chatrian (Émile Erckmann
  and Alexandre Chatrian) 141
ethnicity 3, 5, 16–17, 189–203,
    208–19
expressionism 34, 57–58, 63, 83–84,
    98, 126, 192

Fairy Hill Home 13, 77, 87
Fallon, Gabriel 78, 84, 175
Famine (1840s) 7, 8
Fanu, Alicia Sheridan Le
  Sons of Erin; or Modern Sentiment
    6
Farber, Yaël 16, 203, 207–9, 218
Farr, Florence 8
feminism 13, 16, 26–28, 36, 100,
    170, 200, 208
  see also #WakingTheFeminists
Feuchtwanger, Lionel
  Jew Suss 158

Fianna Fáil 39, 97n22
Fischer-Lichte, Erika 168–69
Fitzgerald, Geraldine 29
Fitzgerald, Mark 15
Fitz-Simon, Christopher 40, 51, 78,
    98, 103, 114
Flotats, Josep Maria 144–45
Flynn, Tara
  Not a Funny Word 10
Foley, Charles 126
Forristal, Desmond 196–98
  Black Man's Country 196–99
Fouéré, Olwen 208
Franco, Francisco 131, 133–34, 137
Frawley, Monica 216
Friedman, Sharon 16
Friel, Brian 139, 145
  Dancing at Lughnasa 138
  The Gentle Island 12
Fülle, Henning 95–96
Furnival, Fanny 208

Gaeilge see Irish language
Gaelic League 14, 113, 116
  see also Irish language
Gaiety Theatre 14, 40, 105, 161n31,
    172–73, 176, 197
Gallienne, Eva Le 29n11
Garde, Ulrike 94
Garner, Steve 212
Garrick, David 6
Gate Theatre see Dublin Gate
  Theatre
Gateway Theatre 171
gay identities 2, 12, 15–16, 28,
    57–75, 108, 114–15, 125, 137, 143,
    152–53, 164
  see also queer identities
gender 1–12, 16–17, 25–37, 39–52,
    58–59, 69–70, 73–74, 85, 88,
    92, 94, 107–8, 138, 142–43,
    154, 170–71, 180, 182, 201, 203,
    207–19

Gender Equality Practice in Irish
    Theatre (2018) 207
Genet, Jean 95
Gibson, Chloe 13, 91–108
Gilbert, James 180
Globe Theatre 99, 193
Goldini, Carlo 139
Goldstone, Patricia 175
Gonne, Maud
    Dawn 7–8
Good, John
    The Antoinetta 93n9
Good, Maurice
    The Antoinetta 93n9
Goodall, Sara 9
Gore-Booth, Eva
    The Buried Life of Deirdre 7
    A Daughter of Eve 7
    The Triumph of Maeve 7
Graells, Guillem-Jordi 138
Graham, Desmond 96n16
Granville-Barker, Harley 141
    Prunella 126
Gregory, Lady Augusta 8, 122, 126,
    141, 145, 152
    Cathleen Ni Houlihan 7, 8
Grehan, Helena 210
Griffith, Elizabeth 6
Griffith, Thomas 6
Grotowski, Jerzy 95, 136
Guitry, Sacha 15, 141
Guthrie, Tyrone 171, 178–79

Hanuszkiewicz, Adam 136
Harmon, Ken
    Done up Like a Kipper 199
Harris, Nancy 16, 210, 212–13, 215,
    218
    Our New Girl 17
    The Red Shoes 207–8, 211–13, 215,
        217–19
Haugh, Irene 152
Haugh, Kevin O'Hanraghan 152

Haughey, Charlie 97n22
Hayes, Mairin 25
Hayes, Michael 102
Haywood, Eliza 6
Heade, Robert 105
Healy, Mary 17, 199
Heath, Edward 104
Hellman, Lillian
    The Little Foxes 17
Henry, Paul 134
The Highland Fair 168–69
Hilferty, Susan, 207, 209
Hill, Lucienne 96n16
Hitler, Adolf 120, 209
Hogan, Robert 1–2
Hogerzeil, Han 80
Holst, Gustav
    The Planets 160–61
Home, John
    Douglas 181
homosexuality *see* gay identities;
    lesbian identities; queer identities
Houlihan, Barry 13
Housman, Laurence 141
    Prunella 126
Howard, Elizabeth 96
Howlett, Angela 49
Hsiung Shih-I
    Lady Precious Stream 190–92
Hughes, Isa 170
Hyde, Douglas 14, 122, 152
    Casadh an tSúgáin 14

#IamIrish 200
Ibbs, Ronald 192
Ibsen, Henrik 15
    Peer Gynt 121, 124, 176
Independent Theatre, 135n13
Inghinidhe na hÉireann 7, 14
Ionesco, Eugène 95, 100
Irish Censorship Publications Board
    39, 45, 51
    see also censorship

Irish Housewives' Association 77, 88
Irish identity formation 4, 57–59, 68, 93, 116, 120, 120, 123, 134, 139, 143, 200
Irish language 2, 5, 10, 13–15 113–29, 131–33, 139–46, 168
Irish Literary Theatre 7, 8, 122
  see also Abbey Theatre
Irish National Theatre Society 7
  see also Abbey Theatre
Irish Republican Army (IRA) 145n37
Irish War of Independence (1919–21) 116, 145n37

Jacobs, Olu 197
Janssens, Maddy 131–32, 146
Jaquarello, Roland 99–100
Jellett, Bay 2, 142, 156
Jellett, Mainie 142
Jessner, Leopold 169, 176
Jesus Christ Superstar 197
Johnston, Denis 145
  A Bride for the Unicorn 15–16, 159–64
  The Old Lady Says 'No!' 159
Jones, Robert Edmund 176
Joyce, James 63
Joynt, Ernest 118

Kafka, Franz
  The Trial 209
Kanin, Fay 196n27
Kanin, Michael 196n27
Kantór, Tadeusz 95
Kaut-Howson, Helena 199n42
Kay, Kwesi 197
Keats, John 123
Kemp, Robert 177, 180
Kennedy, Randolph 180
Kettle, Thomas 154n14
Kilroy, Thomas
  The Death and Resurrection of Mr Roche 12, 108

Kirkwood, Lucy
  The Children 207
Knoblock, Edward
  Kismet 154
Kurosawa, Akira
  Rashomon 196n27
Kushner, Tony
  Angels in America 146
Kwei Chen 190

La Perla Theatre 138
Labiche, Eugène Marin 141
Lally, Des 3
language see Irish language
Lanters, José 58, 61
Larchet, John 152, 156–58, 163
Laverty, Maura 39–52, 145
  Liffey Lane 11, 13, 40, 41n9, 42, 51
  Lift Up Your Gates 39
  Tolka Row 11, 39–52, 93, 107
  A Tree in the Crescent 11, 40n6, 41n9, 42
Lazaridis, Stephanos 102n38
Leeney, Cathy 3, 9, 58–59, 63, 67
Lemaire, Victoire 207–8
Lentin, Ronit 201, 201n53
lesbian identities 2, 11, 25–37
  see also queer identities
Lilliputian Theatre Dublin 6
Lizaran, Anna 139
Lonergan, Patrick 1, 3, 9, 96
Longford, Christine 83, 145, 192, 196
  Mr Jiggins of Jigginstown 9
Longford, Edward 83, 140, 163, 191–92
  Armlet of Jade 190
Longford Productions 40n5, 141n32, 190
Looney, Sarah 172
Lowe, Louise 17
Lyceum Theatre 6

Lyndsay, David 178
Ane Satyre of the Thrie Estaites
177–80
Lyric Theatre 13

MAC (Metropolitan Arts Centre,
Belfast) 10
Mac Anna, Tomás 108n48
Mac Liammóir, Micheál 5, 12, 16,
28, 39, 49–50, 52, 59, 83, 88,
92n5. 96, 97n22, 99, 105–6, 141,
143–45, 154n14, 158, 160n30,
167–71, 173, 175, 180, 182, 192,
194, 199, 202
as actor 41–42, 51, 52, 59, 70, 81,
96n16, 103–6, 120, 151n1, 167,
190–93, 199n42, 202
Diarmuid agus Gráinne 14, 116
'Dul Faoi na Gréine' ('The Setting
of the Sun') 113
Enter a Goldfish 114
and establishment of the Gate
Theatre 1–2, 113, 132, 139,
141, 218
Home for Christmas 172–73
Ill Met by Moonlight 116, 128,
172
The Importance of Being Oscar 16,
103, 113, 128, 167, 172, 195
and the Irish language 14, 83,
113–29, 141
and management of the Gate
Theatre 2, 11, 15, 17, 59, 88,
100, 102–3, 107, 194, 196,
198
The Mountains Look Different
127
Pageant of St. Patrick 177
Prelude in Kazbek Street 12, 125
as producer 13, 77, 92, 126, 141,
196, 198
as stage designer 35, 135n13, 141,
167, 168, 170–75, 178, 182

as stage director 14, 16, 141–43,
178
Where Stars Walk 116, 172
as writer 14, 16, 113–14, 116, 125,
127–28, 172
Macardle, Dorothy
Ann Kavanagh 9
Dark Waters 9
Fenian Snow 9
Witch's Brew 9
MacDonald, Ann-Marie 208
MacEwen, Molly 15–16, 167–83
MacGinely, P.T.
Eilís agus an Bhean Déirce 14
MacGowan, Kenneth 176
Madden, Tom 115
Magdalene Laundries 143
Magee, Heno
Hatchett 107
Mahony, Louis 197
Mamet, David 139
Manning, Mary 2, 5, 9, 12, 29,
57–75, 140, 145
Happy Family 25
Storm over Wicklow 190
Youth's the Season–? 12, 25,
57–75
see also Motley
Markievicz, Casimir 28, 135n13
Marking the Territory 10
Markus, Radvan 14
Marlowe, Christopher
Edward II 136–37
Marrowbone Lane Samaritan Fund
51n52, 77, 87
Marshall, William 194–96, 198
Martin, Édouard 141
Martínez Sierra, Gregorio 15, 126,
141
Martyn, Edward 123, 135n13
Mason, James 102
Mathews, Aidan
Diamond Body 12

May, Frederick 15–16, 151–64
  Scherzo for Orchestra 162
May, Sheila 152
Mayne, Rutherford 141
Mayo Famine (1898) 7
McCrea, Barry 115
McDonagh, Martin 139
McFeely, Deirdre 11
McGuinness, Frank 12
  The Factory Girls 13
  Gates of Gold 12
McInture, Blanche 17
McIvor, Charlotte 4
McKenna, Barney 198
McKenna, James 107
McKenna, Siobhán 208
McMaster, Anew 192–94
McQuaid, John Charles (Archbishop) 51
Meany, Helen 218
Mermaid Theatre 102
#MeToo 210, 217
Meyerhold, Vsevolod 168
Miller, Arthur 102, 199
Mishima, Yukio 139
Mnouchkine, Ariane 95
Moign, Jean 15
Moiseiwitsch, Tanya 178
Molière (pseud. Jean-Baptiste Poquelin) 15, 126, 141–42, 145
  Les Fourberies de Scapin 142–43
Monks, Aoife 167
Montanyès, Josep 139
Mooney, Ria 11, 25, 29, 35, 192
Moore, George 118
Moore, Meriel 2
Morash, Christopher 14
Morgan, Sydney (Lady Morgan, née Owenson)
  The First Attempt of the Whim of a Moment 6
Morrissey, Eamonn 99, 104
Morse, Donald E. 4

Morum, William
  The Late Edwina Black 93n9
Motley 2, 25, 57, 140
Moynihan, Sinead 212
Mullen, Marie 207
Müller, Heiner 139
Mulvany, Kate
  Medea 17
Mumford, Meg 94
Murphy, A.J. 103n39
Murphy, Oonagh 17
  The Children 207
  The Tribes 207
Murray, Christopher 4
Murray, T.C. 141

Na gCopaleen, Myles (pseud.) *see* O'Nolan, Brian
Nakase, Justine 16–17
National Association for Cerebral Palsy 77–78, 87
national identity formation *see* Irish identity formation
National Theatre of Catalonia 144–46
Nazimova, Alla 29n11
Negga, Ruth 16–17, 189, 202–3, 207–8, 210
New York Civic Repertory Theatre 29n11
Ní Ghráda, Máiréad
  An Triail 10
Nic Eoin, Máirín 125
Nietzsche, Friedrich 117
Nijinsky, Vaslav 125
Nikolaisen, Donna Anita 17, 199
Nowlan, David 167
Nussbaum, Martha 85

Ó Conaire, Pádraic 127–28
  Deoraíocht 127
  'Nóra Mharcais Bhig' 127
  The Woman at the Window 127

Ó Conghaile, Micheál
  Go dTaga do Ríocht 115
Ó hAodha, Micheál 114
Ó hÉighneacháin, Tomás 142
Ó Laoghaire, Peadar 125
Ó Lochlainn, Gearóid 1, 142
Ó Murnaghan, Art 162
Ó Siadhail, Pádraig 126
Ó Siochfhradha, Mícheál
  Dia 'Á Réidhteach 145n37
  Hurl 199
O'Casey, Seán 4, 40, 81, 91, 100
  The Shadow of a Gunman 17
O'Connor, Frank 81
  'Guests of the Nation' 145n37
O'Dowd, Ciara 192
O'Farrell, Máirin 182
O'Farrell, Nuala 182
Offenbach, Jacques 139
O'Gorman, Siobhán 16
O'Hara, Mike 7
O'Hea, Jerome, S.J. 48
O'Herlihy, Michael 176–77
O'Keefe, Máire 115
O'Kelly, Donal
  Asylum! Asylum! 199
Old Vic Theatre 174
O'Leary, Philip 116, 118
Olivier, Lawrence 194
Olympia Theatre 12
O'Neill, Charlie
O'Neill, Eugene 141
  Anna Christie 177
O'Nolan, Brian 117
Operating Theatre 12
Osborne, John 15, 104
O'Toole, Fintan 17
Our Country (dir. Liam O'Leary)
  39
Oxford Playhouse 102n38

Pageant of St. Patrick 176–77
Parnell, Charles Stewart 117

Pasolini, Pier Paolo 115
Pasqual, Lluís 135–36, 138, 145–46
  Camí de nit 145
Paterson, Patrick
  The Roses are Real 105
Payne, B. Iden 173
Peacock Theatre 10, 14, 107, 141n32,
  176
  see also Abbey Theatre
Peacocke, John
  The Children of the Wolf 99n26
Pearse, Patrick 28, 119, 127–28
Pepys' Diary (TV programme) 103
Phelan, Brian 5, 98, 100–2, 108
  The Signalman's Apprentice 13,
    93n9, 94–108
  The Tormentors 102
Philips, Katherine 6
Piccolo Theatre 136
Pierse, Michael 4, 98
Pike Theatre 9, 49, 99, 170
Pilný, Ondřej 3
Pine, Richard 135n13, 170–73, 175
Pinter, Harold 95, 100, 139, 199
Pirandello, Luigi 102, 139, 170
Pius XII (Pope) 51
Planella, Pere 135, 138, 139
Plunkett, Edward (Lord Dunsany)
  141
Pole, William 173
Prentki, Tim 77
Preston, Sheila 77
Proust, Marcel 63
Puigserver, Fabià 134, 136
Punchbag Theatre 10
Pushkin, Alexander 125

queer identities 2–5, 9–12, 15, 25–37,
  57–75, 115, 143
Quigley, Godrey 193
Quinn, Antoinette 8
Quintero, Joaquín Álvarez and
  Serafín Álvarez 141

Raidió Teilifís Éireann (RTÉ) 92–93, 97, 102–3, 153, 167, 211
Raine, Nina
   Tribes 207
Rasharc 196
Reddin, Norman 140
Reid, Christina
   Tea in a China Cup 13, 91
Reinhardt, Max 168
Reitzel, C.A. 211
Reza, Yasmina 139
Rhys, Jean
   Wide Sargasso Sea 200
Rich, Adrienne 218
Richards, Shelagh 81, 85
Ridout, Nicholas 208, 219
Rigola, Àlex 136
Rimsky-Korsakov, Nikolai
   Sadko 158
Riordan, Arthur
   The Train 9
Robeson, Paul 193–95
Robinson, Lennox 141, 152
Roche, Billy
   A Handful of Stars 91
Roe, Owen 209–10
Ronconi, Luca 95
Rousseau, Henri 127
Royal Earls, the (band) *see* Zulus, the (band)
RTÉ *see* Raidió Teilifís Éireann
Rushe, Desmond 144
Russell, George 152
Ryan, Phyllis 28, 99

Sacred Heart Messenger 46
Sagan, Leontine 26
Saidléar, Annraoi
   Aintí Bríd 145n37
Saint-Saëns, Camille
   Samson and Delilah 157
Sarks, Anne-Louise
   Medea 17

Sartre, Jean-Paul 15
Schauspielhaus Berlin 176
Schiller, Friedrich 139
Scott, Michael 2
Sears, David 79
Sears, Djanet 208
Serra, Laura 138
Serrano Suñer, Ramón 137
Serrat, Joan Manuel 134
sexuality *see* birth control; gay identities; lesbian identities; queer identities
Shadwell, Thomas 6
Shaffer, Peter
   Equus 98
Shakespeare, William 15, 123, 139, 141, 146, 173, 174
   Hamlet 16–17, 29–30, 57, 189, 202, 208–9
   Henry IV 174
   The Merchant of Venice 172, 174
   The Merry Wives of Windsor 175–76
   Othello 17, 173–76, 192–94, 198–99
   Romeo and Juliet 6
   Timon of Athens 6
Shaw, George Bernard 141, 143, 146
   Arms and the Man 93n9, 141, 143, 174–75
   The Doctor's Dilemma 143
   Fanny's First Play 93n9
   John Bull's Other Island 143
   Man and Superman 143
   O'Flaherty, V.C. 143
   Press Cuttings 143
   Tragedy of an Elderly Gentleman 143
Shepherd, Simon 11
Sheridan, Peter 107
Sheridan, Richard Brinsley 141
   The School for Scandal 174
   St Patrick's Day 190

Sihra, Melissa 4, 8, 85
Simpson, Alan 49n44, 93, 99
Singleton, Brian 12
Sirera, Rodolf 133
Sisson, Elaine 27–28
Smith, Brendan 9
Smock Alley Theatre 6
'Snow White' (fairytale) 215
Snyder-Young, Dani 78–80, 84
Soldevila, Carlota 135
Spanish Civil War (1936–39) 133
St Ann's Warehouse 210
Stafford, T.H. 141
Stanford, Alan 199–201
Stephens, James 152
    'Hesperus' 152
Stephenson, John 158
Stevenson, Sam D. 180
Steyaert, Chris 131–32, 146
Still, George Frederic 80
Stokes, Dorothy 153n10
Stoneman, Patsy 200
Strand Theatre 103
Strehler, Giorgio 136
Studio Arts Club ('the Cabaret') 28
Su Ting Po
    Little Sister 190
    Princely Fortune 190–91
Sutherland, Halliday 45
Swift, Carolyn 93, 171
Synge, John Millington
    The Playboy of the Western World
        182
Sznaizer, Natan 132

An Taibhdhearc 14, 27, 113, 126,
    141, 143
Tapiès, Antoní 134
Taylor, Diana 219
Teatre Lliure 15, 131–46
Tecglen, Eduardo Haro 138
Teixidor, Jordi 133
Teresa of Ávila (Saint) 64, 66–67

Theatre of Ireland 135n13
Théâtre Populaire Breton 15
Théâtre populaire de Bretagne 15
Theatre Royal (Dublin) 6, 193
Thompson, James 78–79
Titley, Alan 123
Tolstoy, Leo 141
Tonelli, Franco 142
Tormey, Anwen 201n51
An Tóstal Festival 176–77
Trezise, Rachel
    Cotton Fingers 10
Trotter, Mary 11
Trump, Donald 208, 210
Trump, Melania 209
Tryater 15
Turgenev, Ivan 125
Turner, Pat 171
Tweedy, Hilda 87–88
Tynan, Katherine 152

Vale, Adrian 93
Valente, Joseph 8
Vallé-Inclán, Ramón María del
    The Barbaric Comedies 145
Van den Beuken, Ruud 3
Vilasarau, Emma 139
Vitrac, Roger 139
Vogel, Paula 208
Vroomen, Grace 12–13

Wagner, Richard
    'Wedding March' 160
#WakingTheFeminists 1, 25n1, 207,
    218
Walsh, Eileen
    The Beginning 207
Walsh, Fintan 4, 58, 71
Walsh, Ian R. 3, 13
Walshe, Eibhear 59
Welles, Orson 120–21, 151, 190, 192
Wesker, Arnold 95, 104
    The Kitchen 102

Westminster Theatre 182
Whelan, Bill
  The Train 9
Whelan, Feargal 15
Whitman, Walt 117
Wickam, James 101
Wilde, Oscar 16, 117, 119, 167
  Salome 29–30
Williams, Ralph Vaughan 15, 153
Williams, Tennessee
  The Rose Tattoo 9, 49
Wills, Clair 77
Wilson, Robert 95
Winsloe, Christa
  Children in Uniform 11–12, 25–37

Woffington, Peg 6
Woman's Life 47–48
Woman's Way 47, 48n36

Yeats, George (née Bertha Hyde-Lees)
  158
Yeats, William Butler 7, 28, 114,
  116–17, 122, 128, 163, 192n12
  Cathleen Ni Houlihan 7–8
  The Countess Cathleen 7
  The King of the Great Clock Tower
    163, 175
  The Resurrection 163

Zulus, the (band) 198